NCAA
INDIANA
all
the
way

Sports editor, Bob Hammel
Photo editor, Larry Crewell

A Herald-Times Book
in association with
Indiana University Press

with stories and photographs by
the Daily Herald-Telephone's
sports and photography staffs

Manufactured in the United States of America

Reprinted by Indiana University Press by
special arrangement with the Herald-Times,
Inc.

LC76-15064
cl. ISBN 0-253-15611-4
pa. ISBN 0-253-15612-2

Indiana University basketball, 1975-76

Contents

Prologue

'For two years, this has been our objective'

The eyes.

Those eyes.

The eyes that blaze laser beams when Bob Knight is burning. The eyes that laugh. That wither. That kid. That humble. That cut. That urge. That command.

The eyes that glazed in numb refusal to let deep pain show through a year before in Dayton, Ohio, relaxed their vigilance in victory and let honesty flood through on a Monday night in March in Bicentennial-happy Philadelphia.

Knight stood on the playing floor at The Spectrum scant seconds after his Indiana University basketball team had made it over the last of a seemingly endless row of hurdles, and the eyes reflected every hurdle, and the rare stumbles.

"For two years, this has been our objective," he said, in the midst of, but not quite a part of, the unrestrained, joyous celebrating going on all around.

His voice was strained, more noticeably so than in that time of crushing defeat a year before. And the eyes were much more moist.

"Not just this year. For two years. All the work that's gone into this.

"I know better than anybody else how hard these kids have worked for it. They're very, very deserving."

And what a long, long road they traveled. They and Knight.

The pages inside look down the last leg of that trip, viewed as it was taken, step by step from Bloomington to Philadelphia via Indianapolis and 31 points in between — a transcribed, next-day look as viewed by Bloomington *Daily Herald-Telephone* writers and photographers all along the line.

It was a sports trip made special by the people who made it, under conditions few champions have faced and conquered. It was a trip almost made a year before, when Fate intervened.

That was a subject Knight could joke about. Fate.

A week before, after his center, Kent Benson, had been forced by fouls to sit on the bench beside him for crucial minutes in a difficult regional game with Alabama, Knight had been asked if the thought might have crossed his mind during that stretch that Fate was working against him in that quest for a championship.

"I don't think Fate has a hell of a lot to do with it," he said, "unless Fate is 6-10 and can hook."

Four fouls on a 6-10 man who can hook may not be Fate, but a broken arm to the best player on the best team in America — a massive, muscular arm snapped in two by a painless, unnoticed blow in the heat of a basketball game — that's something close to Fate. And no one who reveled in the IU events of 1976, *especially* after the events of 1976, will concede that the broken arm Scott May suffered at Purdue Feb. 24, 1975, didn't deprive that Indiana team a bright place in college basketball history.

Knight surely feels that as strongly as anyone, but he moved through the tournament weeks low-key, relaxed, with no sign of a grudge against the world for last year's denial, for putting double pressure on this year and this team lest it be branded the team that won all the games and all the polls and never won the championship.

He showed more anxiety in first-round play at South Bend than at any future stop, readily confessing it. "I just wanted to see these kids get a chance to go beyond the first round," he said.

At Baton Rouge, in the toughest regional known to modern man, he was loose. Around him in handy contact were a number of the men whose counsel he values — Clair Bee, who flew in from New York and stayed with the Hoosier team; Pete Newell and Stu Inman, National Basketball Association executives in town for talent appraisal.

Easing back in a chair when a formal press conference broke up into tableside conversation, he was asked: "Say, do you know if you win this thing you may be the youngest coach ever to do it?"

"You've gotta be talking chronological age," he said, "because I feel like I'm 90."

His straight man went on: "Wooden was 53 when he won his first one."

"You know what I'll be doing when I'm 53? I'll have my butt in a boat somewhere with a fish pole in my hands."

"But you must think about winning it . . .

"Oh, sure, you think about it, but you can't let it consume you. You've got to realize how many

Bob Knight — 'Feel like I'm 90'

Bob Knight — 'Unless Fate is 6-10 and can hook . . .'

hundreds of guys have been in this profession, and only about 22 of them ever won the NCAA championship. The odds aren't very good."

Worse than he thought. Only 21 had, thanks to Wooden's remarkable domination.

At Philadelphia, he was even more open and expansive in a 50-minute question-and-answer session that brought out some coaching philosophies as well as the inevitable Knightian digs.

In recruiting, he noted, "there are three things we feel are involved in basketball.

"First is strength, and I don't mean a guy necessarily has to be 6-5 and 240 pounds. I'm talking about a wiry strength. A guy 6-1 and 170 can have it.

"The second thing is quickness. A slow, plodding team is going to have trouble.

"And the third thing is concentration. There isn't any right way to play basketball. There are a lot of poor ways, but there's not any correct way. We want the guy who can concentrate on the way we want him to play."

He freely admitted to dress codes and regulations on hair length. "What the hell's wrong with looking nice?" he said.

"We tell the kid just what we're going to expect of him when we're recruiting him. I don't care if he goes to Indiana. I want him to be happy where he does go.

"We recruited a kid just this year with hair down to his shoulders. I mentioned to him, 'Now,

Bob Knight

Mike (Miday, of Canton, Ohio), you understand that's gonna be gone if you come to Indiana,' and he said, 'Coach, if you want me to, I'll shave my head.'

"I'll tell you right now, that guy is gonna be a good player for us."

He said he is looking for players who can play all over the court. "We try to get the worst match-up between their defense and our offense," he said. "For example, (Bobby) Wilkerson is the most versatile defensive player we have. He has played every position on the floor.

"You've got to be able to do a number of things to play for us. There are certain things an offense can do that mean you've got to be able to switch men. May has to guard a guard, Buckner a forward."

He was asked if his teams sometimes overpass. "I don't really believe you can overpass," he said. "Passing has to be the key to everything."

And the subject of that coaching future, the one sealed off in Baton Rouge by 53, came up with a query about how he's holding up, physically, under the strain of big-time coaching.

"I don't feel any pressure," he said. "You like to see your kids play as well as they can, sure. But the guy over at Methodist Hospital doing a heart operation has a lot more pressure on him than I have. He's dealing with lives. I'm just worrying about potential.

"I'll tell you, unless I can find a place where the fish are just biting their fannies off, I'll be coaching for a long time."

Twenty-four hours later, it was finals day, and by evening, he had his first national champion.

"Kind of a two-year quest," he called it. A year before, he had a broken dream and shattered ball

---

"This is an extremely good Indiana team. Their passing-game offense is the offense of the times, and it's run as well by that group of players and that coach as any offense ever in America."

— Gus Ganakas
Michigan State coach

---

club, and a morale-propping letter in his possession from Bee, a man 44 years older than Knight but a confidant who urged:

"Take a deep breath. Get your bearings. Set your sights on even greater heights and start all over again.

"The young man, the leader, rebounds swiftly from adversity . . . strengthened by the very blow that cut him down. Now he knows the rough spots that pit the roads and the quicksand that lies so innocently nearby. He knows because he has fought his way up that path of agony — almost to the very top.

"Then, suddenly, refreshed by the driving desire that has always inspired young leaders, he grasps the new challenge with eager hands and races for the starting line.

"He will be back."

"I went into this game thinking about so many people who had invested so much of themselves into our program," Knight said that night in Philadelphia.

"I think of an 80-year-old man (Bee) sitting up in the mountains in New York watching this game on television. Nobody has been more influential on my basketball life than he has been.

"I think of my college coach, Fred Taylor. Not a person out there in the Indiana crowd was rooting harder for us than he was.

"I think of Pete Newell . . . Stu Inman . . . and today, John Havlicek came to our game and spoke to our team in its pre-game meeting on what it's like to play in a championship game and what it would be like to win.

"I went into this game thinking of all those people . . . and our kids. They played five damned good basketball teams in this tournament and won the championship, and more than anything else the way they won it means a great deal to me."

At 35, he is not the youngest man ever to coach a national collegiate basketball champion, but he's among 'em. There's some coincidence in two men who got there slightly earlier — his own coach, Taylor, a winner in 1960 at 33, and the man who coached Indiana to its first two titles, the late Branch McCracken, 32 when his 1940 team won.

"I think it's a goal of any coach to have an opportunity to play in the NCAA, first of all," Knight said. "When you start in it, it's almost beyond the realm of comprehension that you might win it."

He was not grabbed immediately by the joy of victory. "I'm sure it will come to me tomorrow or some other day," he said.

"But I'm going to go right into building for next year. There's a high school all-star game in Washington, D.C., this week, and I've got a reservation on a train to go down to it.

"They pay me pretty well at Indiana, and they don't pay me to relax. We're losing five really strong people, and we'll just have to start in with what we have next Oct. 15 and see how we can do."

Which is what he and this team did last fall. . .

"I don't expect there to be any dropoff in the way we play. I'm not talking about winning games; I'm talking about effort. But you have witnessed as fine a performance over four years by these five seniors as you are ever going to see."

— Bob Knight

Indiana 94, Soviet Union 78

INDIANAPOLIS, NOVEMBER 3, 1975

James Schlesinger may be jobless, but his spirit lives on in Indiana University basketball.

If President Ford really did sack his Secretary of Defense over the weekend for a hard-line defense posture that fuzzed the nation's detente policies, Bob Knight is not the man to consider for the job.

Robert knows defense, and in his 94-by-50 foot world, peaceful coexistence is unacceptable. On his mind at halftime of the Hoosiers' colorful international game against the Soviet national team Monday night was not detente but the dilettante way his team was playing defense.

So the guns barked a bit in the dressing room and the Hoosiers blew the Russians out of a brisk ball game that ended with Indiana a 94-78 winner and a *les majeste* glaze in the eye of the 17,377 who departed Market Square Arena in re-established "We're No. 1" bliss.

The "we" in this case was U.S. basketball vis-a-vis the team (and many of the players) who spirited the Olympic gold medal and immense international prestige away from the Americans at Munich in 1972.

There were times Monday when Munich appeared about to be relived. With 2½ minutes to go in the half, the score was 40-40 and Knight's company on the sidelines included starters Scott May, Quinn Buckner, Bob Wilkerson and Kent Benson, each of them in foul trouble.

Sophomores Mark Haymore and Wayne Radford gave the lead back to IU with close-in field goals, and the lead jumped to 48-42 at halftime when May — hustled back into the game when frisky freshman Rich Valavicius, who gave every sign of enjoying himself in the fierce inside play that marked the game, needed relief in the final minute — and Jim Crews stuck in long jump shots.

May's basket started an all-American finish for the senior from Sandusky. May, who had missed his last two shots before drawing his third foul and sitting down with 6:27 to go in the half, never missed again in a 34-point game.

May was 13-for-15 in this game, and it might have approached a 40-point show under U.S. rules because five of his bullseyes came with Russians clouting him. In international play, that's a foul but no three-point play. The basket counts and play goes on.

It went on sensationally for the Hoosiers in the first 10 minutes after halftime. In that stretch, the lead ballooned to 79-49 as the Russian offense, precise, patterned and polished by years of play together, flew apart under IU pressure.

Some picture plays contributed to the pullaway. Twice, Buckner sailed the ball goalward on a high arc, and centers Benson and Haymore responded with perfectly-timed crams, legal since dunks are permitted in international play.

Once Benson and May combined for a mid-court steal that ended with the night's super-dunk, a two-handed rouser by Benson that let the Soviets know how excited and noisy Hoosier fans can get.

May was a sensational show all by himself. He drew a foul and went ahead with an off-balance shot from the side that glanced through. He barged like a Cadillac through the truckish traffic under the basket and twisted with elan and grace to roll in an over-the-head, left-handed flip. And he zipped jump shots through like they were being outlawed tomorrow.

Benson gave the Hoosiers a board edge over the mountainous Russians with a game-high 12 and added 12 points. Tom Abernethy, the new man in the starting lineup, showed his skills in many ways, including a string of three baskets in the pivotal last few minutes of the first half when he was the only IU regular on the floor.

INDIANA 94

	M	FG	FT	R	A	PF	TP
May, f	29	13-15	8-10	5	2	4	34
Abernethy, f	32	5- 8	0- 0	3	1	4	10
Benson, c	25	5-13	2- 6	12	2	4	12
Buckner, g	20	2-11	2- 4	2	3	4	6
Wilkerson, g	12	4- 6	0- 0	1	2	4	8
Radford	18	2- 3	0- 2	4	4	4	4
Valavicius	18	1- 5	3- 4	6	0	4	5
Crews	20	3- 4	0- 0	0	6	3	6
Haymore	15	4- 7	1- 2	3	0	3	9
Wisman	6	0- 1	0- 0	0	0	1	0
Bender	4	0- 1	0- 2	0	1	0	0
Eells	2	0- 1	0- 0	0	0	0	0
Team				13			
Totals		39-75	16-30	49	21	35	94

SOVIET UNION 78

	M	FG	FT	R	A	PF	TP
A.Belov, f	6	0- 0	0- 0	2	4	5	0
Kozkia, f	26	1- 4	0- 0	2	2	3	2
Tkachenko, c	20	4- 6	0- 4	10	0	3	8
S.Belov, g	25	9-24	3- 4	3	2	1	21
Edeshko, g	21	5- 7	6- 8	4	4	4	16
Harchenko	14	2- 4	0- 0	1	0	4	4
Sharmuhamedov	24	3- 8	10-10	9	0	2	16
Shigili	21	2- 5	2- 4	2	0	5	6
Milosserdov	16	1- 3	3- 4	0	0	4	5
Goncharon	3	0- 2	0- 0	0	0	2	0
Arsamasskov	5	0- 0	0- 0	1	0	1	0
Salnikov	3	0- 0	0- 0	0	0	1	0
Team				13			
Totals		27-63	24-34	47	12	35	78

SCORE BY HALVES

Soviet Union	42	36 —	78
Indiana	48	46 —	94

Errors: Soviet Union 24, Indiana 12

	FG	Pct.	FT	Pct.
Soviet Union	27-63	.429	24-34	.706
Indiana	39-75	.520	16-30	.533

Officials: George Solomon and Louis Stout
Attendance: 17,377 (capacity)

Russians Valeri Milosserdov, Mihail Kozkia 'debate' Wayne Radford

Guards Buckner and Wilkerson shared the biggest Russian problem, 31-year-old Sergei Belov, quick, experienced and good.

Belov lost his primary operating partner, 6-8 forward Alexandr Belov (they're unrelated), early in this game, so Sergei became a one-man offense. His twisting drives accounted for 17 first-half points, but Knight's strong suggestions about more astute positioning eliminated the drives the second half and reduced him to a 2-for-8 jump shooter.

Alexandr, a premier athlete, didn't score in his skimpy six minutes on stage. He picked up four fouls in the first 3:10, the last of those a thwarted attempt to stop May on a breakaway charge to the basket.

From that play came the night's noisiest controversy. Belov and Russian coach Vladimir Kondrashin insisted May's basket shouldn't count, and Kondrashin pulled his team off the floor in protest for a few tense minutes.

Belov left the game after that foul and returned to start the second half. It was barely two minutes along when Wilkerson and Buckner frisked him of the basketball and he fouled out trying to get it back.

Kondrashin did not use Belov's absence as an alibi. Through an interpreter, he expressed conviction that his team played much better than in its opening 67-56 loss at Marquette Sunday morning. "If we played in Milwaukee the way we played here, we would have won the game," the interpreter, player Vladimir Arsamasskov, quoted Kondrashin.

Mark Haymore dwarfed by 7-2 Vladimir Tkachenko

A rematch, maybe, in, say, Leningrad?

Knight and Kondrashin shared a ritualistic handshake after the game, their coaching talk limited by language barriers. But, the two did get together for a few minutes long after the game, a Russian interpreter providing the bridge.

"Tell your coach he has a very well-conditioned team, a very good team . . . and that we wouldn't want to play him in Moscow," Knight said, breaking into a laugh.

Kondrashin gave a smiling answer and Knight beat the interpreter with: " . . . and he says he'd like to play us in Moscow."

"No," the interpreter corrected. "He said, 'How about Leningrad?' "

Knight drew considerable pleasure from the Monday night production that, among other things, shattered the myth that the sporting world lives for its weekly TV-side sessions with Howard Cosell. Put Indiana on a basketball court in Hoosierland and all available seats will fill — even four weeks ahead of the season.

"That was a tremendous crowd (17,377, capacity)," Knight said. Sounded like Assembly Hall, a fellow suggested. "Nothing's like that," Knight said, "but it was really good."

The play was commensurate. Dayton coach Don Donoher, a close Knight friend, was on hand in a scouting role because his team will play the Soviets Saturday night.

"That's a good Russian team," Donoher said. "They'll kill some teams on this tour."

That they didn't kill or even defeat the team they were playing Monday night was another cause for Knight smiles.

IU's Scott May, Kent Benson in an international battle

12

Soviets' Ivan Edeshko — A 'physical' game

Nary a line there about officiating, nor even the accomplished histrionics the practiced Russians delivered to draw some interesting fouls. Not that Knight didn't notice. "I thought there was a somewhat theatrical overtone to it all," Knight said, grinning.

Those smiles came late. In the first half, Knight's succinct sum-up was: "I thought our defense was bad, *really* bad. We weren't staying in with anybody." The second half: "I think I noticed after about seven minutes they had scored just three points."

"We went back to playing our game," Buckner said. "We seemed very anxious at the start — the first time we were going into competition and everything. But when we got that out of us, we were all right." And how was that removed? "I'd say by the coach as much as anyone," Buckner said, grinning.

"When you're playing defense, it opens things up offensively," Knight said.

"The second half, we did a better job of recognizing what they were doing. The first half, we didn't read things. Their offense was doing things our defense is equipped to handle, but we weren't reading it.

"Those guys are big, strong people who can jam the ball places and get it out better than college teams."

Accumulating fouls eased the second half, Knight said, "because we kept ourselves out of the ridiculous positioning that caused the fouls."

"We felt we lost two of our three best all-round shooters. If we're stronger this year, it might be in defensive play, or we may be a little quicker. Maybe Benson has improved a little."

— Bob Knight

Knight was asked if the Monday game bore out feelings of some that the U.S. would be better off sending a champion amateur team to the Olympics rather than a cross-section of national stars.

"I think we should send the winner of the NBA playoffs," he said. "I've always felt that. If they don't let them play, we come home.

"But, no, I'm not sure you could pick any one amateur team. It wouldn't be fair to a lot of kids around the country, not to allow them the opportunity to try to make a squad. And in the case of college teams, you would have the situation where some kids are signing pro contracts.

"I do think we've made some strides to get things going under the auspices of one organization" (the National Association of Basketball Coaches, supervising agency for the current 11-game Soviet tour).

Bring back the dunk, says enthused Benson

No Minnesota, no Michigan and no Kentucky basketball team ever played like the Soviet National team played Monday night.

While the Russians absorbed a defeat, the Hoosiers absorbed some bruises, and felt them afterward.

"I'd say since I've been playing at Indiana, they are the most physical team I've played," said May.

"Definitely," agreed Benson. "They're so much more physical because they've been playing the game so long. Plus they're playing international rules. Minnesota is physical but in a different sense."

What the Soviet team saw, suggested the Indiana players, was not the same IU team that will open against UCLA in three weeks. At least, they hope not.

"I thought at times today we looked very good," said May. "At other times we got a little raggedy on offense, passing, on defense."

When the Hoosiers got going the second half, May said, "it was our defense. I think we spread them out on the court, kept them from the basket."

"I think our pressure might have thrown them off," said Abernethy.

One thing permitted in international ball that needed no explanation was the dunk. "They're a lot of fun," said Benson, author of the night's best dunk.

Kondrashin, the Russian coach, called the Hoosiers "20 points better than Marquette," but he wasn't ready to call Indiana better than the U.S. Olympic team he faced in Munich in 1972. "The team in Munich was much better," he said.

"Indiana is very good, very well prepared. The defense is better than the offense.

"No. 42 (May) is their best player. The whole team is much better with him."

Kondrashin also noted that Benson and Buckner would stand a good chance of making the U.S. Olympic team. He referred to Benson as No. 54, but called Buckner by name. Buckner played in Russia in 1973 and against the Soviet Nationals last spring.

Mission unaccomplished

Scott May wins all-America duel with Richard Washington

There never has been a college basketball opener like it: No. 1-ranked Indiana vs. No. 2-ranked UCLA, before 19,116 at St. Louis Arena, on national television, in a midnight time slot. It was all-Hoosier, on the court and in the stands, as Indiana won, 84-64 — so overwhelmingly that for two months afterward, the Hoosiers were the unanimous No. 1 pick in the national coaches' polls.

Knight, Gene Bartow — 20 points apart, but same stoic look

Laurie Baiden celebrates a St. Louis romp

Indiana 84, UCLA 64

ST. LOUIS, NOVEMBER 29, 1975

Indiana proved its No. 1 ranking to UCLA's defending national collegiate basketball champions and a national television crowd Saturday night with a crushing 84-64 victory before 19,115 at packed St. Louis Arena.

Avenging a 70-59 NCAA tournament loss to the Bruins on the same floor three years before, the Hoosiers bolted ahead for good on a three-point play by Kent Benson that provided a 7-4 lead in the game's early minutes.

The lead steadily widened — to 36-28 at halftime, then a top of 72-46 as all-American Scott May proved his current hardiness and what the Hoosiers missed with him out last March by scoring 33 points, his Indiana high.

It was an all-Hoosier night from start to finish . . . and even longer. Red-clad Indiana fans filled more than half the seats and started chanting 40 minutes before gametime, with more than 30 pro-IU banners blaring messages from every point around the huge cavern.

Fifteen minutes before the game's TV-dictated 10:40 p.m. start, the arena erupted in a chant, "Go, Big Red," and seconds later, the Hoosiers went — off the floor to their dressing room for the last pre-game meeting, drawing a standing ovation from their loyalists as they huddled first in center court and then ran off.

The game's first two baskets were scored on rebounds — by UCLA's Jim Spillane (by far the smallest starter at 5-11) and IU's Tom Abernethy (the Hoosiers' only new starter).

Benson's first five minutes were an all-America application.

Indiana took its first lead at 4-2 when he beat his 7-1 rival, Ralph Drollinger, downcourt on a fast-break for a layup. Spillane tied the game with a backcourt steal and layup, before Benson's three-point play.

After his two free throws opened a 15-8 lead, Benson made a spectacular block on a Richard Washington layup, though the Bruins got the ball back in a flurry and Washington scored.

When the Hoosiers were caught without a man back for the second time in two minutes, Johnson cashing in a layup, Hoosier coach Bob Knight called time out at 10:00, ahead, 19-16.

Buckner scored on Indiana's fourth shot of one offensive burst to demonstrate the way the Hoosiers were storming the backboards, and the impact of their defense showed at the other end when they coaxed the 10th turnover of the night from the Bruins. The misplay blossomed into two May free throws and a 29-20 lead with 5:59 left in the half.

Jim Crews relieved Buckner at 1:59, Indiana's first substitution. Johnson drew his third foul at 1:35 after May's offensive rebound, and 6-10 freshman David Greenwood replaced him, giving the

Bruins a 7-1, 6-11, 6-10 front line. Knight countered by pulling Abernethy for a 6-4 freshman Rich Valavicius as May's free throw gave Indiana its first 10-point lead, 36-26. It was 36-28 at halftime.

Buckner drew a third foul in the first half-minute of the second half but he was scorching on offense. He scored six points as Indiana's lead grew to 44-30 and forced Gene Bartow, UCLA's debuting coach, to take a time out at 18:07.

Wilkerson's first basket of the game widened it to 50-32 as the harried Bruins made four errors in the first 4½ minutes of the half.

When May picked up his third foul at 14:26, the Indiana lead at 52-34, Knight immediately switched Wilkerson onto Johnson.

May's offense wasn't slowed. He squirmed loose twice under the basket for quick feeds that gave Indiana its first 20-point lead, 56-36, bringing the Indiana partisans off their seats with a rousing toast—victory in sight.

With Indiana up, 64-44, Buckner picked up his fourth foul and left with 9:30 to go in favor of Crews — Knight grabbing Buckner in a warm embrace as he reached the bench.

Turned out his evening wasn't over.

May's spectacular feed to Benson under the basket gave Indiana a 66-44 lead and May widened it further with a driving basket. Crews' feed to Benson topped the Indiana lead out at 72-46 as the crowd went wild with 6½ minutes left.

But Washington, the hero of UCLA's 1975 Final Four play that gave John Wooden his final NCAA championship, stayed in all the way and scored 10 straight late points that, with four straight Indiana turnovers, cut the lead to 76-58 and brought Buckner off the bench at 4:17. Another Bruin steal and Washington's basket at 3:30 cut the lead to 76-60.

The Hoosiers put the ball in the freeze, disdaining a shot till Wilkerson's layup at 1:58 broke the

A final word before the take-off in nationally-televised opener.

17

"That was the best half-court defense I've ever seen a team play . . . college or pro. They never let UCLA even start its offense."

— Hank Raymonds
Marquette assistant coach

UCLA momentum. "We're No. 1" cheers rocked the arena as Indiana regained the ball with 1:40 left, and May's final points came on a basket at 0:55. Twelve seconds later, with the lead at 80-62, the Hoosier starters were pulled and greeted with victory hugs on the sidelines and another roaring ovation.

Freshman Bob Bender's first collegiate shot gave the Hoosiers their 20-point winning margin.

Besides May's 33 points, Benson had 17 and Buckner 14 for Indiana. Washington, with 22 last-half points, scored 28 for UCLA, and Johnson finished with 18.

"It was a lot more satisfying than beating Tennessee Tech," Benson said with a broad grin. That was the way Indiana began a 31-1 season in November, 1974.

Kent Benson has a volleyball spiker's look as Hoosiers, Bruins converge on a UCLA shot.

18

Knight's verdict: 'It was a pretty good start'

After the most ballyhooed opener two college basketball teams ever played, Knight was quiet and Bartow a little awed.

"I feel that Indiana proved they deserve their No. 1 ranking, without a doubt," Bartow said. "I think they've got four guys out there who will be first-round pro draft choices, and they're coached superbly.

"But I think there will be some teams in March that will be close to them."

UCLA?

"Yes, I would hope so," he said.

Knight's greatest satisfaction was with the Hoosiers' 39-38 edge in rebounding — an area he had pinpointed in pre-season as a prime target for improvement and one where the gigantic Bruins figured to have an edge.

"I thought Benson (14 rebounds) played the boards very well," Knight said, "and that was one of his major responsibilities."

May finished 15-for-24 after missing 5 of his first 6 shots. "I was a little tight," he conceded. "I couldn't get traction (a common complaint about the floor, laid over the home ice of hockey's St. Louis Blues)."

May called it "the biggest game I ever played in" and admitted to getting personally charged up for his head-to-head match with Johnson.

"He is about the closest thing to my size I've ever played against," said May (6-7, 218, to 6-7, 215 for Johnson). "And we play a lot alike. I was kinda fired up for this one. I knew he was one of the best. And he is. He's a hell of a player."

"I think you saw three all-America forwards out there," Bartow said of May, Johnson and Washington. "Scott May just had a super-brilliant night."

Buckner — "He's been our leader for four years," Knight said — extended Hoosier kudos a little further than Bartow.

"Scott was tremendous," he said. "And Tom Abernethy was steady — he always is. Kent did a terrific job on the boards, and you don't know how many times Bobby (Wilkerson) saved me out there tonight. You can just go down the line."

Buckner was the leader in IU's splurge opening the second half, when the Hoosiers took UCLA out of the game with a combination of superb defense and efficient offense.

"The second half, one of the things we did want to do was try to exploit Spillane's size (5-11)," said Buckner (6-3). "He's smaller than I am, and I'd like to think I'm a little stronger, too."

Defense continues to be the Hoosiers' chief weapon.

"I think any time anybody plays Indiana — with the type of pressure defense Indiana uses — and they don't meet the pressure patiently and smoothly, they're in serious trouble," Bartow said.

"Last season, I believe they were 31-1, so they had many teams that were in serious trouble from their pressure defense.

Gene Bartow — Tough start for the Man After the Legend.

INDIANA 84

	M	FG	FT	R	A	PF	TP
May,	39	15-24	3- 4	7	3	3	33
Abernethy, f	37	4- 9	2- 2	4	5	4	10
Benson, c	39	7-15	3- 4	14	4	3	17
Buckner, g	32	6-18	2- 3	6	1	4	14
Wilkerson, g	39	3- 8	0- 0	4	1	2	6
Crews	8	1- 1	0- 0	0	0	0	2
Valavicius	3	0- 0	0- 0	0	0	1	0
Bender	1	1- 1	0- 0	0	0	0	2
Wisman	1	0- 0	0- 0	0	0	0	0
Radford	1	0- 0	0- 0	0	0	0	0
Team				4			
Totals		37-76	10-13	39	14	17	84

UCLA 64

	M	FG	FT	R	A	PF	TP
Washington, f	40	12-21	4- 4	14	2	3	28
Johnson, f	35	7-14	4- 4	7	1	4	18
Drollinger, c	19	1- 3	0- 0	2	1	2	2
Spillane, g	26	3- 6	0- 0	3	2	4	6
McCarter, g	30	2-10	0- 0	3	3	0	4
Townsend	18	1- 5	0- 1	2	1	0	2
Olinde	10	0- 0	0- 0	1	0	1	0
Greenwood	8	1- 2	0- 0	2	0	1	2
Smith	6	0- 2	0- 0	0	0	3	0
Vroman	8	1- 1	0- 0	1	1	0	2
Team				3			
Totals		28-64	8- 9	38	11	18	64

SCORE BY HALVES

Indiana		36 48	— 84
UCLA		28 36	— 64

Errors: Indiana 16, UCLA 21

	FG	Pct.	FT	Pct.
Indiana	37-76	.487	10-13	.769
UCLA	28-64	.452	8- 9	.889

Officials: Irv Brown, Charles Fouty
Attendance: 19,115 (capacity)

"I thought we could relieve the pressure the first half because of certain things we were going to do. But we didn't, so we shot poorly."

Neither is countering pressure, via the full-court press that was a trademark of John Wooden's early championship teams at UCLA, the answer, Bartow said.

"No," he said, "because I think Indiana is going to handle most presses, with the great experience and the great leadership they have in Wilkerson and Buckner and the kind of shooting that May, Abernethy and Benson will do in the 10-to 12-foot area."

Bartow called the Hoosiers "a good team in mid-season form," but Knight didn't claim that, or want to. "We certainly hope we're a team that, as the season progresses, will improve," he said.

Neither Buckner nor Knight felt the Hoosiers were on an emotional crusade to prove that they, not UCLA, should have won the national championship last year.

"I hate to ruin your psychological ploy," Knight chided newsmen. "You guys sometimes forget that there is nothing as old as yesterday's news. We weren't interested in what happened last year, but we were more than somethat interested in what happened tonight."

"I can't say there was anything special about this one," Buckner insisted. "People keep asking me back home if we're going to be as good as we were last year. That's not one of our goals. This is this year, and we just want to play as well as this year's team can."

Knight's quick evaluation of progress toward that: "Well," he said, grinning, "it was a pretty good start."

Bob Knight — Things weren't all good

'I think we'll see them again' — Washington

Richard Washington and Marques Johnson, the rallying symbols for a UCLA basketball team that is emerging from post-Indiana trauma, see a rematch coming — and they plan to be ready.

"I think we'll see them again — Philadelphia or wherever," Washington said. "And then I'm pretty sure the outcome will be different. We'll give them a little bit better battle next time."

Philadelphia means the NCAA Final Four, and an IU-UCLA meeting would come in the semifinal round. That's too far away for Indiana pondering, but it's the focal point for the bruised Bruins after their 84-64 whipping.

The 6-11 Washington and 6-7 Johnson are the forwards new UCLA coach Gene Bartow calls "super." They may be better than that hackneyed word, and they'll likely bring their team back quickly — on a convenient string of 11 straight games liberally dotted with set-ups. UCLA confidence will be back, and so will UCLA.

The "UCLA mystique," though, might have been a Saturday night casualty. A Los Angeles writer, in questioning Johnson, suggested it was replaced even earlier — on the UCLA practice floor, perhaps — by an awe of Indiana.

"No, we weren't awed by them," Johnson corrected, bruised pride showing. "Not at all. I'm still not awed.

"I had a lot of respect for Indiana, but as far as us being awed . . . as a matter of fact, there's no question in my mind that we're going to have a lot better game next time around.

"I think the main thing that it showed out there was that we just weren't working together. Our offense was staggering at times — it wasn't really good defense pressuring us that much. A lot of it was that we just weren't moving the ball well. We had a lot of turnovers. The floor didn't help. It looked like an ice-skating match at times.

"Everything just added up and added up, and their points just added up and added up."

And the turnovers: How many came from the Indiana defense?

"It's really hard to say — I wouldn't say the majority of them," Johnson said. "I think the floor caused at least half of mine."

He indicated Bartow had described the Hoosier defense in physical terms in trying to prepare UCLA for the game.

"It's not as tough as the coaches had us thinking," Johnson said. "They were physical, but it wasn't a dirty-type thing where they were holding and pushing and elbowing. It was just a clean-type physical game.

"They were good defensively, but I think Kentucky, and Oregon in our own conference, are a lot more aggressive — where they just dive in knocking you down and everything."

Both Johnson and Washington said time is the answer for the Bruins, particularly in this, their first year under Bartow, the successor to John Wooden.

Star-stacking — all-Americans Kent Benson, Richard Washington, Scott May.

"It's not really that tough adapting," Johnson said, "but when you go against a team as good as Indiana, that has had four or five players playing together for four years, practicing together all the time, they can make you look a lot worse than a team that is not as good.

"They have real tough defense. They shot well around the perimeter — that's what hurt us. But once we get used to each other, I think we'll play a lot better ball. I know we will."

Washington pinned his hopes to similar thinking: "Indiana's been playing together a lot longer than we have. I think that was proven tonight.

"That's not saying they're not a good basketball team. They're definitely the best basketball team we've played since I've been at UCLA. Great balance. You make one mistake and, boom, they take advantage of it.

"I think setting the game up this early in the year was a mistake. No one could foresee Coach Wooden leaving.

"If they could, I think it was *definitely* a mistake."

> *"I didn't think it was anything special. I think there are a lot of things we can improve on."*
>
> — Bob Knight

Second-half pullaway: a developing trend?

Bob Knight says he expects it to take about 10 games for the true nature of this Indiana basketball team to evolve. The man has demonstrated an acquaintance with the requisites of a good team, so who's to quibble?

After two games, though, a pattern seems to be forming in which the Hoosiers can be pretty good some of the time but downright fearsome coming out for the second half.

What was true against the Soviet national team was true again when UCLA was the opposition. The first 10 minutes of play after the intermission in those two productions would stock a normal team's highlight film for a season and serve quite well as instructional films — without editing or commentary.

"I thought there were some things we did fairly well," Knight said, "and also some things that I didn't think we did very well.

"We'll sit back now, take a day or so, and evaluate what we didn't do and what we have to work on. This kind of game really gives you a good chance to do that."

Bartow, who watched the 1974-75 Hoosiers twice as the Illinois coach, said Indiana's play in this game didn't alter his opinions.

"I don't see much difference in them now and when I saw them in January and February," Bar-

"They beat Russia to prove
they're the best in the
world. And they beat UCLA
to prove they're the best
in the United States.
Now I'd like to see them prove
they're human and
have a bad game.

— Hugh Durham
Florida State coach

tow said. "They were great last year before Scott May got hurt.

"I think had Scott not gotten hurt, they'd have been in the finals in San Diego, and I think UCLA would have beaten them. Because I just think it was there for UCLA to win."

Bartow's belief in the pre-ordained won't sell in many Bloomington points, just as another of the instant reviews being offered nationally this morning seems questionable. Paul Attner of *The Washington Post* suggested an Indiana-UCLA rematch would find the Bruins better prepared because "it is always easier to play Indiana the second time around. Kentucky, which lost to Indiana by 24 in December last season, proved that in the NCAA tournament." Granted in Bloomington is that it was easier to play Indiana a second time when Scott May wasn't around, a point that Saturday night's performance would seem to have made too clear to have been missed.

It is true that few teams have practice squads available that are capable of simulating Indiana's motion offense and pressure defense, so a live look is educational — but that situation is true for any strong opponent in any sport.

The challenge the Hoosiers would appear to face at the moment is a refocus to normalcy. They have played two games and handled the two reigning champions of amateur basketball — Olympic champ Russia, NCAA king UCLA.

But Knight's application of former Oklahoma football coach Bud Wilkinson's challenge to "play to potential" every time out, however good the opponent, is one carryover from 1974-75 that he is sure to seek. Working against that challenge appeared to be the key that removed peaks and valleys from last year's season to a downright wondrous degree.

An upcoming schedule that parades NCAA hopefuls Florida State, Notre Dame, Kentucky and the like probably guarantees no refocusing problems at all. Wilkinson, Knight and a mature team with its own grasp of realities won't hurt, either.

No. 2 Terps convinced speed would hurt IU

The view from No. 2 — Maryland — was: impressed, but not overwhelmed.

"I watched the game like a scout," Maryland guard Maurice (Mo) Howard told Dave Israel of the *Washington Star*.

"I was impressed with Indiana's defense. It gave no layups, and they had aggressive rebounding that didn't let UCLA get any second shots.

"They were consistent on offense and on defense. They look only for the good shots. May scored a lot of points and shot real well, but virtually every shot he took was uncontested."

Howard's conclusion:

"We're a lot quicker than they are, and they're a lot bigger than we are. That means we might be able to catch them in transition for easy baskets."

Brad Davis, the point guard in Lefty Driesell's three-guard offense (all-American John Lucas the third), felt the Terps' utilization of three small men would hurt IU.

"Wilkerson is tall, but he couldn't keep up with the quickness of Lucas or Mo on defense like he did against the UCLA guards," Davis said. "And Abernethy would be hurt by whichever one Wilkerson didn't cover."

Israel's dry post-quote comment: "It is unlikely that Wilkerson and Abernethy will be hurt by anyone this year, but it is also unlikely that Indiana is as unbeatable as it looked against UCLA. Come March, Maryland and UCLA, as well as Marquette, Tennessee, North Carolina and Notre Dame could be competitive with the Hoosiers."

Lots of teams would have to figure on any "could be" list — and not all for March delivery. If Tennessee belongs, so must Michigan, a one-point loser on the Vols' home court Saturday. There's plenty of time for others to surface, too. Happens every year.

Abernethy outreaches Benson as UCLA's Drollinger watches.

Indiana 83, Florida State 59

Long ago, Bob Knight convinced Indiana basketball zealots that defense is not a nasty word. And now, it's an inadequate word.

Defense connotes wagons in a circle, at best a strike back after being struck. Knight redefined it, IU-style, a few weeks ago: "We just consider it offense without the ball." Florida State learned Monday night the man wasn't kidding.

The Hoosiers stormed at the Seminoles with "How dare you!" outrage each time one committed the gaffe of possessing the basketball. 'Twas done in innocence. The visitors thought rules of the game said it belonged to them after Indiana scores. That part's been redefined, too, in Knight's basketball version of newspeak.

"I'm glad this isn't like baseball," Florida State coach Hugh Durham quipped. "I'd hate to play these guys in a three-game homestand."

The opening tip threw his Seminoles into a hostile backdrop of red, from every direction a blur of white coming their way to slash at the basketball until it was removed with surgical neatness and no blood nor pain. There were those in the 17,526 who filled Market Square Arena Monday night who will pull out the program from this 83-59 Hoosier victory in some far-off day and tell a wide-eyed grandchild, "You should have seen that team play defense."

There will be other programs and other witnesses, other arenas and other victims, because Knight at times seems to be getting close to the ultimate defensive weapon — one icily efficient but raging in emotion, schooled in his demanding techniques and disciplined to outwill humanly tailoffs with pride. Innate, but instilled.

"I knew they only had 6 points kinda late in the game," Hoosier guard Quinn Buckner said, adding with a grin: "But coach Knight doesn't settle for that."

The game was 12 minutes along and Indiana was 18 ahead when Florida State finally got off 6. It had been stuck there for 5½ minutes, and it hadn't been easy getting that far.

Florida State — tall, supple and quick — plays defense, too, and for a time it looked like a game of first-basket-wins. The Seminoles missed their first five shots and Indiana its first seven, but IU was getting them more frequently and finally got one to stick on a close-in Kent Benson hook shot with 3:13 gone.

By then, Florida State already had four turnovers.

Buckner followed with two baskets (one a layup after a steal) and Scott May one in a 70-second spurt that opened a 10-2 lead and drove Durham to a time out. "I would say it was kind of a perilous 10-2 lead," Knight said. "It could have been theirs if they hadn't started off shooting poorly."

Really, it was never THAT bad.

The peril quickly vanished. Buckner jammed in six shots in a row; the May machine went to work and spewed out 14 points; and Benson exploited the middle area for 12 in a first half that, for all of their offense, was memorable for the Hoosiers' defense.

There was a beauty to it, five-man orchestration that blended the sensational and the subtle — steals and interceptions with the slight but dissuading moves that checked advances and created mistakes.

It was all there in this one, stretching beyond five men to include nine players rushed into the assault to guarantee no let-up, no gasping for air.

The pressure stayed on until the Seminoles were thoroughly cracked at halftime, 47-20. The peak was 79-41 — this against a veteran team used to winning and harboring its own NCAA tourney hopes.

"Our defense is moving in the direction we want to go," Knight said. "If we have an objective, it's to be as be as good as we can possibly be defensively."

May finished with 24 points and Benson, hitting 10 of 15 shots, had 22. Buckner also reached double figures with 15 points, plus 6 assists, while Bob Wilkerson had 3 of the Hoosiers' 11 steals and Tom Abernethy (9 rebounds) combined with Benson (9) and May (11) to lead IU's 43-37 control of the boards.

Indiana shot .500 despite its poor start. The Hoosiers even provided Knight with ample fodder for lecturing with 26 turnovers, 16 the last half.

"We got to playing kinda ratty at times," Knight said. "I don't care who we've got out there, I just don't like to see breakdowns like we had at the end of the ball game."

By then, they were affordable, although the committers may find that point argued in Hoosier practices this week.

23

Pressure game puts IU bench in spotlight

Indiana's Achilles heel is supposed to be its bench, but Knight indicated an intent to use his reserves prominently, not bashfully, in battering Florida State.

By the time the game was 10 minutes old, Knight had used nine players. He infused those nine in a multitude of ways with 11 substitutions in the first half — more than he has ever made at Indiana for less than humanitarian reasons.

"We had planned to move people around," Knight said, noting that starting guard Wilkerson had been bothered with flu the last few days and "regardless of what we had wanted to do, we would have had to replace him every three or four minutes.

"But we just wanted to try to play as many as we could to keep the flow of the game going as we wanted it. We're going to have to do that if we're going to be able to sustain what we want to do defensively."

Implicit in it all is a command to hold nothing back when on the floor, with fresh players available to dash in and keep the pressure on when a rest is needed.

Guards Buckner and Wilkerson have the most taxing job, and theirs is the area where pressure means most and relief is most required.

Senior Jim Crews, first man off the bench in the UCLA opener, was first in again Monday, along with Wayne Radford as Buckner and Wilkerson came out. Rich Valavicius spelled Abernethy a minute later, and a third guard, Jim Wisman, returned with Buckner after Quinn's four-minute rest.

Knight blended the nine in combinations that included Abernethy replacing Benson in the middle, and the defensive pressure he seeks was maintained throughout.

Greg Grady, Florida State's three-year starter at center, said every Seminole watched Indiana's nationally-televised 84-64 victory over UCLA.

"It was like homework," he said. They arrived in Indiana "feeling rambunctious," Grady said. "Coming here and playing the No. 1 team, you're bound to be.

"Basically, we just wanted to play the game like we would play against anyone else. But when we got out there, everything was different. We had the same plan and the same ideology, but we couldn't make it work. They played the way they wanted to play, and we didn't.

"That's why they're No. 1. Basically, they just play the game. No tricks. Just the basics."

Another third-year man, Zach Perkins, got the defensive job on IU's May, work he prepared for by watching May's 33-point effort against UCLA.

"I just concentrated on trying to keep the ball away from him," Perkins said. "Obviously, I had trouble doing that." May scored 24 points.

May was standing close by when Buckner, talking with reporters, floated a kidding tribute his way.

"We kept trying to slow our offense down," Buckner said. "One of the things we emphasized the second half was to get four passes before we shot. We *always* emphasize that, but we made a particular point of it then. If we get a good shot, we try to get a better one.

"But we've got this one character on our team who's pretty good, and he gets open so quickly it's hard to do that. When he hits 'em, we don't argue," Buckner said, laughing.

May thought he was cooperating in the discretion. "A couple of times I thought I was open," he said. "But The Man said four or five passes, and I've gotta go with that."

Knight was happy with that phase of the production. "I felt we had Buckner, Benson and May really doing well the things that they do best," he said.

INDIANA 83

	M	FG	FT	R	A	PF	TP
May, f	31	10-19	4- 5	11	5	1	24
Abernethy, f	27	1- 3	1- 2	9	2	1	3
Benson, c	27	10-15	2- 2	9	1	3	22
Buckner, g	25	7-15	1- 2	3	6	3	15
Wilkerson, g	22	3- 8	0- 0	3	4	2	6
Crews	10	2- 2	2- 2	0	0	2	6
Radford	19	0- 0	0- 0	2	2	1	0
Valavicius	13	1- 4	0- 1	0	0	1	2
Wisman	16	0- 2	1- 2	1	1	1	1
Bender	5	0- 1	2- 2	0	0	0	2
Roberson	4	0- 0	0- 0	1	0	0	0
Haymore	2	0	0- 0	1	0	1	0
Eells	2	1- 1	0- 0	0	1	0	2
Team				3			
Totals		35-70	13-18	43	22	16	83

FLORIDA STATE 59

	M	FG	FT	R	A	PF	TP
Perkins, f	21	1- 4	0- 0	5	2	4	2
Thompson, f	26	3- 8	0- 0	7	2	2	6
Grady, c	36	1- 5	0- 1	3	1	1	2
Warren, g	30	4-13	4- 6	4	2	1	12
Smalls, g	27	4- 9	2- 3	1	2	3	10
Smith	19	0- 0	0- 0	1	0	1	0
Davis	19	5- 7	0- 1	2	1	0	10
Harris	20	4- 7	1- 2	4	1	3	9
Allen	5	4- 7	0- 0	0	0	2	8
Team				10			
Totals		26-60	7-13	37	11	17	59

SCORE BY HALVES

Florida State . . . . 20 39 — 59
Indiana. . . . . 47 36 — 83
Errors: Florida State 27, Indiana 26

	FG	Pct.	FT	Pct.
Florida State	26-60	.433	7-13	.538
Indiana	35-70	.500	13-18	.722

Officials: Robert Showalter and Bill Henderson
Attendance: 17,526 (capacity)

'They'd do quite well in the ABA' - Durham

After watching No. 1-ranked Indiana roll over his team, Hugh Durham of Florida State was only partly kidding when he said of the Hoosiers: "They'd do quite well in the ABA. Come to think of it, they might even be the best team in the league."

Durham kept the superlatives coming as he tried to reconstruct the reasons why has team had been "embarrassed."

"Benson is, in my opinion, the best center in the nation," he said. "May is probably one of three or four best forwards in the country, and if Bobby thinks May is the best, then he's probably right.

"You just can't say enough about Buckner, either. He knows his role and he's as good a running guard and floor general as you'll find. That's the kind of guy you want to show off when you're recruiting — all that individual talent and yet he submerges himself completely in the greater glory of the team."

The maze of blocks Hoosiers set for each other sometimes goes unnoticed in the bleachers, observable only in the amazing frequency of open shots.

Opposing coaches notice, though. On a night when everyone else talked of the Hoosiers' defense, Durham said, "Their movement and aggressiveness on offense is really incredible. I got caught in picks twice, and I wasn't even on the floor."

Florida State outscored IU by three points in the last 20 minutes, but Durham wasn't kidding himself.

"We didn't outplay Indiana, the No. 1 team in the country," he said. "We just outscored the people that Indiana put on the floor in the second half."

Durham paused for a moment then and smiled. "I was very appreciative that Knight decided to give those starters a much-deserved rest."

Durham said it's difficult to compare this IU team to the UCLA squad his Seminoles lost to in the final game of the 1972 NCAA tournament

"UCLA was more of a finesse team, while Indiana is an incredibly physical team," he said. "That's a compliment, not criticism. Indiana puts so much pressure on you that they just completely intimidate you."

But Durham did see one definite correlation. "John Wooden was a great coach," he said. "So is Bobby Knight. With talent like Indiana's, you're going to win a lot of games. And with a coach like Bobby Knight, you're not going to get caught in any upsets."

Durham believes there are some college teams in the country this year with the talent to beat the Hoosiers, "but they can't go out and try to play against Indiana's set defense," he said. "You're going to have to be able to run with them and rebound with them. We couldn't, but we're not going to slither back to our hotel and slink home. We gave 'em a good fight."

Tom Abernethy powers inside Herbie Allen for a layup.

"You know it's going to be an intense game on their part. If you don't go out there with equal intensity, you've lost before the game even starts, because they will play that way.

— Hugh Durham
Florida State coach

25

Indiana 63, Notre Dame 60

"Super-team" talk went temporarily out of fashion Thursday night, but Indiana had enough points and poise to escape with a 63-60 victory over Notre Dame before 17,639 at Assembly Hall.

"It was a game that was kind of a struggle for both teams," said Indiana coach Bob Knight.

"And I guess we just outstruggled them."

It's a fair summation, because the Hoosiers didn't outshoot or outrebound the Irish, who pulled off another rare achievement against a latterday Indiana team: a comeback when apparently dead and buried.

The Hoosiers' one assertive stretch of a long, hard evening shot them out front, 51-37, with 11 minutes to go. "Usually when Indiana has a 14-point lead here, it ends up being a 34-point lead," Notre Dame coach Digger Phelps said. "You've got to hand it to our kids for not quitting."

And Knight did. "They deserve a tremendous degree of credit," Knight said, "because over about a three-minute period we were really playing well. But then we made some mistakes and they capitalized on them and really played well down the stretch."

The Irish needed only a couple of shaky minutes by Indiana to strip away the firm command the sudden lead gave IU. Freshman forward Bruce Flowers scored twice in 11 seconds, the second time on an interception with the Irish in a full-court zone press, to move Notre Dame within 53-50 with 8:11 to play.

Those were eight tense minutes.

The Irish never caught up, and never got the ball when they had a chance to, but all-American Adrian Dantley's rebound basket cut the IU lead to 59-58 with two minutes left.

The Hoosiers went into a stall — and survived a major scare when 6-7 Bob Wilkerson dribbled the ball for five seconds with the 6-8 Flowers on him closely enough to get a jump-ball call with 1:26 to play. Tom Abernethy ran down Wilkerson's tip, and the Hoosiers held on again until May hit both halves of a clutch one-and-one with 37 seconds left.

Not the recommended way, but Wayne Radford controls a bouncing ball.

26

When Abernethy drew a charging foul from the determined Dantley eight seconds later, the Hoosiers had the ball, a 61-58 lead and only 29 seconds to kill.

But the cozy feeling left in a hurry. Grabbed by Flowers at 0:23, Quinn Buckner was awarded two free throws. Both missed, and on the second, Kent Benson was called for jumping on the back of Notre Dame's Dave Batton.

Batton hit two free throws, and it was a one-point lead with the ball at the Irish end. However, the Hoosiers cracked the Irish press, and at 0:11, Buckner was back at the foul line in the same situation — two free throws after an intentional foul. This time, he flipped both in, and the Hoosiers at last were in solid shape.

Buckner saw nothing surprising in his successes. "I thought the first two should have gone in," he said. "When I went up the second time, I had the same confidence."

"Sometimes you get the bear, and sometimes the bear gets you," the relieved Knight said. "Statistically, Notre Dame has all the better of it, so I've got to be very pleased with our guys because we came out of the struggle on top.

"Notre Dame has always been a very fine basketball team, and particularly so in games that have some significance."

It was a game that had similarities to the Irish-IU game at Assembly Hall two years ago, the last one Indiana lost at home. Neither team shot well in the first half; errors were frequent. But the difference was that this time, Indiana was the team barely staying ahead and Notre Dame was doing the chasing.

Dantley made what Knight called "two great plays" in the first minute of the game to get Notre Dame ahead, 5-2. Abernethy had opened the game guarding Dantley, but Knight quickly shifted Wilkerson onto him, and Dantley got only one more field goal the first half.

Still, Indiana was down 16-13 and the Irish had the ball four more times with a chance to widen the lead before May hit two free throws and Buckner scored a fast-break basket for an Indiana lead.

Four different Hoosiers contributed to an eight-point streak that helped the Hoosiers to a 29-24 halftime lead ... though the Indiana shooting figure at halftime was a poor .286.

Notre Dame outscored the Hoosiers, 8-2, opening the second half to get ahead again. Indiana's charge didn't really begin until Benson, flu-bugged and scoreless up to then, stole an in-bounds pass in center court and bolted in for a layup that unleashed the noise the packed house had been holding back.

The next 2½ minutes were vintage stuff for Hoosier-lovers.

Benson and May did almost all the scoring as the lead grew to 51-37 — the embattled Phelps drawing a double-technical foul in the process and May converting it into three points by hitting one of two free throws and a close-in hook.

That was the highwater mark as Notre Dame scored on eight straight possessions to tighten things for the nervous finish.

"I really thought our defense was pretty good throughout the Notre Dame game. It enabled us to win the game."

— Bob Knight

May, who had a poor shooting night (7 for 19), led everybody with 25 points and 9 rebounds. Buckner had 16 points, 8 rebounds and 4 assists.

Dantley, held under 20 points only 4 times in 29 games last year, totaled 19 — Abernethy doing the prime defensive work on him the second half after Wilkerson got into foul trouble the first half (3).

Knight, who searched out Dantley to shake his hand after the game, said, "He played as well as he did against us last year (when he scored 32 points). He only took 17 shots, and I think without any question he is more involved with directing the offense this year than he was before."

Indiana was outrebounded, 48-42, and the Hoosiers' .368 shooting average was their lowest in 55 games. Notre Dame didn't excel, either, shooting .393 and outerring the Hoosiers, 19-12.

INDIANA 63

	M	FG	FT	R	A	PF	TP
May, f	39	7-19	11-13	9	1	4	25
Abernethy, f	33	3-4	1-2	2	1	2	7
Benson, c	34	3-10	1-3	6	1	4	7
Buckner, g	40	5-15	6-11	8	4	1	16
Wilkerson, g	28	2-5	0-3	4	0	3	4
Radford	2	0-0	0-0	0	0	0	0
Crews	19	1-4	2-2	2	2	3	4
Valavicius	5	0-0	0-0	1	0	0	0
Team				10			
Totals		21-57	21-34	42	9	17	63

NOTRE DAME 60

	M	FG	FT	R	A	PF	TP
Dantley, f	40	8-17	3-4	8	1	4	19
Knight, f	17	2-2	0-0	2	0	1	4
Batton, c	26	4-10	2-2	5	0	4	10
Paterno, g	26	3-9	4-6	5	1	1	10
Martin, g	20	0-5	0-0	1	2	5	0
Flowers	23	3-5	3-4	5	0	5	9
Laimbeer	14	2-5	0-0	6	0	2	4
Williams	18	0-5	0-0	2	2	3	0
Rencher	6	1-2	0-0	0	1	0	2
Carpenter	11	1-1	0-0	2	2	2	2
Team				12			
Totals		24-61	12-16	48	9	27	60

SCORE BY HALVES

Notre Dame . . . . 24 36 — 60
Indiana. . . . . 29 34 — 63
Errors: Notre Dame 19, Indiana 12

	FG	Pct.	FT	Pct.
Notre Dame	24-61	.393	12-16	.750
Indiana	21-57	.368	21-34	.618

Officials: Phil Robinson, George Solomon and Richard Weiler
Attendance: 17,639 (capacity)

"They're vicious. They're unbelievable the way they go to the boards. I think it's going to be a classical game . . . a super game for college basketball."

— Digger Phelps
Notre Dame coach

'A kid named Buckner'
IU's only edge — Knight

Amid some lecturing and some chiding, Knight delivered a blunt analysis of the shaky Hoosier victory.

"We survived this game for one reason," Knight said, "and that is that we have a kid named Buckner on our team. If we don't have him, we're not even in the game. He is the sole reason we won.

"He directed what we were doing. He played tough. He played smart.

"There has never been a time when Buckner's leadership — which is the best I've ever seen in a player I've coached — was more in evidence than it was tonight."

Buckner heard his coach's words relayed and switched the subject as deftly as he switches hands on a dribble. He spoke in a dressing room that was short on victory talk — an air of not defeat, but chagrin hanging. Buckner pierced it.

"We played against a great team," he said. "We're not happy with the way we played, but we won. What we have to do now is use it as a learning experience. Usually you say that after you lost a game. I think that's the way we look at this one."

The lessons learned, Knight suggested, should involve the virtues of concentration and defense.

"This is a team that has to be better mentally than any team I've ever had if it's going to reach its full potential," Knight said.

"You've got to learn to read a team. You've got to realize that this year we don't have Steve Green in one spot and John Laskowski in another and Scott May someplace else — three exceptional shooters.

"So our concentration and defensive play have got to make up for it."

"We took some shots we didn't need at that particular time, and that showed a lack of awareness of what we have to do. We committed some fouls that bothered me, from the standpoint that there wasn't any concentration there."

Knight obviously has chafed at some of the bouquets thrown at the Hoosiers already this year — "awesome" . . . "vicious" . . . "would do quite well in the ABA."

"Tonight we were a team that shot 21-for-57 — 37 per cent. You're not a great team when you shoot 37 per cent.

"All I read about is how physical we are. We got outrebounded (48-42).

"You can't separate one team from another at this level. They all have big players and they all have good players. They all work hard, and they're all well-coached. No team is just going to pound the others.'

Why, Knight was asked, would two teams ranked in the Top 10 each shoot under 40 per cent in a showdown?

"There weren't a great many shots taken out

there without a hand in the face," he said. "Both teams were aggressive on defense, and, because of that, nobody but Dantley really got off to a good shooting start, so everybody got a little tight, perhaps.

"I think you saw two teams that work hard and two teams that really like to beat each other. But I think you could see from the reaction on the floor after the game that the kids know each other and like each other, just as Digger and I are good friends. I have tremendous respect for the job he does in getting a team ready for a game."

Buckner felt the Hoosiers got into their playing groove only once all night — after Benson stole a pass and converted it into a layup that sparked the Hoosers' pullaway to a 51-37 lead.

"Bennie was having a tough night," Buckner said. "When he did that (the steal), he started loosening up, and I think it helped the rest of us, too. Bennie's capable of doing a lot of things other guys his size can't.

Abernethy, a native South Bender who got a long-term assignment on Dantley for the second straight year, lost the job in the first minute of play when Dantley stung him for five quick points.

But, most of the last half, Abernethy was on Dantley, including the time when Dantley, hurrying to get a shot away with 29 seconds left and the Irish down by three, was called for charging.

"He spins a lot, and I just happened to be in the right spot," Abernethy said.

When the whistle blew, "I knew it couldn't be on me," Abernethy said. "It could have been one of those situations where no foul is called at all. And, I did a little acting, I think."

'Know I can play better,' dismayed Dantley says

In the quiet Notre Dame dressing room, Dantley was, at once, both proud and embarrassed.

He sat clad only in his trunks, his fingers idly crushing little dents into a soft-drink can, his chest muscles rippling ever so slightly as he talked.

"I had a hell of a night with Wilkerson on me," he said. "I got two quick fouls on him, then that was it. I had open shots, but they wouldn't go in."

Dantley, averaging 29 going into the game, realized he wasn't the only player on the floor who didn't sparkle to everyone's expectations.

"Benson might have had a bad game," he said. "I *know* I did. I know Benson can play much better, and I *certainly* know I can put on a better performance than I did today."

Scoreless in the first half, Benson finished with seven points and six rebounds against Irish centers Batton and freshman Bill Laimbeer.

"He's a great player," Batton said, "so I got a little more up to play against him than some other guys.

"All week long we worked on their offense. I just knew where he was going to be all the time. His

A time for silence

game is to go to the ball. So I just waited for him."

Benson was the key man, though, when Indiana put on its second-half spurt that opened a 14-point lead. "His shots started going in," Batton said. "He started playing the game he's capable of."

Phelps said the three freshmen he used — Laimbeer, Flowers and Bernard Rencher — "are going to help us before the year is over. I thought Flowers (9 points, 5 rebounds) did a super job tonight."

"Part of our plan was to keep May and Benson from scoring," Flowers said. "And to box out. We had signs all over the locker room saying to box out. We did a pretty good job of it."

Neither Flowers nor Phelps was outwardly perturbed at losing. "I'm not worried about polls, I just want to get a bid," said Phelps. "I just want a bid to the (NCAA) tournament."

"It really comes down to March," said Flowers. "This is not really that big a deal. March is the time.

"I think we'll get them (in a rematch). I think it will be a little different next time."

All-Americans Adrian Dantley, Scott May tangle

Indiana 77, Kentucky 68

LOUISVILLE, DECEMBER 15, 1975

Indiana was good and lucky Monday night, so college basketball's version of the No. 1 gun survived another shoot-out with a frisky young challenger.

The lucky part was the way the Hoosiers scrambled to get into overtime with Kentucky. The good part was that, once there, they finally asserted the command that had eluded them for 40 frustrating minutes and they put the Wildcats down, 77-68.

It took an indiscreet shot by Larry Johnson, one of the Kentucky heroes, and a fluke basket by Kent Benson to pull the Hoosiers back from Boot Hill.

Johnson tried an off-balance, driving shot from about five feet with 1:10 to go in regulation time and Kentucky ahead, 62-60. It missed. "We didn't want to take that shot," Kentucky coach Joe Hall winced. "We wanted to keep the offense moving, try for the inside shot."

"I had confidence I would make it," Johnson said. "I've taken shots like that before."

A Scott May jump shot tied the game, but Rick Robey, another Wildcat standout, untied it with a quick inside move and basket at 0:29.

Quinn Buckner — just passin' by Truman Claytor

A couple of quick passes inside the 1-3-1 Kentucky zone defense gave Tom Abernethy "an opening to the basket so I took it." He shot from four feet, but Robey came flying across to get a hand on the ball before it could get to the basket — goaltending, in IU eyes, but not in the officials'. "I was jumping up about the goaltending," IU coach Bob Knight admitted. "I almost missed the tip-in."

It wasn't one to miss. Benson, partially blocked out on the play, stuck out a hand barely more than waist high — primarily to bat the ball in the air and give him a chance to go up after it for a tip-in. "I hit it with my full hand, right in the palm," Benson said. The ball arched high in the air and swished neatly through with nine seconds left, tying the game, 64-64.

Getting to the overtime was a lift for IU, a body blow to Kentucky which had a precious victory in its hands. The difference showed quickly as the Hoosiers coolly and precisely put Kentucky away.

They had things under control before the first minute of the overtime was gone. Benson broke the tie with two free throws, then twice in a row swept off defensive rebounds to set up Indiana scores — by Abernethy on a close-in jump shot and Quinn Buckner on a breakaway after he took an uncharacteristically long outlet pass from Benson at midcourt and outsprinted Kentucky freshman Truman Claytor to the goal for a layup.

Suddenly, it was 70-64 with 4:04 to go, and the Wildcats never got closer than that the rest of the way as IU poise produced an error-free possession game.

Benson and May, who shared game honors with 27 points apiece, did all of Indiana's scoring as the Hoosiers moved to a 17-7 lead in the first six minutes.

It was 23-11 after 10 minutes, Kentucky guards Johnson and Claytor breaking down repeatedly in backcourt under pressure from Buckner and May — May the surprise assignment on Claytor while Bob Wilkerson took on high-scoring forward Jack Givens.

At a time when it could have taken charge, Indiana missed four potential free-throw points, committed two turnovers and missed a couple of good shots, and that was all the encouragement Kentucky needed to work back into the game.

It was 32-24 with 1:40 to go in the half when a Kentucky blitz cut the edge to 34-32 by halftime and made irreverent rascals out of the young Wildcats.

Indiana eased out again to 48-42 as May stuck in three straight jump shots, but sophomores Givens and James Lee ignited the Wildcats again by refusing to quit on the Wildcat offensive board until Lee stuck in a basket on Kentucky's fifth shot.

The effect of that flurry was newfound Wildcat zeal. Robey roamed in free for an uncontested rebound basket seconds later to cut the IU lead to 54-53 with 8:23 to go. May, firing blanks by then in an 0-for-7 streak, had open invitations to score on most of the tries. But he tried to force one with the one-point lead and Givens (1) leaped high to block the shot, (2) recovered the ball along the sidelines near midcourt, and (3) eluded an attempted cutoff by Wilkerson to get the layup that put Kentucky ahead, 55-54.

After May's sixth and seventh misses of his dry spell, Claytor and Lee shot Kentucky into a 60-56 lead. But another UK upset wasn't to be.

"We hurt ourselves with mistakes," Hall said, "but I'm totally pleased with the effort, the courageousness.

"The tip by Benson had to be the luckiest I've ever seen."

Abernethy (10 points) was the only Hoosier besides May and Benson to make double figures. Buckner had a tough time with fouls and shooting in regulation time, but he directed the overtime production smoothly and scored five of his seven points in it.

Givens had 20 points and Johnson 16, and Givens (12 rebounds) and Lee (10) gave Kentucky 47-40 board control. Benson led Indiana with 14 rebounds.

INDIANA 77

	M	FG	FT	R	A	PF	TP
May, f	45	11-28	5- 8	8	0	3	27
Abernethy, f	42	4- 5	2- 4	7	2	4	10
Benson, c	45	11-19	5- 7	14	1	4	27
Buckner, g	24	3- 7	1- 4	4	4	4	7
Wilkerson, g	44	2- 7	0- 0	5	4	1	4
Wisman	1	0- 0	0- 0	0	0	0	0
Valavicius	17	1- 1	0- 0	1	0	0	2
Crews	7	0- 1	0- 0	0	1	0	0
Team				1			
Totals		32-68	13-23	40	12	16	77

KENTUCKY 68

	M	FG	FT	R	A	PF	TP
Givens, g	31	9-21	2- 2	12	1	1	20
Robey, f	23	3- 5	5- 7	8	0	4	11
Hall, c	15	0- 1	0- 0	3	0	2	0
Johnson, g	41	8-15	0- 0	7	3	2	16
Claytor, f	41	2-12	0- 0	0	3	2	4
Phillips	15	3- 5	3- 5	4	0	1	9
Lee	33	3- 9	0- 0	10	1	3	6
Casey	7	0- 3	0- 0	0	1	2	0
Fowler	13	1- 2	0- 0	1	0	1	2
Haskins	5	0- 1	0- 0	0	0	0	0
Warford	1	0- 1	0- 0	1	0	0	0
Team				1			
Totals		29-75	10-14	47	9	18	68

SCORE BY PERIODS

Indiana	34	30	13 —	77
Kentucky	32	32	4 —	68

Errors: Indiana 11, Kentucky 16

	FG	Pct.	FT	Pct.
Indiana	32-68	.471	13-23	.565
Kentucky	29-75	.387	10-14	.714

Officials: Jim Bain and Burrell Crowell
Attendance: 16,615

So much for hatred; Knight visits, hails UK

Stern and unswerving, Knight strode out of the winning dressing room and headed for the losers' on an errand of tribute.

The losing team was Kentucky, supposedly high on Indiana's hate list. After Knight left the Wildcats, Johnson said, "He told us we really played hard and aggressive. He wished us good luck and said he was really glad he didn't have to run into us again in their conference season."

"I thought it was a very nice touch," Hall said.

So much for hatred. The rivalry that was refought before 16,615 fans was a college basketball showpiece, a classic not so much for brilliant or sensational play as for superb competitiveness. Effort. Desire. It was not what oddsmakers thought it would be. It was what college basketball ought to be, and Knight could have been expected to recognize it.

"I thought they played a very fine basketball game," Knight said of the Kentuckians. "They play hard. Since Joe's been there, I think they've always played really hard, and there isn't anything that I respect more than that."

He was not, however, an apologetic winner. "The thing people have just got to understand — and I hope they'll listen pretty soon — is that there are a lot of good basketball teams in America," he said. "We played one tonight, and we won on what is really their court.

"I've got to feel very pleased that our kids beat a damned good basketball team away from home. This team (Kentucky) plays as hard as anybody we play. By the same token, we've got some kids who play that way, too."

It seems to have come as a shock in some places that this Indiana team has showed itself to be something less than unbeatable. Meanwhile, at a time when gentlemen like Hall and Notre Dame's Digger Phelps publicly bemoan the ruggedness of their schedules, this same Indiana team has gone 4-0 against the toughest start of all — UCLA, Florida State, Notre Dame and Kentucky. It's also the No. 1-ranked team in the nation, by unanimous vote of United Press International's coaches' panel — and by that string of victories alone, not by past deeds or reputation or anything done off-court, it deserves the ranking . . . because nobody else has done more.

And it could be beaten Friday, or Saturday, or both times and some times in the future, because the tag of No. 1 doesn't convey invincibility — it guarantees a whole long line of Notre Dames and Kentuckies out there ahead, primed to fire their very best shot when No. 1, Indiana, is the target.

This Indiana team does have some developing to do, hardly an uncommon state for mid-December. Twice in a row, it has squandered solid leads that might have been springboards to more

"That (Kentucky's 92-90 victory over Indiana) was last season and that ended there. We don't play last season's games this season. We lost, we made no excuses, and that is that. This is a new season and we're trying to play it as best we can."

— Bob Knight

Kent Benson — A Big Red snuff

Bob Wilkerson — 'Good job of running things'

decisive victories. The missing element is not a "killer instinct" but what most commonly passes for that: long periods of concentration that stretch bursts into blowouts . . . if the other team isn't matching the concentration. What results if it is is a very good game. One winner. One loser.

There is no shortage of desire showing in the Hoosiers. Benson scored 27 points and wrote his night off as a disaster. "I wasn't satisfied with my offensive movement inside," he said, "and I wasn't blocking out on rebounds the way I should.

"So many things went wrong, and maybe some things we did do right we might have been over-conscious of. In the overtime, we just got our concentration back and went out and played the way we should have been playing all the time."

"The thing I was most disappointed with was our defensive board play," Knight said. "You get them to take a bad shot or two and then they wind up getting the basket anyway, on the boards." Forest fires aren't as irritating to Smoky the Bear as that situation is to Knight.

May brought out the same word Benson did to describe the rebounding problem. "I would call it a lack of concentration," he said. "The guys inside were trying to screen their guys off, but that's not enough. You can't just block out; you've got to go after it yourself."

Buckner, who picked up four quick fouls and spent lots of observation time on the bench

("That's a nice way of saying it," Buckner said, grinning), said Kentucky "crashed the boards really hard."

Buckner had other observations. He came back on the court when May was shaking his head and mired in an 0-for-7 late-game shooting slump. He made a point of talking to May immediately. "I just wanted him to keep trying," Buckner said. "You could see his stroke was right."

It is fashionable now to say that zoning Indiana is the answer, because the Hoosiers aren't blessed with lots of good outside shooters. Overlooked is that Knight never has attacked a zone with long shots . . . and that, when the Hoosiers did destroy the Kentucky zone in the overtime, they didn't do it with bombs. More Buckner bench-notes: "We weren't penetrating very well. Bobby (Wilkerson, who spent most of the night as the Hoosiers' point man and earned Knight's praise) did a good job of running things, but we had to get some other penetration into the zone."

In the overtime, Knight said, "we got a little better movement and got the ball inside. And we were able to do some things then to pull them out that you can't do unless you're ahead. I may have made a mistake midway in the second half when we were up seven and I didn't bring them out. But we were getting the shots we wanted so we stuck with it."

"At times we got a little bit sloppy, but you

always tend to think negatively — what you didn't do or what you wanted to do but didn't. You forget the other guy may have been doing something right. Kentucky did a really good job on its offensive board and that got them back in the game — that and their fast break. We got caught with that a couple times."

Another fear the panicky raise is that the Hoosiers are a one- or two-man offense, that May's 0-for-7 stretch came because he felt he had to deliver and consequently pressed.

"I feel like I'm one of the guys who has to make the *play*," May said, "whether it's making a pass or a shot or a rebound or a steal, whatever it takes. I don't think I have to get the basket.

"I did let it (missing) bother me in the Notre Dame game, so this time I just kept telling myself, 'Forget it.' I just wanted to concentrate on the hole and go up and stick it in. I thought they were on target. They just didn't go in.

"Then I hit one and that got my confidence back. That's all shooting is — confidence."

Interesting point. And another, especially for the worrisome: May didn't take a shot in the overtime when Indiana hummed away from Kentucky.

"I think experience paid off in the overtime," Johnson said. "They kept calm. They kept banging away and got quick baskets."

And won, over a good and spirited rival. Wasn't easy. Seldom is.

Bob Knight, SEC official Burrell Crowell chat one-sidedly

Eventually, IU experience made the difference — Hall

The difference between Kentucky's regulation-game success and its overtime problems on defense was basically a matter of veteran Indiana finally catching youthful Kentucky in costly mistakes, Hall decided.

Some sharp passes snipped through the UK zone that had bothered Indiana all night, leading to a couple of quick overtime baskets and forcing the weary Wildcats to abandon the zone altogether and go chasing against IU's freeze. They chased, but never caught up.

"We just broke down," explained Hall. "We had a couple of bad breaks. We made a couple of bad passes. Those are youthful mistakes we're going to make."

"They caught us off-guard in the zone," added one of UK's youths, 6-10 sophomore Rick Robey. "They capitalized a couple of times on it, and we had to go from the zone. Then they made a couple of good moves."

Those moves came after some IU frustration against the Wildcats' collapsing 1-3-1 zone, a defense Kentucky likes to use and one Hall thought could be especially effective against Indiana.

"Indiana likes to move from the guards to the post man," said Hall. "So we dropped our point man back and denied them that flat pass."

Hall added that wrinkle after some special study, said Givens.

"We watched some films from last year," he said. "We saw where they hurt us when we made mistakes, and we changed our defense just a little. It hampered them a lot.

"They lobbed a lot to Benson last year up at Indiana. They couldn't tonight. I think that's what hurt — on the back line there."

For all his work on defense, Givens, a 6-4 leaper, was counted on for Kentucky's offense. He provided it mainly in the second half, getting 13 of his team-high 20 points then. Not all the second-half motivation was self-motivation, Givens admitted.

"Coach got on me a couple of times, told me I was not in the game," Givens said. "I knew he was right. It helps a lot when coach gets on you. I know sometimes it can bother you when he gets on you. But that's his job.

"He just wanted us to go the boards 'cause they were going to be there. We wanted to get some cheap baskets. I just wanted to get in there and deflect the ball if nothing else.

"Sometimes it takes a game like this to show what you have to do to correct the mistakes. This represents a lot of progress.

"We had a couple of chances to beat them. That's all you can ask for."

Indiana 93, Georgia 56

Bob Knight and his Indiana basketball team were treated to cake when they entered their dressing room after opening the second Indiana Classic with a 93-56 bouncing of Georgia Friday night.

'Twas a special cake, decorated in tribute to Knight's 200th college coaching victory. "Very nice," Knight said, bitingly, "considering you've just had since the game to get it ready."

Given a vote, Knight would have vetoed any sort of cake-baking that smacked of anticipating a victory. That's a definite Knight no-no. But, in truth, there was plenty of time to get a cake baked, iced and sliced between the time No. 200 was clinched and the game officially ended.

Indiana was firmly in charge at halftime, leading 44-24. And the Hoosiers ended any remaining doubt by scoring the first 22 points of the second half to open a 66-24 lead and give the reserves a chance for a busy evening.

Before they left, a couple of starters made some plays that Knight liked a lot — Tom Abernethy and Bob Wilkerson, who have had some trouble getting started this season.

Wilkerson scored a little (six points, including a stop-and-zoom drive off the baseline for a self-opened layup) but contributed to lots more. He had eight assists and combined with Quinn Buckner for some harassment that stopped Georgia before it could get started.

Indiana shot ahead, 7-0, because Georgia had no answer to the backcourt challenge. "Our guards were obviously jittery and nervous," Bulldog coach John Guthrie said. "When you play against that 94-by-50 basketball, you'd better be ready for it. You've got to handle the pressure or they'll take you right out of your offense. They do a great job of keeping the pressure on you. That's their whole philosophy, and they implement it."

Wilkerson and Buckner combined for seven steals, five by Buckner, who played only 12 minutes because of foul trouble. Wilkerson stayed around 18 minutes, longest of the regulars (Kent Benson matching him). "Bobby really played well," Knight said.

Abernethy scored 12 points and had 5 rebounds in only 16 minutes of use, going 5-for-5 from the field and 2-for-2 on free throws in cashing in two three-point plays.

Abernethy also got the defensive duty on Georgia's 6-7 sophomore, Jacky Dorsey, and he made it the toughest night of Dorsey's college career. Jacky was never below 12 and under 20 only twice in a brilliant freshman season. He scored seven in a game this year when he played only seven minutes before being hurt.

Friday, he played all he could — 23 minutes before fouling out — and scored just five points. "I didn't think Jacky was nervous," Guthrie said. "We just couldn't get the ball to him."

That was the fault of Abernethy and the two guards, sometimes others. "I had lots of help — especially when he'd get the ball and start backing in," Abernethy said.

"I thought Abernethy played extremely well," Knight said. "He did an excellent job in the overtime Monday night, and it carried over into this one."

He went into the game determined to get himself open for more of a scoring contribution than

INDIANA 93

	M	FG	FT	R	A	PF	TP
May, f	17	8-10	2- 2	6	1	2	18
Abernethy, f	16	5- 5	2- 2	5	1	1	12
Benson, c	18	1- 3	4- 6	3	0	0	6
Buckner, g	12	4- 6	0- 0	2	3	4	8
Wilkerson, g	18	3- 6	0- 1	4	8	0	6
Valavicius	16	2- 4	0- 0	1	1	3	4
Wisman	27	2- 7	5- 5	0	1	4	9
Radford	23	2- 5	6- 8	5	0	2	10
Crews	11	2- 5	0- 0	3	1	1	4
Roberson	8	2- 3	2- 2	6	0	2	6
Bender	12	0- 1	3- 4	1	2	2	3
Haymore	17	3- 9	1- 2	6	1	4	7
Eells	4	0- 1	0- 0	0	0	0	0
Team				7			
Totals		34-65	25-32	49	19	25	93

GEORGIA 56

	M	FG	FT	R	A	PF	TP
Dorsey, f	23	2- 9	1- 2	4	1	5	5
Jackson, f	20	4-10	4- 4	3	0	3	12
Foster, c	34	6-16	6- 9	13	0	5	18
Flanagan, g	32	1-10	2- 3	3	1	4	4
Daniels, g	34	4-13	4- 4	3	0	3	12
Fusi	16	0- 2	1- 2	4	2	0	1
Drafts	9	1- 2	0- 0	0	0	2	2
Hicks	8	0- 1	0- 0	0	0	3	0
Thorne	9	0- 0	0- 0	0	0	0	0
Slonaker	8	0- 0	2- 3	2	0	2	2
Team				9			
Totals		18-63	20-27	41	4	27	56

SCORE BY HALVES

Georgia	24	32 —	56
Indiana	44	49 —	93

Errors: Georgia 39, Indiana 29

	FG	Pct.	FT	Pct.
Georgia	18-63	.286	20-27	.741
Indiana	34-65	.523	25-32	.781

Officials: Charles Fouty and Mike Mathis
Attendance: 13,157

Tony Flanagan of Georgia bounds and rebounds

he'd been making (30 points in the first four games).

"I had a little more confidence in my shooting," he said. "You can't rely on one or two to score.

"The main thing was concentration — trying to do as much as I can. That's what we all wanted to do in this one."

The Hoosiers were no happier with their play in narrow victories over Notre Dame and Kentucky than Knight was. "We had a team meeting after practice — right here in the dressing room," co-captain Scott May said.

"You could see it in the films. Everybody thought they were hustling and going 100 per cent, but as we played, we'd get tired and go into a shell. We weren't doing the little things.

"But I thought everybody concentrated pretty well in this game." May's contribution was packed into just 16 minutes, and he exploited them for 18 points, hitting 8 of 10 shots.

IU's Bob Bender, Jim Roberson (43) sandwich Georgia's Walter Daniels

Among the reserves, sophomore Wayne Radford had the best night with 10 points. "We made some mistakes the last half," Knight said, "which is to be expected when you're going with young kids in there. But I was really pleased with the way Radford played. He did a lot of things well."

Jim Wisman had 9 points, Mark Haymore 7 and Jim Roberson 6 to flesh out a box score that saw the regulars score only 50 points and shoot .700 (21-for-30).

"I thought we played with the kind of intensity we want to have," Knight said. "Now, if we can take this as a foundation and build on it, it'll be a big help."

Friday's crowd was 13,157, up about 3,000 from opening night of the first Classic a year ago—and a little better than expected.

No. 200 a piece o' cake for precocious Bobby K.

Milestones have come to Knight at a ridiculously early age, starting with his debut as a major college coach at 24.

Now, at 35, he has won 200 games, and a quick scan of the records, aided by National Basketball Hall of Fame executive director Lee Williams, doesn't find any other coach who reached 200 major-college victories at so tender an age.

College basketball's all-time biggest winner, Adolph Rupp of Kentucky, finished at 879, but Adolph turned 36 with only 116 of those logged.

No. 2 on the victory list, Dr. F. C. (Phog) Allen, Rupp's coach at Kansas, was well over 200 after his 35th year, but the feat demands an asterisk.

Allen did it by winning 74 games in one year — when he coached simultaneously at Baker College (22-2), Haskell Indian Institute (27-5) and Kansas (25-3). Baker is 15 miles south of Lawrence, and Haskell Institute is in Lawrence with KU. By no means should the feat be demeaned; just asterisked. A 15-mile trip in those days (1908-09) must have demanded real dedication.

For the record, Allen was 234-30 when he turned 36, doubling at Baker (24-0) and Kansas (18-6) the year before his triple. His "major" college victories through 35 totaled 161.

Another all-time coaching great from the Big Eight, Henry Iba, also made it past No. 200 at 35, with small-college assistance. "Mr. Iba," a veritable idol of Knight's, was 101-14 at Marysville State Teacher's College (now Northwest Missouri) before an 11-8 year at Colorado that preceded his brilliant career at Oklahoma State. At 35, overall, he was 201-53.

Another of Knight's revered people, Clair Bee, won games at a better percentage than anybody, but he didn't get started in college coaching until

Co-captains Quinn Buckner, Scott May pass milestone cake to Bobby Knight, flanked by son Tim and former Army coach Tates Locke

28 and didn't play enough games per year to get to 200 so soon.

Among the people who came close to 200 by 35 was IU's Hall of Famer, Branch McCracken, who became a college coach even younger than Knight. Mac was 22 when he began at Ball State in the 1930-31 season. At 35, he was 180-58 and headed into World War II duty after winning an NCAA championship and launching his 378-victory IU career with a 93-41 start.

That other super-winner, John Wooden? Victory No. 1 in college hadn't come his way yet; John turned 36 coaching at South Bend Central High School, making up for lost ground with amazing speed once he got going.

"Quinn Buckner has probably played in 200 games in the last six years, and with the exception of his freshman year at Indiana, he's been the captain of every one of those teams. And they probably haven't lost 20 of those games."

— Bob Knight

A DeVoe-ted disciple has team ready, eager

"We've played three fine ball games in a row. If there's any time you're ready to play the nation's No. 1 team, it's now."

Virginia Tech's Don DeVoe peeked ahead to the championship game of the second Indiana Classic with eagerness and confidence, but it was a lot more fun for him to look back a second at the game that got him there — a shocking 87-60 whipping of Pacific-8 Conference power Oregon.

Most shocked of all were the good folks in the opening-night crowd who headed home at halftime of the second game, with Indiana safely in the final game and Oregon apparently headed there.

The Ducks had Tech down, 42-36, and looked formidable in doing it. All-America guard Ron Lee was playing the part, the brawny Ducks bossed the backboards, and things appeared in hand. "Now, we weren't a good ball club out there in the first half," Oregon coach Dick Harter said, "but we showed signs of playing well.

"In the second half, we just didn't play. They played well; we played terrible."

The change came with a lightning strike — 18

straight points by Tech that changed a 10-point Oregon lead into a Gobbler game and started Virginia Tech's 51-18 domination of the second half.

Forward Russell Davis of Virginia Tech tied the tourney scoring record with 27 points (IU's May set it against Nebraska last year) and set one by going 13-for-13 at the free throw line. That even broke the two-game record, as did Sensibaugh's 12 assists.

DeVoe considers himself more than just a friend, a former teammate and former assistant to Knight — more like a disciple. "Bobby has been a tremendous influence on my coaching career, especially in strategy of defense," DeVoe said.

"And I've long been an admirer of his ability to motivate players and his overall knowledge of the game.

"Nobody is more aware than he is of what's going on. I personally feel there are at least a half-dozen teams in the country with as good or better talent which aren't getting nearly the mileage out of their players that he is from his."

Oregon's game plan is founded on defense, too, and the Ducks play it aggressively. "Indiana plays the defense without fouling," DeVoe said simply. "They have the type of kids who follow the ball with their eyes better.

"They just demolished Georgia. It could have been a shutout."

Scott May is a wide, 6-7 screen as Quinn Buckner sweeps by

Indiana 101, Virginia Tech 74

There's no need to quibble over whether it was the best basketball Indiana has played this year or just some of the best. It *was* the best an IU team has ever shot and, overall, it was good enough to blow a solid, smart, poised and inspired Virginia Tech team into disarray and give the Hoosiers a successful defense of their Indiana Classic championship, 101-74, at Assembly Hall Saturday night.

The issue was over much, much earlier than folks who watched Virginia Tech destroy a good Oregon team on the tourney's opening night would have suspected. The game wasn't a quarter along when Quinn Buckner's second 3-point play hoisted the Hoosier lead to 32-15 — followed in quick order by nine more points to put the lead at 41-15.

By then, Virginia Tech coach Don DeVoe had spent three time outs trying to reorganize the attack that Indiana had destroyed. The Gobblers stabilized and almost matched points with the Hoosiers the rest of the way, but they never made any hint of a comeback against an Indiana team that, on this night, was taking no survivors.

IU's Scott May, who scored at better than a point-a-minute pace and hit 19 of the 23 shots he took in the two nights, was a one-sided choice as most valuable player in post-game press balloting.

For the second year in a row, Indiana's superiority was so overwhelming that the Hoosiers put four men on the all-tourney team — guards Bob Wilkerson and Buckner and center Kent Benson joining Georgia center Lucius Foster on the honor team with May. It was a repeat for Buckner (last year's MVP), Benson and May.

DeVoe's first time out came 74 seconds into the game, after Indiana had whooshed away to a 7-1 lead. The points came on May's jump shot 10 seconds after the opening tip, a driving 3-point play by Buckner, and a mid-court steal and breakaway for a layup by Wilkerson.

Virginia Tech got the lead back to 7-5 by wrapping baskets around May's only miss of an 18-point first half. But Tech had no more answers at either end of the floor for the next few minutes as Indiana scored virtually every time it had the ball and stopped Virginia Tech just as frequently.

The Gobblers had 10 turnovers, 5 of those on steals or interceptions, when the 41-15 lead was reached.

There were some Hoosier plays in there that put the tourney-record crowd of 14,641 up in the air howling.

IU was running as never before in the Bob Knight coaching era — Wilkerson and Buckner repeatedly centering the ball on fast breaks and dealing the ball off perfectly for layups.

"I thought we got the ball out and got it down the floor in a break situation as well as in any game since I've been here," said Knight, whose disdain

for a running game vanished long ago — when he got running players.

Indiana hit 50 with 2:20 left in the half on two free throws by Tom Abernethy — the one Hoosier starter who didn't make all-tourney despite two solid performances.

The lead was then 50-25, and by the time IU hit halftime with a 56-34 lead, all five starters had been pulled.

They came back to start the second half and delighted Knight by scoring the first six times they had the ball. The lead was 79-46 when four of the starters came out, and peaked at 87-52 with 9:17 left when the last one — Buckner — was pulled.

Freshman walk-on Jim Roberson was the man who put the Hoosiers over 100 for the first time this year, the seventh time in the Knight era and the

VIRGINIA TECH 74

	M	FG	FT	R	A	PF	TP
Davis, f	34	4- 5	4- 4	3	2	2	12
Thieneman, f	10	0- 1	0- 0	1	0	2	0
Wansley, c	28	1- 4	0- 0	6	1	2	0
Cooke, g	28	6-12	3- 4	3	3	2	15
Sensibaugh, g	23	1- 4	0- 1	1	1	1	2
Thorpe	20	7- 9	2- 2	3	0	3	16
Edwards	7	0- 3	0- 0	0	1	3	0
McKee	15	0- 7	2- 2	7	1	1	2
Ashford	22	2- 5	2- 5	0	4	4	6
Collins	16	6- 8	7- 9	5	0	2	19
Team				5			
Totals		27-58	20-27	34	13	28	74

INDIANA 101

	M	FG	FT	R	A	PF	TP
May, f	23	11-13	5- 6	6	1	2	27
Abernethy, f	22	3- 5	3- 4	2	3	0	9
Benson, c	27	7-12	1- 1	6	0	2	15
Buckner, g	21	4-10	4- 6	3	6	3	12
Wilkerson, g	23	8-11	0- 0	3	6	3	16
Radford	16	1- 1	1- 2	0	1	2	3
Wisman	18	1- 4	1- 2	4	1	0	3
Crews	10	3- 5	0- 0	0	1	2	6
Valavicius	8	0- 0	0- 0	0	0	5	0
Roberson	10	1- 1	0- 0	1	0	2	2
Haymore	11	2- 3	0- 1	4	1	3	4
Bender	6	1- 1	2- 2	0	1	2	4
Eells	3	0- 0	0- 0	0	0	0	0
Team				7			
Totals		42-66	17-25	36	21	26	101

SCORE BY HALVES

Virginia Tech	34	40 —	74
Indiana	56	45 —	101

Errors: Virginia Tech 28, Indiana 21

		FG	Pct.	FT	Pct.
Virginia Tech	27-58	.466	20-27	.741
Indiana	42-66	.636	17-25	.680

Officials: Charles Fouty and Mike Mathis
Attendance: 14,641

fourth time at Assembly Hall. He took a pass from Mark Haymore for a layup at 0:54 to get the basket.

Indiana shot .742 in the sensational first half (23-for-31) and .636 for the game — an all-time Hoosier record. It beat the .633 the Hoosiers hit in 1959 against the alma mater of both final-game coaches — Ohio Staters Knight and DeVoe.

May played 23 minutes and scored 27 points, after an 18-point, 16-minute showing when Indiana beat Georgia Friday night, 93-56.

Wilkerson hit 8 of 11 shots, including a couple of tip-ins, to hit his season high with 16, while Benson had 15 points and Buckner 12. Each guard contributed 6 assists.

Reserve Mike Collins led Virginia Tech with 19 points, 14 in the last half. Russell Davis, who scored 27 against Oregon, was shut off from the ball so effectively by May that he managed only 12 points in the title game.

The victory balanced an old IU account with Virginia Tech, which won the only other basketball meeting of the two schools, 79-70, in a first-round Mid-East Regional game in the 1967 NCAA tourney.

Spotlight finally finds Hoosiers' 'Spiderman'

It was, among other things, a triumph of the work ethic. Collectively and individually.

May admitted to understandable and genuine elation when he was named as the most valuable player of the 1975 Indiana Classic basketball tourney Saturday night. And just about as high on May's pleasure scale was an announcement that came seconds later — that Wilkerson, so often the forgotten man in Hoosier basketball davastation the last two seasons, at last had made an all-something team.

"To be honest, I thought a couple of our guys might deserve the MVP award a little bit more than I did," May said.

"Bobby for one. I thought he played a real good tournament. It would have been a tremendous award for him to win."

There was an implication of sympathy for past Wilkerson voting snubs. "It really did bother me," May said. "I guess we all felt pleased for him tonight, because he really played hard."

"I thought Wilkerson played extremely well in these two ball games," Knight said.

"He has worked very hard for the last couple of days in practice, and I thought in the tournament, he did an excellent job for us at both ends of the floor."

The word "work" kept popping up — again in Wilkerson's own reaction to the Hoosiers' victory over Virginia Tech, their second straight Indiana Classic championship, his all-tourney selection . . . and the best basketball the Hoosiers have played for a while.

The last one took precedence. "Coach has really been on us," Wilkerson said. "We know

Bob Wilkerson — Reaching potential, and finding fame

we've been loafing lately, and he really worked us hard — two-a-day a couple of days ago (Wednesday). We knew we can't play on a roller coaster the way we have been playing, up and down like that. It really helped us.

"I think what happened in the tournament shows it's what *we* do that determines how we play — not what the opponents do."

Wilkerson, the 6-7 guard with the wrap-around arms that won him the nickname "Spiderman," set a tourney record with 14 assists in the two nights, and he also shot well (11 for 17) and rebounded. "I was just going to the boards better," he said. "I knew I had to go inside."

His board play may have influenced Virginia Tech's concentration on going to its own offensive board, and the result was a series of times when the Hoosiers got the rebound anyway and wheeled out alertly to beat the Gobblers with a fast break.

"It wasn't anything we went into the game figuring on," Wilkerson said. "It just happened, and we were able to take advantage of it."

Wilkerson's ballhandling role was a bit more prominent than usual because Buckner, usually the Hoosiers' assist leader, was bothered by flu during the week and limited in playing time during the tourney. "We tried to get him out every four or five minutes," Knight said. Buckner played only 33 minutes in the two games, scoring 20 points with 9 assists and 8 steals in that time.

"I thought everyone seemed to fit into the role he's responsible for filling," Knight said.

"I thought Tommy Abernethy (the Hoosier starter left off the all-tourney team) played extremely good basketball for the two nights.

"Benson played very well. And I thought our reserves played better as a team in this game than they did last night.

"Virginia Tech is a tremendously well-coached team. Don has done a fine job with them. That's a team that's going to win a lot of basketball games.

"Things just went our way tonight. They played very well last night against Oregon, but this time things went our way at the start of the ball game and we got them down.

"The best we've played? Oh, I don't know. I thought we played pretty well the first half of the Florida State game, too. These kids have played well a lot of times the last couple of years.

"I was really pleased the way we came out the second half and maintained the way we were playing."

The Classic is basically Knight's "baby," a goal of his from the time he came to Indiana and a production he is involved with in all phases of planning in the weeks leading up to its play.

"I was very pleased with the turnouts," he said. "It was up about 5,000 total from last year, and I think that's awfully good."

It was even a little better than that — up 6,407, or about 30 per cent.

The final-night games drew 14,641, giving the tourney a two-night total of 27,798. Last year, in the inaugural Classic, the total was 21,391 with a high of 11,233.

Bob Wilkerson — 22 points, 14 assists, and all-tourney

Indiana 'far superior' to Tar Heels — DeVoe

"We couldn't stop the avalanche," said DeVoe, whose once-fond upset hopes turned quickly to a desire to imitate the Hoosier team that hammered his Virginia Tech club.

"We've just *got* to do things Indiana is doing the rest of our schedule," said DeVoe.

What Indiana did to win is everything, said DeVoe, totally impressed.

"It would take a great effort to beat them," he said. "This is the most talent offensively and defensively I've ever played against.

"Indiana just handled us. They would not allow us to run our offense. They took the ball away from us at midcourt and beat us down the floor. But the most disappointing thing to me was that we didn't force them to take any outside shots.

"They are a great team, tremendously coached. They just didn't show me any flaws in the top six people. We were just overpowered at both ends of the court. It's a miracle to me Kentucky and Notre Dame could stay with them."

DeVoe said there is no comparison between the ways North Carolina (an 88-75 winner over Tech) and Indiana handled his team. "Indiana is a far superior basketball team," he said.

Gobblers Davis and Ernest Wansley were likewise impressed with the Hoosiers. Davis scored 27 points Friday but got just 12 against Indiana, and the 6-11 Wansley scored just 2 points while contending with Benson in the middle.

"Indiana is much more aggressive than North Carolina," Wansley said. "Indiana plays better defense and executes its plays better.

"They put pressure on all over the court. I never thought it would happen to us."

"Indiana really pressures the ball," Davis said. "I didn't get the ball as much as I did last night."

There was Gobbler trouble at the other end of the court, too. "They screen away from the ball real well," Davis said. "We had problems getting over the picks."

Tom Abernethy — A rebound, a position in good hands

IU's Classic balance, depth please Knight

Despite playing time shortened by the one-sided scorers, all five Indiana starters averaged in double figures for the two Classic games.

Benson and Wilkerson had to survive six-point games to do it, but Benson and Abernethy averaged 10.5 in the two games, Buckner 10.0, Wilkerson 11.0 . . . and tourney MVP May 22.5.

"I've said before this is a team that could be a little more unbalanced than some of our other teams, simply because of May's ability," Knight said.

"But it is good to see the kind of balance we got in the tournament because it means you had pretty good offensive movement."

The Hoosiers also got 65 tournament points out of reserves, and that pleased Knight. "Any time kids beyond your first seven can play a lot, it helps you for the future," Knight said. "It's something of value to us, perhaps a long way down the road."

Kent Benson shuts off the whole world to Virginia Tech's Dave Sensibaugh

Indiana 106, Columbia 63

Tom Penders, Columbia's 29-year-old coach, had a one-word greeting for Indiana's Bob Knight when the two shook hands late Friday afternoon: "Thanks."

"Sure, I told him that and I meant it sincerely," Penders said after the top-ranked Hoosiers' 106-63 victory over his team on opening day of the 24th Holiday Festival at Madison Square Garden.

"He could have buried us by 70 if he'd have wanted to," Penders said. "I really appreciate what he did."

What Knight did was keep his opening lineup together for only about 13 minutes, during which the combination outscored Columbia, 43-16.

On the day May became the 15th Hoosier to score 1,000 points in his career, Penders sought to make things as tough for him as he could by throwing a box-and-one at Indiana — a four-man zone with the fifth defender assigned solely to May.

"The people who scheduled this game must also have booked Custer and the Indians.
When I heard the pairings, I felt like I had just chosen the wrong door on 'Let's Make a Deal.'"

— Tom Penders
Columbia coach

So, May played only 16 minutes and — special defense and all — scored 12 points. His 1,000th point came on a baseline jump shot at 10:55 of the first half, opening a lead that had started out 14-0 to 26-8.

"Hey, that's pretty nice," said May, who has 1,007 points. "I didn't know anything about that."

May showed the Columbia defense was vulnerable by breaking free for an inside shot only 2:15 into the game. That came in the middle of IU's game-opening cruncher, during which Quinn Buckner — closing in on 1,000 points himself (he's at 991) — had three interceptions, Bob Wilkerson one and Kent Benson the first of two mid-court steals he made and cashed in with impressive gallops to the IU end.

"I was surprised at Benson's agility," Penders admitted. "We thought if we took him outside, he might get a little overaggressive and get in foul trouble. But he can really go outside and play." Buckner agreed: "Bennie likes to play out there. He loves those steals."

"He could play forward in the pros," Penders said. "I think he could match up and play most people. They all can. They're incredible on defense."

Columbia is in for a lean season, and Penders knows it. Hoosier reserves proved it by continuing to add to the margin long after taking over. Indiana had six men in double figures and came fairly close to having all 10 it brought along in there. Benson led the five starters with 15, and freshman guard Bob Bender was the reserve who made the double-figure list with 12 points — officially 6 for 6 shooting, although he (and others) remembered two of his shots that missed. "Late Christmas present," he said of the charitable scoring.

Indiana finished at .597 (46-for-77) and was outshot. Columbia officially was 25-for-40 which is .625. That's the highest an opponent has shot in the five Knight years at IU, years that reached a milestone of their own Friday with Knight's 100th coaching victory with the Hoosiers.

Columbia had almost as many turnovers (33) as shots, and the ratio was reversed when the starters were in.

Manhattan coach Jack Powers, whose team hurdled St. Bonaventure, 76-65, for a second-round shot at Indiana, wasn't as pleased about Knight's charitibility as Penders was, Powers's scouting chance hampered by the starters' skimpy playing time. "They weren't in there long enough to really see anything," he said.

Powers didn't have that situation in his own game. St. Bonaventure appeared to have things under control, ahead 51-47 when its leading scorer for the season, 6-7 Bob Rozyczko, drew his fourth foul. Manhattan caught up at 63-63 with 5½ minutes left and took the lead for good on a basket by its best shooter, 6-7 Tom Lockhart, who averages 22 and scored 20 in this one. Guard Ricky Marsh had 18 for the Jaspers, whose 5-3 record includes a 78-71 loss at Louisville and a 79-72 loss to St. John's.

South Carolina and St. John's are the other semifinalists, St. John's boosting its record to 8-0 by beating Temple, 67-59; and South Carolina routing Villanova, 95-86.

St. John's, a three-time Festival winner and the Garden crowd's darling, was down 40-32 three minutes into the second half before 5-9 guard Frank Alagia got the Redmen going. They caught up at 43-43 and, once ahead, never were caught.

A New York natural: Hoosiers vs. muggers

Indiana's basketball players, elite in their own social circle, were billeted in elegance for their stay in New York City. Their hotel rooms looked out over 800-acre Central Park, which was showing at its loveliest in the Hoosiers' early hours in town — brightened, not buried, by a light snow that arrived with them Thursday afternoon, before a Friday rain that washed the brightness away and left gray where white had been.

The reality of the park's beauty was conveyed by the New York-wise Knight, who advised drily in a first-day team meeting: "If you're going to walk over there, do it in groups of 10."

The Columbia basketball team would probably pay to see that match-up: Knight's 10 vs. the parkful of muggers legend says is out there, particularly at night. There must have been times, some of them as recently as Friday's thumping of Columbia, that the hands of Buckner, Wilkerson, et al, seemed sufficiently larcenous and quick to be capable of snatching the glove off Muhammad Ali in mid-jab. A mugger's knife or gun should be no problem.

Not far away, either, are the bright lights of the city, or the tourism "musts." However, May allowed when he and fellow co-captain Buckner shared the grilling area with Knight at a post-game press session, "We didn't get an opportunity to see anything yet."

"You won't, either," one of the Knight-wise in the New York gallery quipped.

"We didn't come here to go downtown and see the sights," May answered, evenly. "We came here to play basketball."

The Hoosiers proved that — and for one more time, the efficacy of and their adherence to the Knight-adopted challenge to play each game against personal potential, not live opponents — in their relentless destruction of Columbia's outclassed sophomores. Such a situation won't be thrust upon them again in this tournament or season. Columbia is, without any question, the weakest of Hoosier opponents this year. "It is to their credit, considering the opposition, that the Hoosiers played full throttle," Phil Pepe wrote in *The New York Daily News.*

Even Penders enjoyed the experience. Sort of. "It's kind of like going to the dentist, I guess," the Columbia coach said.

"Really, it was a great experience for our kids and a great experience for me. Our kids were talking in the locker room afterward: 'Did you see the way Benson dived on the floor?' " Big for a mugger at 6-11 and not normally thought of in the purloining group, Benson was the Hoosiers' leaders with four steals Friday.

"They're so tough," Penders said. "They scored 14 points in the first half off great defensive plays. Their defense is their offense. We knew that.

"They could have a psychological problem along the line, but Bobby will never let them take anyone lightly. Like, some people said they might come in here overlooking us. Knowing Bobby the way I do, I said, 'No way.' I knew they wouldn't."

Knight noted that Columbia didn't approach the game negatively. "They had an excellent plan — a box-and-one on Scott," he said. In effect, that provided a double-team on the Hoosier all-American each time he got the ball.

Excellent plan, but it didn't work. "It left open shots for the other guys," May noted. "Bennie was killing them inside, and Quinn and Bobby were getting wide-open shots on the wings." All five starters finished above .500 for the day — a cumulative 26-for-37, .703.

"It's the first time I've had that done to one of my teams since 1967," Knight mused. Didn't work that time, either.

Benson's play produced different opinions oncourt and off from his first tournament match-ups.

"I never played against that many big people," sad Columbia center Ed Shockley. "Not only big, quick, too. Benson, man, the dude is really fast."

But Steve Grant, Manhattan's 6-7 center, said, "His defense seems a little shaky on the drive."

INDIANA 106

	M	FG	FT	R	A	PF	TP
May, f	16	4- 6	4- 4	4	1	2	12
Abernethy, f	26	6- 8	2- 2	7	1	3	14
Benson, c	16	7- 9	1- 1	3	1	4	15
Buckner, g	14	5- 8	0- 1	0	4	4	10
Wilkerson, g	25	4- 6	3- 4	5	8	1	11
Crews	23	4-15	1- 2	2	5	1	9
Radford	21	3- 5	3- 4	4	5	2	9
Wisman	28	4- 9	0- 1	1	2	4	8
Valavicius	13	3- 5	0- 0	2	2	5	6
Bender	18	6- 6	0- 0	1	4	2	12
Team				4			
Totals		46-77	14-19	33	33	28	106

COLUMBIA 63

	M	FG	FT	R	A	PF	TP
Love, f	29	4- 6	4- 8	4	1	4	12
Collins, f	22	2- 4	2- 3	1	1	2	6
Shockley, c	22	3- 4	0- 3	6	1	1	6
Bentz, g	24	3- 5	4- 6	5	1	1	10
Combs, g	21	3- 5	0- 0	1	0	3	6
Scott	25	2- 4	0- 1	3	5	4	4
Wilhite	14	4- 5	2- 5	1	1	4	10
Crew	12	0- 1	0- 2	2	1	0	0
Hassan	23	3- 4	1- 2	5	1	0	7
Dellicarri	8	1- 2	0- 0	0	1	0	2
Team				7			
Totals		25-40	13-30	35	13	19	63

SCORE BY HALVES

Indiana . . . . 56 50 — 106
Columbia . . . . 27 36 — 63
  Errors: Indiana 11, Columbia 33

	FG	Pct.	FT	Pct.
Indiana	46-77	.597	14-19	.737
Columbia	25-40	.625	13-30	.433

Officials: Joe DeBonis and Clark Folsom
Attendance: 11,073

Indiana 97, Manhattan 61

NEW YORK, DECEMBER 27, 1975

Scott May put on an all-American performance Saturday night to get top-ranked Indiana winging away as the Hoosiers overwhelmed Manhattan, 96-71, to gain the finals of the 24th Holiday Festival basketball tourney.

Now 8-0, Indiana will play St. John's (9-0) for the tourney championship.

May scored 32 points, 22 in the first half, as the Hoosiers — breaking their all-time shooting mark for the second time in a week — zoomed away from the Jaspers in the opening minutes, then emerged from a wobbly stretch to take a 48-30 halftime lead. They made it a blowout by outscoring Manhattan in the first four minutes of the second half, 11-2.

May went out of the game with 7:05 left after getting his fourth foul. The Garden crowd of 13,339 gave him a standing ovation on departure, and Manhattan coach Jack Powers must have felt like joining in.

"What can you say when you see a kid like that?" Powers said. "He looks like he could step right into the pros and keep on going.

"He just keeps playing — he's strong, he's quick. We tried to keep a fresh man on him all the time, but we didn't have anybody who could handle him."

Just as the Hoosiers dusted off Columbia with a 14-0 takeoff in their first Festival game Friday, they stung Manhattan with a 22-4 knockout blow opening this one.

There were two keys — May's shooting and Tom Abernethy's defensive work on Manhattan's scoring star, Tom Lockhart.

After Quinn Buckner's layup got Indiana ahead, 2-0, May hit his first two shots to open a 6-2 edge. Jasper guard Larry Frazier cut it to 6-4 with a baseline jump shot, and then the Hoosiers strung together 16 straight points — shutting off Manhattan on 12 possessions in a row, 5 of those without a shot.

Lockhart, whom Hoosier coach Bob Knight had described as "one of the best offensive forwards we'll play all year," didn't get his first basket until the game was 12 minutes old and Indiana was leading by 20, 31-11. At that point, it was only the second shot he had managed with Abernethy over-playing him to keep the Jaspers from getting the ball to him.

Meanwhile, May was exciting the Garden populace with a variety of drives, jump shots and rebounds. His 3-point play at 7:38 countered Lockhart's basket and gave Indiana a 34-13 lead.

Then, after Indiana temporarily went dry and Manhattan clicked for eight points in a row to take life, it was May who shut the door with 10 points in the last four minutes of the half to keep the lead fat.

When May and Kent Benson, the Hoosiers' junior center who celebrated his 21st birthday with a 19-point game, each hit twice and Buckner once in the first three minutes of the second half, the Indiana lead was 58-32 and Manhattan was convinced.

Buckner's second-half basket was his fourth of the night, but he came out after drawing his fourth foul at 14:04 — his career point total temporarily stalled at 999.

Hoosier reserves again logged considerable playing time and competed well, although Lockhart celebrated the removal of Abernethy by flashing his superb offensive skills at the expense, chiefly, of hard-working freshman Rich Valavicius.

Knight lifted Abernethy with 10:39 to play and Indiana's lead at 70-39. Lockhart at that point had three field goals and eight points, but he exploded

INDIANA 97

	M	FG	FT	R	A	PF	TP
May, f	33	13-21	6- 8	13	2	4	32
Abernethy, f	26	2- 3	0- 0	7	1	0	4
Benson, c	16	9-16	1- 2	7	3	2	19
Buckner, g	14	4- 6	0- 0	3	5	4	8
Wilkerson, g	26	5- 6	0- 0	1	5	4	10
Crews	22	3- 4	2- 2	3	5	0	8
Radford	11	3- 4	4- 5	1	2	1	10
Wisman	14	1- 1	0- 0	1	4	2	2
Bender	5	2- 2	0- 0	0	2	1	4
Valavicius	10	0- 2	0- 0	1	0	0	0
Team				9			
Totals		42-65	13-17	46	29	18	97

MANHATTAN 61

	M	FG	FT	R	A	PF	TP
Lockhart, f	29	9-19	3- 3	9	4	1	21
Pope, f	14	2- 5	0- 1	3	1	3	4
Grant, c	33	6-11	0- 0	8	0	0	12
Frazier, g	20	1-10	1- 2	0	1	3	3
Marsh, g	32	5-18	4- 4	1	0	2	14
Bruno	14	0- 3	0- 0	1	0	4	0
Hurley	8	0- 4	0- 0	1	0	1	0
Dye	14	1- 2	0- 0	0	0	1	0
Mattias	3	1- 4	1- 1	1	1	0	3
Courtney	8	0- 1	2- 2	2	1	0	2
Team				5			
Totals		25-77	11-13	30	7	16	61

SCORE BY HALVES

Indiana	48	49	— 97
Manhattan	30	31	— 61

Errors: Indiana 13, Manhattan 17

	FG	Pct.	FT	Pct.
Indiana	42-65	.646	13-17	.765
Manhattan	25-77	.325	11-13	.846

Officials: Tom Birch and Austin MacArthur
Attendance: 13,339

for four baskets in the next two minutes. By game's end, he had almost matched his 21.9 average with 21 points.

The Hoosiers finished 42-for-65 for a .646 shooting mark that beat the .636 they posted against Virginia Tech in breaking a 17-year-old school record. May was 13-for-21, making him 17-for-27 in this tourney and 36-for-50 for the last four games — .720.

Besides May and Benson, the Hoosiers got double-figure scoring from Bob Wilkerson and reserve Wayne Radford with 10 points each. Ricky Marsh was second-high for Manhattan with 14. The Jaspers shot only .325 with a quick-firing plan that did keep their turnover count low (17) but didn't produce any more points.

> *"Nothing is hopeless. My kids*
> *respect Indiana. They're a good*
> *team, a great team, but our kids are*
> *not awed by them. These are*
> *city kids. You don't awe city kids.*
> *They may be beaten by a team with*
> *more talent, but they*
> *won't be awed."*
>
> — Jack Powers
> Manhattan coach

Hoosiers break, re-break shooting mark with .636, .646

Carnesecca puts IU 'in a class with greats'

Knight had his second straight chance to relax — to the point he allows himself — as his team crunched Manhattan, and it left him in a bantering mood by the time he met the New York press. He wound up getting in some jabs and delivering an earnest lecture that, essentially, said he expects a rugged test when the Hoosiers meet unbeaten St. John's for the Festival championship.

St. John's coach Lou Carnesecca, a friend of Knight's going back to Knight's days as Army coach and Carnesecca's as an assistant to the late Joe Lapchick at St. John's, touched off the debate by commenting after his team had gained the finals that he was looking forward to meeting Indiana — a team, he said, "I would put in a class with the Jabbar and the Wicks teams at UCLA and the great Ohio State teams he (Knight) played on."

"Yeah," Knight said when the quote was relayed. "I've heard that stuff before. Usually from a coach just *before* he played us."

Asked how he would rate his current team against the Jerry Lucas and John Havlicek-led Buckeye teams he played on from 1960 to '62, Knight declined deftly.

"That's something I can't do," he said, smiling sweetly, "because I've never seen them play each other. And the thing I don't have that you people have is the ability to judge something I haven't seen."

"I'll bet you do it in other sports," a New York writer challenged.

"Okay," Knight conceded. "I watched the Colorado-Texas football game today and I did reach the conclusion that there was no running back on the field that compared with Jimmy Brown.

"Really, I'm the worst judge in the world of how my team is. You'll think I'm lying, but it honestly amazes me every time we win because I always figure we could lose this way or that way or this could go wrong.

"As I watched St. John's play two games in this tournament, I can honestly say I don't think there's a physical difference between our club and theirs.

"Our center (Benson, 6-11) is a little bigger than theirs (6-7 George Johnson) but Johnson's a hell of a jumper. Okay, our guards (Wilkerson, 6-7, and Buckner, 6-3) are bigger than one of theirs (5-9 Frank Alagia), but show me a kid anywhere who's quicker than Alagia is.

"I think they've got a hell of a basketball team, and I have always felt that Carnesecca was an outstanding coach. The only thing he's ever done that I wondered about was coach in the pros (with the New York Nets, between stints at St. John's) and he did whatever he had to do to get himself straightened out after that mistake, so I just respect him as an excellent basketball coach."

Knight's greatest pleasure with Saturday's semifinal game came when the Hoosiers opened the game with a 22-4 rush and nailed it down with an 11-2 start in the second half.

"Manhattan's kids came out and played hard," he said. "Except for that start we got, the rest of the half was dead even.

"I thought Tommy Abernethy did a good defensive job for us (on Lockhart) and that was a key for us to the way we got started. If he had the same kind of spurt at the start as he had later in the game (13 points in the last 10½ minutes), it would have been a different game."

Powers praised the Hoosiers as "definitely one of the finest college teams I have seen," but he suggested the game would have been much tighter if the Jaspers had met the Hoosiers fresh, rather than a day after their taxing 67-65 first-round victory over St. Bonaventure.

"We couldn't get a second shot," he said. "Our kids were tired. I feel we definitely would have given them a stronger game on the boards if we had been fresh, and I think that's where the key was tonight.

"I know Bobby's coaching, and I knew they were going to take our inside game away.

"But we started out the game getting five good shots and we couldn't get them to stick. After that, we probably started forcing some."

Powers had suggested Friday he might try a patient attack against Indiana, but he said after the Saturday night game that the tempo was about what he wanted.

"We weren't going to hold the ball," he said. "We took a few shots we shouldn't have taken, but part of it was that our kids were tired. Indiana was just too much for us to play on our second game in two nights.

"We've played some good basketball against good teams. We came back in the second half and tied Louisville at Louisville (ultimately losing by only seven). But that time we were fresh.

"For one stretch in this game, we played fairly well. We took away the ball and took away the wings and did a pretty good job inside. But then we got tired and they pulled away."

It was Indiana's second victory over Manhattan at the Garden — but there was a long time, and a move of Garden sites, in between. The other Hoosier victory over the Jaspers was in December of 1936 by a 42-34 score.

Indiana and St. John's also have met once — the Redmen claiming a 65-55 victory at IU in the 1951-52 season.

A championship lineup — from left, Scott May, Quinn Buckner, Kent Benson, Bob Wilkerson, Tom Abernethy

Indiana 76, St. John's 69

NEW YORK, DECEMBER 29, 1975

Indiana got clutch plays from front-liners and subs Monday night to beat back St. John's, 76-69, and win the 24th Holiday Festival basketball tournament.

The biggest college basketball crowd in New York history, 19,694, packed Madison Square Garden to see the two unbeatens tangle, and another 3,500 people were turned away. "People screamed for this game, and they got their money's worth," said St. John's coach Lou Carnesecca. "It was a great, great game."

All-American Scott May won a silver bowl as the tourney's most valuable player, and he earned it with seven points in the last five minutes after St. John's had rallied from eight down in the second half to tie the game, 65-65.

May, held to only three shots in the first 15 minutes of the second half, shook loose on an out-of-bounds play to drill the tie-breaking basket from the corner with 4:47 left.

May rebounded Frank Alagia's miss seconds later, and the Hoosiers freed Tom Abernethy — another of their standouts in this one — for a shot from the baseline that gave them operating room, 69-65.

St. John's never again had the ball with a chance to tie, Indiana going into a freeze in the last three minutes after reclaiming the ball with the 69-65 lead still on the board.

There was one interruption. Quinn Buckner, directing the freeze, drove for the basket with 2:24 to go. "It was open to the basket," Buckner said, "but somebody got in front of me, amazingly. I thought the guy was sliding, but when we hit, I didn't even want to look at the official. I knew there was no way he could call it any other way."

The charging foul was Buckner's fifth, eliminating him and turning the ball over to the charged-up Redmen. They capitalized on it quickly with a driving layup by center George Johnson, the leader of their upset bid.

This time, Indiana held on until May was fouled with 1:24 to go, and he hit both free chances to put the lead at four again.

Senior Jim Crews, Buckner's replacement, sagged back in on Johnson for a surprise double-team that produced a St. John's turnover with 1:11 to go — "one of the real key plays of the game for us," Knight said. May hit one free throw at 0:38 after a 33-second freeze to put the margin at five, and after Alagia drilled two free throws at 0:31, May was back at the foul line with 21 seconds left to clinch things with two more — his 28th and 29th points of a big night.

Crews boosted the winning margin with two free throws with three seconds to go.

Indiana never trailed in the last half — indeed, never again after Abernethy's jump shot from the key with 12:38 to go pulled the Hoosiers around St. John's, 16-15, in the middle of a 10-point streak that changed the Redmen's biggest lead into a 22-15 hole.

Fouls started building then, however, and they changed the game — for both teams. Kent Benson, who scored only four points in the game, drew his third foul and sat down with 10:26 to go in the half. Buckner's third came with 4:58 left in the half, after his one-and-one conversion had re-established the cushion at 32-25. Just 56 seconds before halftime, Bob Wilkerson got his third — and May had two, putting the Hoosiers in trouble even though they took a 39-36 edge to the dressing room.

In the first three minutes of the second half, both Buckner and Benson drew their fourth fouls and went out — Johnson, who scored 23 points, hitting both free throws on Benson's exit to tie the game, 45-45.

Reserve Wayne Radford, Buckner's replacement, broke that tie with two free throws, and the restructured lineup (freshman Rich Valavicius, at 6-4, filling in for the 6-11 Benson) surged to an 8-point lead that appeared to hit 10 when Radford worked free for a layup — only to be called for backing in on the shot and lose the points.

St. John's roared back quickly and tied the game at 61-61 on two more Johnson free throws with 7:12 to play. By then, Wilkerson and May had their fourth fouls, but they, Buckner and Benson were all back, as were St. John's Alagia, Beaver Smith, John Farmer and Johnson, all in foul trouble, too. "With eight minutes to go, you go with your best," Knight said.

St. John's got tying baskets two more times before the May and Abernethy goals that gave the Hoosiers the command they needed going into the final seconds.

The defeat was the first for St. John's after nine straight victories that had moved the Redmen into the national rankings. It made Indiana 9-0, the first Big Ten team to win the Festival title since Illinois did it 13 years ago.

The Hoosiers had their fifth straight .500-plus shooting night, hitting .532, but their victory margin came at the free-throw line where they had a 26-15 edge. Much of that came in the last 84 seconds when St. John's fouled four times trying to break the stall.

The Redmen shot .482, outrebounded the Hoosiers, 30-28, and came much closer than almost any other Hoosier opponent in the last two years to coaxing as many turnovers from Indiana as the IU defense produced (17-16).

Buckner, charged with a first-half foul Wilkerson committed in a scoring snafu, played only 24 minutes but scored 14 points — including the basket only two minutes and 32 seconds into the game that made him the 16th 1,000-point scorer in Indiana history. May became No. 15 earlier in the tournament.

Abernethy scored 12 points, while Wilkerson had 8 and matched May with 8 rebounds as the Hoosiers' co-leaders. Besides Johnson's 23, St. John's got 16 points from Alagia and 14 from guard Glen Williams. Johnson also led both teams with 10 rebounds.

Earlier in the evening, Manhattan, a 97-61 victim of Indiana in the semifinals, took third place by blasting the South Carolina team that had given St. John's problems, 87-73. Manhattan's Tom Lockhart scored 33 points to give him a 74-73 edge over May as the tourney scoring leader.

May joins the greats
on Festival MVP list

There are some nonentities on the list, but there are also some of college basketball's golden names of the last quarter-century: Bill Russell of San Francisco, Oscar Robertson of Cincinnati, Jerry Lucas of Ohio State, Bill Bradley of Princeton, Lew Alcindor of UCLA, Tom Gola of LaSalle, to dash off six who went on to win about a dozen Player of the Year awards.

And that list skips solid pros like Bob Lanier of St. Bonaventure, Jimmy Walker of Providence, Guy Rodgers of Temple, Wally Jones of Villanova and Jim Price of Louisville.

May moved into some choice company when he was named the most valuable player of the 24th Festival.

May stood on the sidelines with his Indiana teammates when, after the championship trophy was put in Hoosier hands, announcement of the MVP came. A cluster of Indiana fans behind him was yelling, "May ... May ... gotta be Scott May!" He was asked later what his reaction would have been if another name had been called out.

"Nothing," he said. "We won the tournament. No way I could have cared."

It was a popular choice, toasted with a loud ovation by the St. John's-leaning crowd and by both coaches afterward. "I certainly thought he deserved it," Knight said. "He had a great tournament."

Carnesecca noted he was pleased with the work a series of players he alternated on May did against the Hoosier senior. "And he still got 29 points," Carnesecca said. "That goes to show you what a great player he is. He certainly deserved the MVP."

"I thought it was the greatest thing in the world," said Buckner, Hoosier co-captain with May and a selection with him on the all-tournament team (along with IU's Benson, Manhattan's Lockhart, and Johnson and Alagia of St. John's).

"Scott's a great player who played a great tournament, and he's going to keep on doing great things," Buckner bubbled on. "I'm kinda high on Scott."

"Sure, it's a thrill," May said. "It means a lot to me. It means a lot of people liked the way I played and the way our team played.

"I just think motivation is always important, and if you think as a coach that a game is going to take care of itself in getting your team ready to play, you're making a mistake. In our Kentucky game last year, I started Scott May just because I thought he was ready to play. It was as simple as that. But I'm not so sure that our kids didn't think, 'We've got Scott back now; everything's OK,' and maybe we went into that game without the edge we should have had. And we were one of the eight teams left in the NCAA tournament, playing for a chance to go to the national finals."

— Bob Knight

INDIANA 76

	M	FG	FT	R	A	PF	TP
May, f	38	9-14	11-12	8	3	4	29
Abernethy, f	40	5- 8	2- 2	3	2	0	12
Benson, c	24	2- 4	0- 0	4	2	4	4
Buckner, g	24	4-13	6- 7	0	3	5	14
Wilkerson, g	40	4- 7	0- 3	8	6	4	8
Crews	6	0- 0	2- 2	0	0	1	2
Radford	18	1- 1	3- 4	3	1	1	5
Wisman	5	0- 0	0- 0	0	1	1	0
Valavacius	5	0- 0	2- 2	1	0	2	2
Team				1			
Totals		25-47	26-32	28	18	22	76

ST. JOHN'S 69

	M	FG	FT	R	A	PF	TP
Smith, f	26	2- 6	2- 3	6	2	5	6
Farmer, f	39	1- 3	0- 0	1	1	5	2
Johnson, c	40	10-17	3- 4	10	1	5	23
Alagia, g	40	5-12	6- 8	3	4	4	16
Williams, g	39	6- 9	2- 2	1	2	3	14
Rellford	25	3- 7	2- 2	6	0	4	8
Weadock	3	0- 0	0- 0	0	0	0	0
Clarke	1	0- 0	0- 0	0	0	0	0
Winfree	1	0- 2	0- 0	0	0	1	0
Robertson	1	0- 0	0- 0	0	0	0	0
Team				3			
Totals		27-56	15-19	30	10	27	69

SCORE BY HALVES

Indiana	39	37 —	76
St. John's	36	33 —	69

Errors: Indiana 16, St. John's 17

	FG	Pct.	FT	Pct.
Indiana	25-47	.532	26-32	.812
St. John's	27-56	.482	15-19	.789

Officials: Ed Cartotto and Norm Van Arsdalen
Attendance: 19,694 (capacity)

Scott May — Joins Robertson, Alcindor, Lucas, Gola on Festival MVP list

"St. John's has a great basketball team — I was really impressed with them. They're gonna be a tough team the rest of the way."

May's night included the defensive assignment on the leading St. John's scorer, Smith, who fouled out with only six points. "I knew he was a great basketball player and I had to do a good job on him," May said. "Defense was a big part of our ball game."

Two things happened to May that hadn't happened in the first eight Hoosier games — he got in foul trouble, and he ran into a stretch where he couldn't get free from the determined Redmen's defense for a shot.

The two factors were related.

The no-shot stretch lasted 10 minutes, during which a 51-45 lead (reached when May was fouled attempting his last shot before the dry spell and he converted both free throws) vanished. And in the middle of it all, he picked up his fourth foul, a charging call.

"I couldn't take a chance after that," he said. "We weren't setting very good screens, so we weren't getting open very well, and they were doing a good job — you've gotta give them credit. I couldn't just power my way in again and take a chance on getting a fifth foul, so I just didn't get anything."

That ended with one of the biggest baskets of the night, a bullseye he threw in from the deep right corner with the game tied, 65-65, and St. John's and the packed house sniffing an upset.

The last five of May's 29 final-game points came at the free-throw line in the last 84 seconds, clinching victory. He looked in total command of the situation in throwing the free throws through mechanically. Looks may have lied. "My hands were going like this the first time," May said, grinning as he held a huge, shaking right hand.

There's another list, a new one with one name on it — men who have played on a Festival champion and coached one.

Knight became the first, Monday night's victory going alongside the 1960 championship the Ohio State team he played on as a junior won by beating St. Bonaventure in the final game.

Knight isn't given to personal comments, but winning a major title in the Garden had to have its special satisfactions.

Seven times he had brought teams to the Garden — to two Madison Square Gardens, in fact — his Army teams in the 1965 Holiday Festival and the 1966 National Invitation Tourney at the "old" Garden and his '68, '69 and '70 Army teams and his first Indiana club (1972) in the NIT after the switch was made to the current building in February of 1968.

The other times, Knight was battling odds when he arrived. He landed some choice punches with those scrappy Army clubs, but Monday was the first time one of his teams played for a championship in the Garden. It also was his 102nd victory at IU, exactly the number he had when he left the state of New York and West Point. This time, he got there in 1½ fewer years and 30 fewer games.

St. John's a Big Ten warm-up, Buckner says

A New York questioner sought to be philosophical in asking Buckner: "What is the Indiana basketball team taking back from having played in this tournament?"

"Are you kidding?" pragmatist Buckner responded. Pointing to a silver championship trophy not far away, he said: "What's this?

"No, really, it's a good start for us going into our conference season, because that's just the kind of games we're going to be running into."

"Minnesota's pretty rough, I hear," the newsman said.

"Man, you're talking about a game way out in the season," Buckner said. "I'm talking about our first game (Saturday at Ohio State)."

As a senior, Buckner is more likely to remember the 70-69 and 85-79 missteps the Hoosiers had at Ohio State his first two college years than Indiana's 72-66 victory there last year — the Hoosiers' first at St. John Arena since 1967 and a game in which they trailed with eight minutes to go. Similarly, he is more likely to remember the St. John's game for the victory and the tourney championship than for the 1,000th point of his Hoosier career, picked up in progress.

Not that the achievement is insignificant. He's only the fifth Hoosier guard and 16th player to do it.

But for a few seconds during the game, Buckner thought he might remember the night for something else.

With 2:24 to go and Indiana leading, 69-65, Buckner glumly went to the bench after fouling out on a charging call that turned the ball over to St. John's.

As he reached Knight on the sidelines, Buckner said, "That may have been the dumbest play in the history of basketball."

An hour later, on the merry Hoosier team bus

Quinn Buckner — 16th Hoosier to score 1,000

headed back to their hotel from the Garden, Knight yelled to Buckner: "Hey, Quinn — did you expect me to argue with you?"

"I figured you'd give me support one way or the other," Buckner said as both laughed.

Knight had reacted to the remark at the time with a quick pat and a command. "He told me to keep on the guys who were out there — to keep them going," Buckner said. "I did, but they were getting along just fine."

Buckner on the sidelines is an impatient sitter, eager to bounce up with warnings or reminders or encouraging words to someone on the court. The same New Yorker who asked the opening question wondered if Knight approved of such sideline direction.

"Oh, yeah," Buckner said, "except, first of all, I shouldn't have been on the bench directing things. I should have been on the *floor* directing things."

Another post-game questioner asked if Indiana was "particularly up, with your goal of an undefeated season on the line."

"That's not what our goal is," Buckner said. "Our goal is to do the best job we can.

"St. John's didn't surprise us. They had to be up for this game.

"We have to be prepared for that every game because of the position we're in. Every team we play now — they all have good players and they've all got a sense of pride."

Garden jitters, fouls don't shake Hoosiers

They laugh and call them "Garden Jitters" in New York, the tendency of good teams and great players to play below par the first time they're tested in the most famous arena in America: Madison Square Garden.

They didn't see them in an Indiana team that had all sorts of pressure on it Monday night — a full house heavily weighted with backers for underdog St. John's, the quick and talented Redmen inspired for their shot at the nation's No. 1-ranked team, and fouls tapping Indiana's starters as never before in the last few seasons, forcing the Hoosiers to go to a bench considered suspect by even the people who were ranking this as the best college team to come along in a while.

Carnesecca, who gave the Hoosiers one of the glossiest pre-game build-ups, took back none of it after his 9-0 team chased the Hoosiers to the end before losing in what the Garden announcer called "one of the greatest games ever played here."

"I will say it — I consider it one of the great teams," Carnesecca said of Indiana. "Another team would have folded, the trouble they were in. They had Buckner, Benson and May in foul trouble and they never lost their poise. That's the kind of team that is."

There was opportunity for self-serving in the

comment; clearly, the better Indiana is rated, the better Carnesecca's own team is because there was little difference in the two good clubs Monday night. But superlatives were dropping all over the Garden for the intense way the two teams went at each other — the exceptional St. John's quickness against Indiana's strength, a match-up that produced offsetting edges at each end of the court throughout a tense night.

Knight was finishing his post-game press remarks when he noticed Carnesecca sitting at the side of the room, waiting to go on. "I didn't even see you sitting there when I called you a great coach, you little jerk," Knight needled.

"But let me tell you something — you've got a hell of a team, and they're really, really well-coached."

After Knight left, Carnesecca said, "I have nothing but high praise for my kids.

"They're down a little right now, naturally — the sting of defeat and all that.

"But I told them after the game: 'Look, I hope this game is going to make you a better club. Let's use it for our advantage. I've seen St. John's teams win this tourney and go downhill after that.'

"What does it mean to me to lose? I lost 50 games one year (as coach of the American Basketball Association New York Nets). I can live with one."

Carnesecca said he had hoped his team's quickness could get IU in foul trouble. "The only way a cruiser can beat a battleship is with a couple of torpedoes," he said, grinning.

"But everybody was in foul trouble tonight, and I thought we still maintained our aggressiveness to the end. That was one thing we said before the game: we were never going to sit back."

Carnesecca reveled in the Garden-record crowd. "That was New York people who came from all over the city to see city kids play the No. 1 team in the country," he said. "And there are people who say college basketball is dead in New York."

As for the "Garden Jitters," Carnesecca wasn't counting on them. Saturday night, after his team had beaten South Carolina to gain the finals and he was sitting in the stands watching IU against Manhattan, a well-wisher suggested, "Maybe they'll get the Garden Jitters." It was halftime then, and IU led, 48-30. "Yeah," Carnesecca responded, "48 points in a half and they didn't even break a sweat. The Garden sure scared them."

'Fifth-man' Abernethy takes turn as IU star

Writing in *The New York Daily News* Monday, Phil Pepe said: "Tom Abernethy is a 6-7 forward. To future generations, he is destined to be 'the fifth man on that great Indiana team.' On most other teams, he would be called a star."

Abernethy didn't change teams, but he was a star of the Indiana conquest of previously-undefeated St. John's that made the Hoosiers champions of the 1975 Holiday Festival tourney.

Twice in little more than a minute after stand-outs Benson and Buckner had gone to the bench with four fouls in a tied ball game, it was Abernethy who stuck in jump shots and kept St. John's from taking control of the game.

He had four of those in all, plus two free throws, in a major second-half contribution to the scoring side of the narrow victory. "If you're talking about offense, yes, this may have been his best game," Knight said. "But he's been doing an excellent job on defense and rebounding the whole tournament."

Abernethy roomed with Buckner in New York, and he got a Sunday night lecture from Buckner on his ability to contribute more to the Hoosier offense. "He was propping up my confidence," Abernethy said, smiling. "He kept telling me I could hit the shots."

Early in the game, Abernethy worked his inside moves precisely and blackboard-perfect and slipped in for two easy baskets. Each time, Johnson, an excellent jumper, clouted the shots back in his face — and neither one was ruled goal-tending.

The blocks inevitably inspire a hometown crowd, and sometimes they have a devastating effect on the blockee's psyche. "They told me I'd better move outside," Abernethy said, grinning. And he did it without scars. On two of his jump shots, he just got the shot away when Johnson came leaping at him, missing the ball each time by inches.

"I knew if I hit a few it would take some of the load off Scotty," Abernethy said. May was the focal point of the St. John's defense and difficult to spring at times, especially after he, too, got in foul trouble.

Earlier this year, Abernethy said, he probably wouldn't have taken the shots he hit. "I was a little too conscious of setting screens and not looking for how I could get a shot myself," he said. "And then, too, I've been shooting pretty well, and that helps the confidence." He's hitting so well that his 4-for-7 (.571) Monday lowered his season percentage. He went in shooting .667. "He can shoot but he won't," Buckner said. "If there's been any chance he would miss, he hasn't been taking it."

Benson would have liked to take some of the load off May, too, but Benson had his toughest evening of the season.

Only 1½ minutes into the game, Johnson scored a 3-point play that drew Benson's first foul. A minute later, Johnson scored again, and two minutes after that, Benson drew his second foul on offense.

"Any time you get in foul trouble, it hurts the way you play," Benson said. "I didn't play him the way I was supposed to, and I didn't go to the boards the way I should."

"We were very, very fortunate to win a game with only four points from him," Knight said. "We would normally figure on 18 to 20." Buckner became the first Hoosier starter to foul out of a game this year, and he did it with four fouls. An official's miscall charged an early-game foul to him (No. 21), rather than No. 20, Wilkerson, the guilty party.

The result of the foul problem was sudden prominence for Crews, Radford and Valavicius in the second half, with Jim Wisman filling in for Buckner for five minutes in the first half.

"This, as much as any game we've played this year, was a real team achievement," Knight said. "I really don't ever remember having to make so many changes since I've been in coaching. I don't remember ever doing that much jockeying around."

Wilkerson had another night when he guarded a forward, a center and a guard. Abernethy did just as much switching when new situations came up, and every other Hoosier on the floor had his assignment changed at least once. "I thought both Wilkerson and Abernethy did a good job defensing the post," Knight said.

Tom Abernethy — 'Doing an excellent job'

Indiana 66, Ohio State 64

Indiana got a lesson in Big Ten realities Saturday but squeezed through with a 66-64 victory over Ohio State in the two teams' Big Ten opener.

In the end, it was two free throws by Kent Benson with 19 seconds to go — the only points Indiana managed out of four one-and-one chances in the last 63 seconds — that let the Hoosiers get past the upset-sniffing Buckeyes before the first capacity crowd of the year at St. John Arena, 13,489.

The Hoosiers didn't make all their own breaks in this escape. Buckeye sophomore Jud Wood, a leader in the upset try, had a great play blow up in his face when he missed a layup after a mid-court steal with 1:16 to play.

The game went down to the final second. Ohio State cut the IU lead to 66-64 with Wood's shot from the corner at 0:04 and called time out before Indiana could get the ball in bounds.

One second ticked off when the Hoosiers completed the in-bounds pass to Quinn Buckner, who was fouled. Another ticked away when Buckner missed the free throw and Buckeye Craig Taylor rebounded and called an immediate time out.

That left 0:02 on the clock, and Ohio State tried a floor-length pass that just missed connecting with fleet Larry Bolden along the baseline on the right side of the court. Bolden dropped the ball out of bounds at 0:01, and the game ended with a 60-foot pass from Buckner to Benson, Indiana's offensive leader in this one.

"He was the only one we had who could throw the ball in the ocean the last half," Indiana coach Bob Knight said.

Benson finished with 23 points, second-high to Scott May, who had 24. But it was Benson who hit the big points at the end, working inside against a Buckeye zone specially tailored for IU — with the 6-0 Bolden playing in the middle to give Ohio State taller players on the perimeter (an anti-May device).

Indiana fell behind, 52-50, on Wood's basket with 10:36 to play, but two straight Benson baskets inside the zone and over Bolden switched the lead back to IU — for good, as things turned out.

Three more Benson points helped moved the Hoosier lead to 58-52, but Mike Daugherty's jump shot off the baseline cut it to 64-62 with 3:37 to go.

The Bucks had the ball back three more times, including Wood's attempted layup. Jim Crews, victimized by Wood on the steal, averted another chance by picking off a mid-court pass, and the Hoosiers rebounded Buckeye misses to survive the other two threats.

Bolden finished with 20 points, hitting 9 of 13 shots and Daugherty, playing the game of his

Buckeye life, had 18 on 8-for-9 shooting. The Hoosiers outrebounded Ohio State, 40-27, Benson having edges of 23-8 in points and 12-9 in rebounds in the renewal of his three-year duel with Taylor.

The Hoosiers gave the scrappy Buckeyes life by blowing a series of chances to take control of the game in the first half, which ended with Indiana a shaky 40-38 leader.

May, who missed his first four shots and didn't score until he wrestled in a rebound basket with nine minutes gone in the game, heated up fast to scored 18 points in the half, but Bolden matched him point-for-point.

May's three-point play with 6:19 to go broke a 24-24 tie, but two free throws by freshman Fred Poole and a breakaway basket by Bolden — 8-for-8 in the half — gave Ohio State its first lead, 28-27, and turned on the capacity crowd, relatively docile till then.

A five-point Hoosier sequence, wrapped around a technical foul assessed against Ohio State coach

---

INDIANA 66

	M	FG	FT	R	A	PF	TP
May, f	40	10-24	3- 3	9	2	2	24
Abernethy, f	33	4- 8	0- 0	5	3	2	8
Benson, c	40	9-12	5- 7	12	0	2	23
Buckner, g	34	2-10	0- 3	3	8	3	4
Wilkerson, g	33	2- 4	0- 2	3	2	3	4
Crews	8	1- 1	0- 1	0	1	1	2
Radford	5	0- 0	0- 0	1	1	1	0
Valavicius	7	0- 1	1- 2	0	0	1	1
Team				7			
Totals		28-60	10-19	40	17	15	66

OHIO STATE 64

	M	FG	FT	R	A	PF	TP
Poole, f	33	2- 9	2- 2	3	1	3	6
Daugherty, f	39	8- 9	2- 2	2	2	5	18
Taylor, c	40	3- 9	2- 2	9	4	4	8
Wood, g	32	5-12	0- 0	5	4	3	10
Bolden, g	40	9-13	2- 2	2	1	4	20
Bayless	10	0- 0	2- 2	2	0	1	2
Cline	6	0- 1	0- 0	0	0	1	0
Team				4			
Totals		27-53	10-10	27	12	21	64

SCORE BY HALVES

Indiana	40	26 —	66
Ohio State	38	26 —	64

Errors: Indiana 19, Ohio State 24
Technical foul: Ohio State bench

	FG	Pct.	FT	Pct.
Indiana	28-60	.467	10-19	.526
Ohio State	27-53	.509	10-10	1.000

Officials: Richard Weiler, George Solomon and Phil Robinson
Attendance: 13,489 (capacity)

55

Fred Taylor when he thought May charged after hitting a go-ahead jump shot, put Indiana back in front, 32-28.

But Ohio State caught up again on two Bolden baskets. Two field goals by May and one by Benson opened the Hoosiers' widest lead at 40-34 with only 1:23 to go in the half, but Ohio State nibbled back to cut the halftime edge to two.

Knight was unhappy with the Hoosiers' error total (19, 14 in the first half). "There's a lack of concentration when you have that many errors," he said. Shooting wasn't a bright spot for the Hoosiers in their 10th victory, either. Ohio State outshot Indiana, .509 to .467.

'We get used to it or we start getting beat'

"We outstruggled 'em," Knight said, the same comment he made seven games earlier in an escape from Notre Dame. Originality was not a pressing concern for the man who was not the least elated over his team's first Big Ten victory of the year.

This was a game with some significance that will be noted around a league never known for its servility. The Hoosiers may be top-ranked, but they can be had, and Knight made it clear he hopes the message is read as well at home as it will be around the conference.

"This team played like hell against us," Knight said of the Buckeyes, who came into the game with a 4-4 record. He indicated conviction future conference opponents are sure to be coming at the Hoosiers just as hard.

"Sure they are," he said, "and we either get used to it or we start getting beat. It's as simple as that. And I don't see any signs that we're getting used to it."

The Hoosiers have been No. 1 in the polls going into their last 31 games, so the experience of being a prime target is not new. Neither, as Knight noted, is it new in Columbus.

"There is a tremendous advantage in looking up and playing above you," Knight said of Ohio State's underdog role. "You saw it not too long ago." It was a reference, not a needling one, to Ohio State's plummet from No. 1 in its Rose Bowl upset by underdog UCLA Thursday.

"This was a lot like the game in Los Angeles," Knight said. "People came in to see their team play the game, and once they sensed they had a chance to win, they were like sharks smelling blood."

The blood-letting in this one came late in the first half when Ohio State went ahead for the first time, 28-27. The Bucks stayed ahead only 24 seconds that time and led only one other time in the game (for 32 seconds). But that was enough for the crowd to get charged up for the night, and the Buckeyes rode along with them.

"I don't think there's any question it was our best total effort of they year," Taylor said. "But if you can't get excited about playing the No. 1 team in the country, you're in real trouble."

"They always play like that against us," said Knight, who has won two of five IU visits to the gym that was home for him in college days — all five of those games decided by eight points or less.

"If they play like that all year long, they're going to be tough for anybody to beat," he said.

Bolden, a key man on both offense and defense, was the reason the Buckeyes came back as he hit all eight shots he took in the half and totaled 18 points. "His first half was unreal," Taylor said.

Taylor said the Buckeyes hadn't played the particular zone defense they used most of the way against IU, with Bolden tucked in the middle of it to cut off the quick pivot passes to Benson and to take Bolden off the top of the zone in favor of taller players.

"We tried to get a little size around the perimeter because May just shoots over you," Taylor said, smiling as he added:

"I don't think you can play one thing against Indiana. Bobby's living high on the hog because he can with the kids he has.

"They really power the boards. There were about three instances where we were in perfect position and they took a swipe and knocked it loose. We've got to get a little more size somewhere."

Knight said the thought of running into zone defenses regularly the rest of the way didn't worry him. "We've played 10 games and won 10 and seen some zone in just about all of them," he said. "Let 'em zone. We can't be doing all that bad against them."

He indicated some compassion for Wood, who stole the ball and appeared headed for a game-tying layup with 1:16 to go when his unchallenged shot rolled off. "It's too bad the poor kid has to live with that," Knight said, "but if we make some free throws (the Hoosiers missed three one-and-one chances after going to a stall with a four-point lead and four minutes to go) it doesn't make any difference. There were a lot of other points that got away, too.

"We made three or four really bad passes there at the end, but we had to make some good plays, too. Jimmy Crews stole the ball after we threw it away once, and we did some good rebounding on the defensive backboard at the end."

"It was a 'W,' " a Columbus newsman said, and Knight agreed: "Yeah, in the end it was. We've got to feel lucky to get out with it."

Indiana 78, Northwestern 61

In one of the classic blowouts of the 1974-75 Assembly Hall season, Indiana amassed a 46-12 lead in the first 19 minutes against Northwestern on the way to an 82-58 victory.

It's hard to improve on that, but Monday night the Hoosiers stung a better Wildcat team with a 43-18 wallop in 18 sweet minutes that made things easy in a 78-61 Hoosier romp — No. 11 this season, No. 21 in a row in Big Ten play to set an all-time IU record, and No. 26 in the live string at Assembly Hall.

The blowout stretch came in mid-game this time, after the Hoosier faithful — a paltry 15,923 in the hall where all 17,000 seats were sold, some obviously to students who haven't made it back to campus yet for second-semester classes — worried a lot in the first 13 minutes.

Billy McKinney, whose reported knee pains apparently never reached his darting feet, was the man who kept the pressure on Indiana early.

Billy caught IU guard Quinn Buckner with both of his wheels ouchy — a toe injury on one side

Wayne Radford looks penitent as official Mike Mathis signals a foul and James Wallace (55), Tony Allen (15) and Bob Wilkerson watch

and a bruised knee on the other leaving Buckner in a position where McKinney had all the edges and Buckner all the fouls.

No. 3 came for him with 10:42 to go in the half, and Bob Wilkerson — out of the starting lineup for the first time in 43 games, chiefly because of defensive problems against similarly swift Larry Bolden of Ohio State Saturday night — came in as Buckner's replacement. IU's lead then was 18-15, and McKinney had 11 of the Northwestern points.

The 6-7 Wilkerson mastered 6-0 Billy twice last year, obviously bothering him with his enveloping size. This one made it three times for Wilkerson, for McKinney scored just three points the rest of the night, the key to the pullaway and victory. "I thought Wilkerson played very poorly at Ohio State," Hoosier coach Bob Knight said in a plainspeaking review. "Tonight, he probably played as well as I've ever had a guard play on defense."

The other Wildcat guard, Tim Teasley, took over with long-range bombing for a few minutes to keep Northwestern close at 22-19 with seven minutes left in the half.

But free-throw shooting, the phase of the game that went so sour it almost killed the Hoosiers at Ohio State, provided the pry that lifted Indiana to a 40-27 halftime lead.

At that point, Hoosier free throwers were officially 20-for-20, including seven perfect one-and-one exploitations.

Tight defense was what made that productivity into net profit. Four times in the last four minutes of the half the Hoosiers coaxed Northwestern turnovers, one of those when Wilkerson engulfed McKinney so completely the little lefty couldn't shoot or pass and thus wound up in a jump ball with Wilkerson. He couldn't control that, either. Few in college ball could.

"The guys we had in there at the end of the half took us from the lead of about 4 points that they inherited to a 13-point lead at halftime," Knight said of Wilkerson, Wayne Radford, Jim Crews, Tom Abernethy and Kent Benson.

"Then the combination we used at the start of the second half (Scott May, who drew his third foul with 5:22 left in the half and sat down for Crews, back in with Wilkerson, Radford, Abernethy and Benson) gave us very good basketball and enabled us to build up a pretty good lead."

The lead topped out at 65-37 on Abernethy's jump shot with 9:04 left. Knight already had started pulling his front-liners by then.

Contributions came in all ways. May had a rare unproductive night, scoring only two field goals and 13 points and taking a rap on the right side of his head that opened a cut to match the one he got on the left side of his head at Ohio State. "I think Scott was just not feeling right," Knight said. But he topped both teams with 10 rebounds in only 21 minutes, and he drilled 9 of 10 free-throw chances.

This night, the scoring came from the other two men on the Hoosier front line, Benson (22 points) and Abernethy (16).

Radford teamed with Wilkerson for effective backcourt play at both ends of the court. Each scored 8 points, Wilkerson hitting Radford twice for fast-break cash-ins and Radford dealing off 6 assists of his own.

McKinney, who sat out nine minutes after the game was clinched, topped Northwestern with his 14 points, and Teasley had 12.

The Hoosiers' second Big Ten victory went with 18 last year and one over Purdue closing out the 1974 season for the 21 that beat the old IU record of 20 straight conference victories, put together by Branch McCracken's 1952 and '53 teams. The only longer streaks in Big Ten history are 23 by Wisconsin in 1912 and '13 and the record 27 by the Ohio State teams of 1960-62.

INDIANA 78

	M	FG	FT	R	A	PF	TP
May, f	21	2- 7	9-10	10	0	3	13
Abernethy, f	26	7-13	2- 2	7	4	1	16
Benson, c	35	10-16	2- 3	2	1	2	22
Buckner, g	9	0- 1	2- 2	0	1	3	2
Wisman, g	14	0- 1	0- 0	1	1	5	0
Valavicius	13	0- 2	2- 2	4	1	3	2
Radford	25	2- 3	4- 4	3	6	4	8
Wilkerson	25	2- 6	4- 4	4	4	4	8
Crews	9	0- 0	0- 0	1	0	1	0
Haymore	9	1- 4	1- 4	4	0	3	3
Bender	8	1- 2	2- 3	1	0	1	4
Roberson	1	0- 0	0- 0	0	0	1	0
Eells	5	0- 1	0- 0	1	0	1	0
Team				3			
Totals		25-56	28-34	38	18	33	78

NORTHWESTERN 61

	M	FG	FT	R	A	PF	TP
Boesen, f	11	1- 3	0- 0	2	1	5	2
Svete, f	18	1- 3	7- 9	2	0	4	9
Wallace, c	31	2- 5	0- 0	5	0	3	4
McKinney, g	31	4-10	6- 9	1	2	2	14
Teasley, g	30	5-10	2- 2	1	0	1	12
Allen	20	1- 6	3- 4	3	0	4	5
Fields	19	0- 2	0- 0	1	0	4	0
Hildebrand	7	1- 2	0- 0	1	0	4	2
Klaas	22	2- 3	3- 3	3	0	0	7
Endsley	20	1- 3	2- 4	2	1	2	4
Team				10			
Totals		18-47	25-33	33	4	28	61

SCORE BY HALVES

Northwestern...................	27	34 —	61
Indiana.......................	40	38 —	78

Errors: Northwestern 29, Indiana 24
Technical foul: Indiana bench 2

	FG	Pct.	FT	Pct.
Northwestern	18-47	.383	25-33	.758
Indiana	25-56	.446	28-34	.824

Officials: Charles Fouty, Tom Rucker and Mike Mathis
Attendance: 15,923 (sellout)

Abernethy turns shooter
with injured May down

Benson was feeling pretty good about his contributions Monday night until someone came around with a statistics sheet.

His eyes slid across to the rebound column, then bulged in disbelief.

"Two?" he shouted. Turning to IU assistant coach Harold Andreas, he asked: "I have two rebounds? Can that be right?"

"I don't think so," Andreas said soothingly. "I only remember one."

Benson's concern — on a night when he played well enough at both ends of the court to outscore his match-ups from Northwestern, 22-4 — reflects the growing Hoosier concern for specific roles they know to be theirs if the pieces are to fit together as well as possible for this 1975-76 Indiana team.

Some things are taken for granted. Everyone on the floor will work at defense, though some will draw tougher assignments than others, *i.e.*, Wilkerson's mid-game cooling of Northwestern star Billy McKinney.

On offense, there are variances in responsibilities, too, and Abernethy appears comfortable in a newly stressed role as a scorer — though not

Tom Abernethy swoops in on Northwestern's James Wallace

ready to claim marksmanship on a par with graduated Hoosier forward Steve Green, the most accurate shooter in IU history. "One game is no comparison with him," Abernethy laughed.

Still, Abernethy's sniping in the 15-to-18-foot range was one of the Hoosier highlights Monday. He ultimately took 13 shots and hit 7, after averaging fewer than 6 shots a game in Indiana's first 10 victories.

He was acting under orders Monday. "Abernethy can score," Knight said. "With him, it's just a matter of his getting himself in position to score. Perhaps he was a little too conscious of giving the ball up in the past."

"I had some open shots and I was definitely looking for some," Abernethy said. "I've been shooting a fairly good percentage (.660 going into the Monday game), and he wanted me to get as many good shots as I could.

"I remember forcing one a little (a shot approaching 20 feet)." That's long for any Hoosier and well beyond the normal range of Abernethy, a high school center for current IU assistant Bob Donewald when both were at South Bend St. Joseph's.

There was a time earlier in the year when Abernethy probably wouldn't even have strayed that far out on the floor, confining himself for the most part to an under-the-basket role as a blocker and passer for Benson and May.

"I guess my kind of shot is a little different from what it used to be," he said. "Before, if I came out that high, it probably was just to relieve pressure on one of the guards. Now, I'll take the shot if I have it."

Benson's individual challenge came a few nights earlier, in Columbus, Ohio, against a longtime nemesis: Craig Taylor. "I knew I had to do a job against Taylor, especially after what he had done to me the last two or three times," Benson said. "If I didn't, I was letting myself down, I was letting my team down and I was letting the coach down."

Benson had 23 points and 12 rebounds that night (to 8 points and 9 rebounds for Taylor). "Then tonight (against Northwestern), I knew I had to continue playing well," he said.

James Wallace was the latest of many centers who have sought to take Benson off the defensive backboard by moving well out on the floor — sacrificing a big man for the opposition, too, while leaving Benson in good operating room.

"I like playing out on the floor," Benson smiled. "That does make it a little tougher to rebound, naturally. I just try to block out my man and make sure Scott or Tommy can get the ball.

"But they had me down for one rebound the first half, and if that's true, it's ridiculous. I should be getting a lot more than that. There's no reason I can't go to the boards even if I do start out on the court."

Knight bucked the tradition that "you don't break up a winning combination" by making his first starting lineup change of the year — Wisman at guard for Wilkerson.

Knight denied the intent was a shake-up. "We're just trying to play basketball with the best basketball players we have," he said. "It's not that you're searching for something in particular. If we have someone out there who for one reason or another is not getting done what we feel we have to have done, then there are other players on our team who are working just as hard in practice and they deserve a chance to see if they can do it.

"In this game, though, I thought Radford and Wilkerson gave us really good defensive pressure on the guards."

Buckner, who normally teams with Wilkerson, played only the first nine minutes Monday before drawing three fouls and sitting down. "Buckner's got a bruised knee, and he hurt the big toe on the other foot," Knight said. "Once he got in foul trouble, we took him out and when the lead got pretty big, there was no need to bring him back in."

May also was sub-par physically after cutting a deep gash on one side if his head Saturday at Columbus and nicking the other side Monday.

Wilkerson takes all fun out for NU's McKinney

A chance to play against Buckner excites Chicagoan McKinney.

And little Billy, a sprightly sort, got the match-up he wanted when Buckner picked him up on Northwestern's first possession.

"I get up for him," said McKinney, who has a history of good games against Buckner. "Don't get me wrong, I think he's a great player, but I think I'm good too, I think I'm kind of underrated. So if I play well against Quinn Buckner, they have to give me recognition.

"I've been kind of misfortunate. He's been a good player and he's been on a championship team."

McKinney flits around a basketball court, playing peek-a-boo behind screens, flying down the lane or lofting soft left-handers. Against Buckner early, it worked, and McKinney's 11 points in the first nine minutes kept Northwestern within 18-15. But Wilkerson, benched for the first time in the last two years, shadowed McKinney all over the court after fouls took Buckner out.

"I don't think it made that much difference at first," said McKinney. "The first few times he (Wilkerson) was in there, I drove around him, penetrated. I didn't want to make it seem like I was going one-on-one. I wanted to penetrate, but not all the time. I wanted to get my teammates involved."

That didn't work either, even though both McKinney and Wildcat coach Tex Winter had hoped it would. "We're not looking, we never have looked for McKinney to carry the whole load," said

Winter. "You just can't ask a 6-0, 150-pound player to carry the load in the Big Ten. We want to get everybody involved in the game."

None of McKinney's teammates ever got sufficiently involved in Northwestern's offense to do much good. Teasley had a dozen points, the most help any Wildcat could give McKinney.

And Wilkerson finally mastered McKinney, too.

"Wilkerson's 6-6 (actually 6-7) and very quick," said Winter. "He's the kind of big guard that Billy can't even see over. Billy's always had trouble with him."

"His height helps him," said McKinney, a 6-footer only by the grace of a generous yardstick. "He can excite you. He's all spread out. He can force you into doing a stupid thing, like making a charge.

"I wasn't intimidated by him. No one gets me intimidated."

Northwestern found out about charges. The Wildcats were called for seven offensive fouls in the first half alone, when Indiana hit all 20 of its free throws to take a 40-27 halftime lead. "We never anticipated that," said Winter.

Indiana was tagged with a flock of fouls, too—33 in all, to Northwestern's 28. The fouls weren't lost on Winter, who expected Indiana to be physical. The Hoosiers were a little more than that, he said.

"You can be much more physical at home than on the road," Winter said. "Most teams can be.

"Sure they can. But we can't comment on the officiating."

That was far from Northwestern's only problem. The Wildcats hit only 38 per cent of their shots in the game, had only seven rebounds at halftime, and made 29 turnovers. In one second-half stretch, Northwestern did get off six hurried shots—two of them blocked—but made seven turnovers and fouled on another shot attempt. Net result? Two points in the first seven minutes of the half as Indiana surged ahead, 54-29.

"They got a spread on us and it gave them some breathing room," Winter said. "They kind of relaxed and started hitting well, which they haven't been doing too well lately."

"I was impressed with Michigan's muscle. I would like to see the Michigan-Indiana game. They'll need four referees for that one."

— Frank McGuire
South Carolina coach

60

Indiana 80, Michigan 74

Indiana blitzed Michigan opening both halves Saturday and hurdled the Wolverines, 80-74, in a game billed as the top-ranked Hoosiers' biggest road test of the season to date.

Indiana ran up a 16-2 lead in the first six minutes. Then, after Michigan had closed it to 36-33 at halftime, the Hoosiers grabbed firm control with a 10-4 spurt opening the second half. The lead that surge provided (46-37) never shrank below 6 points until the last three minutes.

Michigan's closest penetration then was 4, but it took a smothering block by Kent Benson on a layup attempt by Michigan's Steve Grote to shut off the Wolverine comeback in the last 75 seconds.

The Benson block, which produced a jump ball that the 6-11 Benson easily controlled against the 6-2 Grote, came with 1:10 left and Indiana's lead at 74-70.

The Hoosiers held the ball for 15 seconds before Bob Wilkerson worked free for a layup. Wilkerson was knocked to the floor after the shot by Michigan's standout freshman center, Phil Hubbard, who fouled out on the play.

Stunned by the fall, Wilkerson was replaced by Jim Crews, whose two free throws ran the lead to 78-70 with 0:55 left, clinching things.

Benson closed his shooting day 16-for-18, the best shooting percentage ever for a Hoosier scoring that many field goals. He had one miss each half as he led IU to a .596 shooting performance (34 for 57) that goes into the books as eighth-best ever by a Hoosier team — four of those by this year's team.

Indiana's defense was the key to the Hoosiers' fast start. Michigan's may have contributed to the second-half spurt.

The Hoosiers fell behind in the first 10 seconds when fleet Rickey Green dribbled away from Wilkerson for a layup.

But that was the last defensive mistake the Hoosiers made for a while. Michigan got only two more shots in the next six minutes, losing the ball six times to steals and another two times on mistakes as Indiana ran in 16 points in a row to stun a Michigan-record crowd of 14,063.

Benson was IU's offense after Quinn Buckner dropped in three layups in the first 2½ minutes. The redhead hit his first six shots, missed a jump shot from the baseline, then drilled three more in a row.

In the process, he helped work Hubbard into foul trouble, drawing three in the first 6½ minutes, before Hubbard picked up his fourth in pursuit of a rebound that Wayne Radford had in his hands.

However, little-used Tom Bergen gave Michigan a surprise lift. The 6-10 transfer from Utah hit a jump shot and two free throws after replacing Hubbard and maneuvered into position to draw a charging foul that put Benson in trouble with three personals just 25 seconds before the half.

Hubbard's problem prompted Michigan coach Johnny Orr to open the second half in a zone defense, the first time the Wolverines have used one all year. It wasn't preplanned, Orr insisted. "Gosh, no," he said, "if Hubbard had only had three fouls, even, we wouldn't have done it."

However, Orr admitted the Wolverines have been practicing the defense since the start of the season and said of the Hoosiers, "I didn't think they were a particularly good shooting team . . . until today."

Planned or not, the zone was a 6½-minute disaster for Michigan. It ignited the Hoosiers, particularly Scott May, shut off until then by Michigan

INDIANA 80

	M	FG	FT	R	A	PF	TP
May, f	39	6-15	3- 4	9	2	3	15
Abernethy, f	40	4- 6	1- 3	8	4	3	9
Benson, c	39	16-18	1- 2	4	2	3	33
Buckner, g	32	5- 9	1- 3	1	5	5	11
Wilkerson, g	39	3- 7	2- 2	5	14	3	8
Radford	5	0- 2	2- 2	1	0	2	2
Valavicius	3	0- 0	0- 0	0	0	0	0
Crews	1	0- 0	2- 2	0	0	0	2
Team				4			
Totals		34-57	12-18	32	27	19	80

MICHIGAN 74

	M	FG	FT	R	A	PF	TP
Britt, f	37	2- 5	0- 0	0	5	4	4
Robinson, f	27	2- 4	2- 2	3	0	4	6
Hubbard, c	34	11-17	1- 1	5	0	5	23
Green, g	38	8-16	2- 2	1	4	3	18
Grote, g	31	4- 8	5- 6	4	4	3	13
Baxter	11	2- 4	0- 0	0	1	1	4
Thompson	15	1- 3	0- 0	6	2	1	2
Bergen	6	1- 1	2- 2	0	0	0	4
Team				5			
Totals		31-58	12-23	24	16	21	74

SCORE BY HALVES

Indiana . . . . 36 44 — 80
Michigan . . . . 33 41 — 74
Errors: Indiana 27, Michigan 19

	FG	Pct.	FT	Pct.
Indiana	34-57	.596	12-18	.667
Michigan	31-58	.535	12-13	.923

Officials: Art White, Gary Muncy and Carel Cosby
Attendance: 14,063 (capacity, Crisler Arena record)

senior Wayman Britt's remarkably dogged defense.

May, 1-for-9 the first half, missed another shot opening the second half. Then, freed of Britt by the zone, he jammed in three jump shots in a row.

When Orr removed the zone, IU's lead was 53-44, and the Hoosiers and May were sizzling. The whole team missed only two more shots — one of those an open jump shot by Benson five feet in front of the basket that broke a string of eight straight hits for him.

Hubbard enjoyed notable offensive success himself, shooting over the foul-conscious Benson and driving well, too, in a 19-point second-half splurge that gave him Michigan scoring honors (23) and kept the game from becoming one-sided.

Even with him in high gear, Indiana pushed its lead to 68-54 on Benson's 3-point play at 8:45, and the lead was still 72-60 with 4:57 left after Buckner's layup cashing in an Abernethy interception.

But the Hoosiers wobbled down the stretch with five turnovers as Michigan scored seven of the last nine times it had the ball — the exceptions a driving layup by Grote that rolled out with 2:15 left and IU up 73-68, and the baseline drive by Grote that Benson blocked.

Benson's 33 points matched his Hoosier career high. May finished with 15, Buckner 11, Abernethy 9 and Wilkerson 8 (plus 14 assists, tying the "modern" IU record set by Buckner at Illinois in 1974).

Flaws in control game spoil big win for Knight

All around the Big Ten eyes were on Crisler Arena Saturday, because this was when and where Indiana's hold on the rest of the league was supposed to be ended by a hot and fast Michigan team.

Didn't happen. Indiana instead put the No. 13-ranked Wolverines in league trouble by winning, a defeat with a double-sting for Michigan since it came at home.

But it could have come more easily for the Hoosiers, who played dominant basketball for long stretches of the game but couldn't make their possession game work at the end. The perfectionist in Bob Knight made him almost as upset with that flaw as Orr was with losing.

The Hoosiers took a time out with the basketball in their hands and a 72-60 lead on the scoreboard with 4:29 to play. No mystery; freeze time. But, in those last 4½ minutes, the Hoosiers lost the ball six times, in six different ways — a three-second violation, a half-court pass picked off by the pressing Wolverines, a missed one-and-one, a jump ball whistled after five-second defensive pressure, a traveling violation and an errant inbounds pass at the Hoosier end.

"Our defense made some plays that put us in

Quinn Buckner barks bench orders, with Jim Crews (left), Bob Weltlich, Harold Andreas alongside

pretty good position where we could hold the ball," Knight said, "but we didn't do that very well. If you have the ball stolen or intercepted, that's one thing, but you just can't have an illegal block (that came earlier) or a three-second call when you're holding the ball. That kills us."

The late-game breakdowns weren't fatal because the Hoosiers had lots more minutes when they played very well against an opponent generally considered the best the league has sent against them in the last two seasons.

Benson's shooting was record stuff. May (9) and Abernethy (8) had almost as many rebounds (17) as Michigan's eight players (19). Strong team play offset a sub-par scoring day by IU's usual No. 1 weapon, May, who was 6-for-15.

And there were 12 Indiana steals, 4 by Abernethy and 3 each by Benson and Buckner — half of those coming when the Hoosier defense plainly shocked the free-wheeling Wolverines at the start.

"Our game plan is to get away 18-0," Knight deadpanned. "At least, I'd sure like to see it.

"But basketball flows in spurts. You're not going to keep something like that going unless the other team is totally outmanned, and that certainly wasn't the case in this one."

The jump-ball call on the smothered shot enraged Orr, who had to be restrained after the game when he tried to get to official Gary Muncy, who made the call. "I just wanted to ask him some questions," Orr said later with a peaceful smile. "I guess I'll have to ask him some other time.

"I'm only human. You can sit there only so long, and then you've got to defend your players. I wanted that foul so badly . . ."

He implied that the four first-half foul calls against his center, Hubbard, were debatable. "I think if I officiated, I could foul Kent Benson out any time I wanted to," he said. "In a big game like this, I'd let 'em go a little bit.

"But Benson was tremendous. He played a great game. So did Hubbard, considering he had four fouls in about eight minutes.

"They're certainly a good team, there's no doubt about that. I told our kids they have nothing to be ashamed of. They fought 'em all the way.

"I thought we did a pretty good job of pressing them at the end. If Grote's layup would have gone in or if they had fouled him there at the end, we would still have had a chance to win the game.

"But we didn't, so I guess that's why they're No. 1."

Michigan returns the visit to IU's Assembly Hall in a nationally-televised game Feb. 7. A dramatic fellow with a microphone asked, "Will this one eat at you until then, John?"

"I'm too old for that," Orr scoffed. "They were good. I thought it was a good game."

"A good basketball game between two good teams," Knight put it. If it had ended 4½ minutes earlier, Knight might have graded it great.

Benson's 16-for-18 'hellacious' to Orr

Orr mentioned only one Indiana player in his post-game comments, but he raved about that one — Benson.

"He just made some hellacious shots," Orr said. "That's why he's an all-American, I guess."

"I was just taking the type of shots I could hit," Benson said. "I never dreamed I'd shoot that well."

The game continued an auspicious beginning to his junior Big Ten season for Benson, who was 19-for-28 and averaged 22.5 in IU's first two league games. Saturday's performance made him 35-for-46 as a shooter in Big Ten play (.761).

"Now I've just got to think about Michigan State," said Benson, whose day would have been brighter with a few more rebounds (he had four as his Michigan counterpart, Hubbard, continued the recent pattern of Hoosier opponents by keeping Benson out on the court most of the game).

The tactic worked all right in Hubbard's scoring (23 points).

But if it was designed to give Michigan a rebounding advantage by taking Benson out of the picture, it failed, because IU forwards May and Abernethy had a wide edge over their match-ups.

That's been the key each of the three Big Ten games IU has played, for while Benson has been confined to a 6.0 league rebounding average, Indiana has had three of its best team margins of the season — 40-27 at Ohio State, 38-33 over Northwestern and 32-24 Saturday.

Benson faulted himself for Hubbard's 19-point second half, which came after Benson drew his third foul in the last half-minute of the first half.

"I played him too loosely," Benson said. "I was worrying more about the lob pass then, and he hit some outside shots."

Knight said Benson "played really well" and denied the Hoosiers sought to protect him the second half by dropping him off Hubbard more than normal. "We did change a little bit at the end of the first half and maybe he thought we were still doing some things differently," he said.

Both Orr and Knight noted the defensive work of Britt, who held May to three field goals while playing him man-to-man.

"It's to May's credit that he was having a tough time scoring and all of a sudden he got some shots and he was able to hit them," said Knight. "Britt did a hell of a job on him. He's a fine basketball player. I've said that since the first time we played him."

"He did do a good job," May admitted. "I thought he was holding me, but they didn't call it, so I guess he wasn't. He was tough to get away from.

"I let it bother me in the first half and forced some shots. I tried not to do that the last half."

Indiana 69, Michigan State 57

Since the Big Ten started piggy-backing its basketball road trips a year ago as an economy move, eight conference teams have spent 0-2 weekends in the state of Michigan.

That's every team that has tried it ... except Indiana, which completed another sweep over the state Monday night by tacking Michigan State to the wall alongside Saturday victim Michigan — the Spartans losers by a 69-57 score.

There was a capacity crowd at Michigan State's Jenison Fieldhouse (9,865), and the locals were vocal — Terry Furlow the cause for upset dreams. He stirred Spartan imaginations as few basketball players ever have by scoring over 40 points three different times last week — games of 50, 48 and 42 points that set all-time two-game, three-game and one-week scoring records for the league of Rick Mount, Gary Bradds, Jim Rayl and other noted gunners.

When Furlow, upon introduction as a Spartan starter, ran onto the floor with a finger pointed cockily at the previously introduced Hoosiers, his audacity was toasted with loud and long applause.

And, when he defied the Hoosier defense by sticking in his first two shots from well out on the court, the noise was overpowering and the optimism pervasive.

Indiana responded with a 10-point surge in barely over two minutes to take a 10-4 lead that shrank a few times but never totally disappeared the rest of the night.

Furlow kept 'em yelling — and close — with 18 points in the first half as Michigan State chopped Indiana's lead from a peak of 14 (38-24 with 3:01 left in the half) to 44-36 at halftime.

"An eight-point lead's a little shaky," IU coach Bob Knight said, "particularly if they get the second-half tip and score and maybe come back with another bucket."

Instead, the Hoosiers turned momentum their way. Indiana got the second-half tip and scored, on a rebound basket by Kent Benson. And, on the first trip to Michigan State's end, Hoosier Quinn Buckner, who inherited the defensive job on Furlow in a halftime switch, stuck out a hand and stole the first Spartan pass aimed at Furlow. "Big play," Knight noted later.

Seconds later, Furlow started upcourt with a long rebound and had a teammate well ahead of him, behind the IU defense. The Spartan captain waited a dribble too long to throw toward him, though, and Buckner slipped up from behind to steal the ball in mid-dribble.

State managed one more big try, after Scott May — who carried Indiana's offense in the first half with 16 points against a defense specially rigged just for him — drew his fourth foul with 17:41 to go and sat down, replaced by Jim Crews.

The Hoosier lead reached 48-36, dipped to 48-40, then hit a new peak at 56-41 with 14:15 to play.

Minus both Buckner (his fourth foul came at 15:22, and Wayne Radford took on Furlow) and May by then, Knight brought out his old Army game — "not really an all-out stall at the beginning," he said, "because we were able to get the ball to Benson so well."

It was the possession game that crumbled in the final minutes Saturday and made a clinched game into a close one. This time, the Hoosiers ran their lead to 64-47 and then shut off shooting entirely, though Benson and Buckner worked loose for layups in the last 1½ minutes.

"They're a patient team," Spartan coach Gus Ganakas said. "They're the *epitome* of patience."

The Spartans were something less. Furlow never did score a second-half basket off the MSU offense, his three field goals in the half coming on two steals and the early tip-in. Without his contributions, the Spartan offense went bankrupt.

INDIANA 69

	M	FG	FT	R	A	PF	TP
May, f	21	8-15	2- 2	6	2	5	18
Abernethy, f	40	4- 6	0- 0	5	3	1	8
Benson, c	40	11-20	1- 2	9	3	2	23
Buckner, g	21	2- 8	1- 2	0	2	4	5
Wilkerson, g	38	3- 6	1- 2	5	3	3	7
Crews	18	2- 2	0- 1	0	1	0	4
Radford	9	1- 1	0- 0	0	1	1	2
Wisman	13	0- 0	2- 2	1	1	0	2
Team				2			
Totals		31-58	7-11	28	16	16	69

MICHIGAN STATE 57

	M	FG	FT	R	A	PF	TP
Furlow, f	40	11-20	4- 4	7	0	0	26
Wilson, f	33	2- 4	1- 2	7	1	4	5
Kelser, c	39	5-10	0- 1	13	1	3	10
White, g	38	0- 6	2- 2	2	1	2	2
Chapman, g	33	5-14	4- 4	4	3	3	14
Nash	14	0- 0	0- 0	1	0	4	0
Wiley	2	0- 1	0- 0	0	0	0	0
Rivers	1	0- 0	0- 0	0	0	0	0
Team				2			
Totals		23-55	11-13	35	3	16	57

SCORE BY HALVES

Indiana	44	25 — 69
Michigan State	36	21 — 57

Errors: Indiana 13, Michigan State 20

	FG	Pct.	FT	Pct.
Indiana	31-58	.534	7-11	.636
Michigan State	23-55	.418	11-13	.846

Officials: Robert Burson, Ray Doran and Fred Jaspers

Attendance: 9,865 (capacity)

"We went into a one-pass-and-a-shot offense," Ganakas said. Furlow finished with 26 points, high for both teams. Guard Robert Chapman hit his 14-point average, but he built it shooting .536 for the season and he got it this time with just .357 accuracy (5-for-14).

Freshman center Greg Kelser's 13 rebounds gave Michigan State a 35-28 board edge, the first time the Hoosiers have been outrebounded in Big Ten play this year. Benson had 9 rebounds plus a team-leading 23 points. May was the only other Hoosier in double figures with 18.

Two other figures offset the rebound deficit: IU shot .534 and cut its turnovers from Saturday's 27 to 13.

Indiana kept the Big Ten lead at 4-0 (Purdue staying just behind at 3-0 by whipping Wisconsin, 91-81).

Kent Benson — Likes that crowd noise

'Cheering hypes me up,' says Benson of key goal

Indiana has played in front of capacity houses on virtually every road trip the last two years, and the setting is getting familiar. Each time, there is a pre-game moment in which the home team's lineup is introduced, the crowd roars at its wildest, adrenalin obviously flows in the players being introduced in the starting lineup . . . and Hoosiers stand by and wait.

Dave Matthews of the *Lansing State Journal* described that sort of scene in the Ann Arbor game:

"Michigan has never seen anything quite like it. An upset-crazed Crisler Arena record throng of 14,063 stood and screamed as its beloved band of basketball-playing Wolverines was introduced.

"The foe that had aroused Michigan's backers to such an unprecedented frenzy, top-ranked Indiana, stood quietly, waiting for the noise to subside and the action to begin.

"It was a beautiful scene, portending memorable moments to come. And it didn't take long at all . . . but it was Indiana, not Michigan, that rose to the occasion."

Occasionally the moments of truth come later, as at East Lansing Monday night.

Michigan State played at the top of its game in the first half and simply stayed within eight of Indiana. Early in the second half, though, when the Spartans dropped 12 down and appeared to be fading out, May drew his fourth foul and sat down, and the man who turns Spartan crowds on, Furlow, did it with a soaring, perfectly-timed leap over Benson for a tip-in. When he followed with two free throws to cut the margin to eight again, the crowd sensed "Charge!" time, and, when the Hoosiers ran through some offensive maneuvers and couldn't shake a man free for a shot, the din in the stands grew to a scream that demanded IU panic.

Instead, after 44 seconds and countless passes, Benson popped open just long enough to get a pass from Crews and convert it into a basket with a short jump shot. IU's lead climbed to 50-40 and never again got under 10, and Knight pinpointed that play as the night's backbreaker.

"That was probably the last time they could have gotten back into the game," he said. "Under those circumstances, I was probably as pleased with that as any possession we've had all year."

For all their equanimity, the Hoosiers aren't oblivious to crowd noise.

"The cheering just before the game starts really hypes me up," Benson said. "It helps me as much as it does them.

"Once the game starts, though, the noise is more one-sided, but it still makes us play better. You just want to concentrate on what you're doing so you can stick it to 'em and shut 'em up."

Buckner served the same function with Furlow the night before the game.

Normally, outside phone calls don't ring into IU players' rooms on the road, but Buckner said Furlow got a call through. "He just wanted to get together and talk — not even about basketball," Buckner said. "He seemed like a nice enough guy.

"But," Buckner said, grinning, "we don't do that with the opposition before a game. I just kinda ended that conversation in a hurry."

Buckner wound up meeting Furlow at close range starting the second half Monday, and he was just as abrupt. Buckner intercepted the Spartans' first pass aimed at Furlow in the half, and he continued to try to keep himself in line of any possible passes to Furlow until two quick fouls gave him four and sent him to the bench.

"Guys like that you can't let touch the ball," he said. "I've been impressed with his shooting since I saw him up here three years ago.

"It wasn't anything different from what we were trying to do with him the first half (when Bob Wilkerson was assigned to Furlow), only the rest of us weren't talking too well to help Bobby. You've got to have help against a guy like that. He can really shoot."

Wilkerson switched to Michigan State's No. 2 scorer, Chapman, the last half, after Chapman had worked May into his foul trouble in the first half.

May was the object of a special defense Ganakas called "almost like a box-and-one only we were playing man-to-man."

"I didn't notice anything special," May said. "They had (Edgar) Wilson on me most of the time, and he did a good job. The only difference between this game and the one at Michigan (when the Wolverines' Wayman Britt stayed with May most of the day) was I worked harder to get open."

May had 16 first-half points before picking up his second and third fouls 53 seconds apart late in the half — then adding No. 4 just 2 minutes and 19 seconds into the second half. He ultimately fouled out for the first time this year, scoring 18.

Ganakas was left to wonder what might have happened if he had played things straight. "The first half, he got his points, anyway," the Spartan coach said in clearly impressed tones.

"But it was kinda ironic, really. When he went out in the second half (with only 2½ minutes gone and IU leading by 10), we kinda relaxed.

"It was like a boxer who makes one mistake and gets knocked out. We fought a good, hard, smart fight and then got knocked out in the 13th. That's the kind of team they are."

"They actually control the tempo of the game through their offense. They're so patient they wear you out defensing them. And then, of course, their defense comes into play."

— Gus Ganakas
Michigan State coach

Furlow passed around by IU and 'held' to 26

Furlow's string of three 40-point games made Indiana's defense against him the primary subject of speculation before the game.

"Indiana and Bob Knight are defense-oriented," Ganakas had mused. "They may take up the challenge of stopping Terry." Furlow proclaimed no fear. "We can beat them, I know that," he said. "If I can keep my concentration . . . if all our guys keep our concentration . . . we've got a splendid opportunity."

It turned out that no one Hoosier took terrible Terry; he was passed around so freely among Hoosier defenders that everyone but Benson had him at least once, and even Benson was aware of him.

"I tried to help on him whenever I could," Benson said, "but I wasn't supposed to switch on him." The thought of the 6-11 Benson chasing the swift, 6-5 Furlow around in Furlow's prime scoring regions — nearly 20 feet from the basket — clearly was not one that entranced Knight, who claimed no major achievement for the Hoosiers in stopping Furlow's 40-point string. Just relief in winning.

"I can remember when he came in against us as a freshman up here," Knight said. "He scored about 10 points and immediately impressed us as being an excellent shooter.

"He's worked hard on his game, and he doesn't just catch it and shoot it now. He can create a shot for himself after he gets the ball. I'm just glad we're getting him out of here." Furlow is a senior.

"Terry kept us in the game the first half," Ganakas said. "I actually had the feeling we had control of the tempo in the first half.

"I told our guys I was proud of them. I feel we played physically hard and mentally hard. We were very intent in this game, particularly in the first half.

"But they're a great team. It's hard to pick out players. May and Benson are very outstanding, but the whole team complements each other. They have such a team-operating basis that individuals don't mean anything.

"But May and Benson are the two most expressive."

The Hoosiers also were obedient in this one. After they lost the ball six times in the last 4½ minutes at Michigan Saturday, Knight said "I just talked to them very briefly about our shooting percentage and our turnovers.

"We shot 59 per cent at Michigan. If we cut our turnovers in half, and that wouldn't seem to be asking too much, and we maintain the same shooting percentage, then we're throwing away 12 to 14 points with those turnovers." Monday, the turnovers dropped from 27 to 13 . . . and the winning margin was 12. Good timing.

Indiana 83, Illinois 55

The first sellout crowd in five years at Illinois' Assembly Hall had little to cheer about Saturday . . . and blew it when it did.

Indiana's No. 1-ranked Hoosiers were moving smoothly toward their 14th straight victory when sophomore Audie Matthews scored a second-half basket for Illinois, then stole a Hoosier pass and raced in for a layup.

All the flurry did was cut IU's lead to 56-40, but the hungry Illini fans in the crowd of 16,128 read rally into the situation and leaped to their feet, roaring — the noise building in volume and fervor as Indiana brought the ball downcourt.

The effect on IU was not at all what the roarers had in mind — more like a gloved slap in the face to a pack of Zorros.

The Hoosiers worked Scott May free for a basket; stole the ball back and cashed in a Kent Benson layup; fielded an Illinois miss and popped Jim Crews free for a jump shot . . . and on and on and on for a 13-point zap in four shiny minutes that really were not particularly atypical of the whole day that ended with IU an easy 83-55 winner.

It sent the Hoosiers into their Monday night Assembly Hall meeting with Purdue with both teams unbeaten in Big Ten play — Indiana 5-0 and Purdue 4-0 after its 84-80 victory at Ohio State Saturday night.

It was a demoralizing day, though, for new Illinois coach Lou Henson, who didn't promise anyone an upset but got a little that way himself when the pieces of the machine he has been patiently building came flying apart in front of him.

The game was only 32 seconds old when Henson made his first substitution, and he kept wheeling players in so frequently it appeared to be a calculated attempt to confuse the Hoosiers and wear them down with manpower.

Wasn't that at all, Henson said. The man was just miffed. Much.

"If a player doesn't play team ball, I can't permit him to stay out there," Henson fumed. "I was very unhappy with our team. We played a selfish game."

Baskets by Nate Williams and Rich Adams broke the Illini in front at the start, 4-0, but from 6-2, Indiana discouraged a build-up in Illini frenzy by blanking the home team on eight straight possessions and running in 10 points in a row.

Things never got too shaky again for the Hoosiers in one of their most authoritative thumpings of a road opponent this year.

Tom Abernethy was the leader as Indiana opened a 45-28 halftime lead. Abernethy had 15 points by then, with maximum efficiency. He was 6-for-6 from the field, 3-for-3 on free throws.

Abernethy's high for the season before the game was just 16 points, but Henson wasn't fooled.

"He's a player — he is *really* a player," Henson said. "Sometimes when a good player — I won't even say 'good'; when an outstanding player like that is in with people who are better publicity-wise . . . a great player can get lost." Casey Stengel couldn't have said it better.

Abernethy finished with 17 as the IU front line combined for 60 points — 27 by Scott May, his Big Ten high this year, and 16 by Kent Benson, who pushed his conference shooting over .700 with 8-for-11 despite a sprained left wrist picked up in a scary first-half fall.

Illinois center Mike Washington decked Benson as the Hoosier center was cashing in a layup after a mid-court steal. Benson made a one-point landing on the wrist but played the second half with the wrist heavily taped.

Bob Wilkerson added 8 points, 8 rebounds and 8 assists — with only one turnover — for one of his best all-round performances.

INDIANA 83

	M	FG	FT	R	A	PF	TP
May, f	38	12-22	3- 6	10	5	3	27
Abernethy, f	30	7-10	3- 3	2	2	2	17
Benson, c	32	8-11	0- 1	9	4	3	16
Buckner, g	16	1- 3	1- 2	3	2	4	3
Wilkerson, g	27	3- 5	2- 2	8	8	3	8
Wisman	8	1- 1	0- 0	0	5	0	2
Crews	18	3- 5	2- 2	0	3	1	8
Radford	13	1- 1	0- 0	1	0	1	2
Valavicius	14	0- 0	0- 0	1	0	0	0
Bender	6	0- 1	0- 0	2	0	0	0
Team				3			
Totals		36-59	11-16	39	29	17	83

ILLINOIS 55

	M	FG	FT	R	A	PF	TP
Adams, f	23	8-16	0- 0	7	1	4	16
Matthews, f	29	4- 7	0- 0	3	2	1	8
Washington, c	15	0- 5	2- 2	3	1	0	2
Williams, g	33	4-11	3- 4	1	2	1	11
Tucker, g	23	1- 4	0- 0	5	2	4	2
Leighty	17	1- 4	0- 0	2	2	2	2
Ferdinand	20	4- 8	0- 0	2	2	2	8
Lubin	19	2- 5	2- 4	1	1	2	6
Gerhardt	18	0- 1	0- 0	1	1	0	0
Team				4			
Totals		24-61	7-10	29	11	16	55

SCORE BY HALVES

Indiana	45 38 —	83
Illinois	28 27 —	55

Errors: Indiana 14, Illinois 16
Technical foul: Illinois bench

	FG	Pct.	FT	Pct.
Indiana	36-59	.610	11-16	.688
Illinois	24-61	.393	7-10	.700

Officials: Jerry Menz, Bob Brodbeck and Bob Showalter

Attendance: 16,128 (capacity)

The Hoosiers also got lots of production at the other guard, from lots of people: Quinn Buckner, then Jim Wisman, ultimately Jim Crews — ironically, all three of them Illinois all-state players who left the home state for Indiana. Crews had the best scoring day of the three with 8 points and a couple of superb assists.

Indiana shot .610, the sixth-best one-game mark in Hoosier history, three of those six and five of the top nine entries on that list coming in this season that just passed the halfway mark Saturday.

Adams had 16 points and Williams 11 for the Illini, who had an eight-game home-court winning streak ended.

Knight sees deficiencies, but Henson sees more

Knight dropped a surprise on the impressed Illinois press Saturday: the Hoosiers have "deficiencies."

"Could you tell us what those 'deficiencies' are?" an Illinois newsman asked.

"I think we have them," Knight said.

"What are they?"

"I think about them a lot," Knight said, smiling, "but I'm not going to think about them publicly."

Henson agreed with Knight . . . to a point. "I think any ball club has weaknesses," Henson said. "But it's going to take an expert, and he's going to have to look a long time, to find out what they are on Indiana's team.

"I do think there are some teams in the league that can play Indiana better than we can. It has to be a sound team. The Illinois basketball team is not a sound team."

It came across as a harsh indictment of Illini talent, and, on this day, Henson intended it that way.

"It's certainly not a disgrace to get beat by the No. 1 team in the country — and I feel Indiana is that," Henson said. "The worst thing you can do is expect a team to do something it can't do. I didn't think we would beat Indiana — we wanted to try, but I didn't honestly think we would beat them.

"And I'm also aware that a good team can make you play poorly. But it's ridiculous to put a team on the floor and have them play individual basketball.

"We won't even win a game the rest of the year if we don't play team ball. We can't line up and beat anybody."

"Individual play" has never been a Knight complaint — especially not in recent Champaign appearances against the Illini.

Saturday's victory gave the Hoosiers a five-game winning streak over Illinois on the road, and the last three of those produced enough teamwork for shooting performances that rank in the six best IU has ever had in Big Ten play — .579 in a 101-83 victory there in 1974, .573 in a 112-89 win there last

year, and .610 Saturday. That's a three-year average of .585 that indicates the Hoosiers can shoot pretty well in any and every Assembly Hall.

"There were some aspects of the game we obviously have to be pleased with," Knight said. "I thought our defensive play was pretty solid — maybe as good as it's been in a while.

"Illinois got into a difficult situation at the end of the first half (IU jumping its lead from 35-24 to 45-26 in the last 4½ minutes of the half).

"I thought they came back with good character at the start of the second half, and they scored the first four points. Then they again found it difficult to keep those things going."

The game was the 10th on the road for the Hoosiers in their 14-0 start, six of those on nominally neutral courts that ranged in pro- or anti-Hoosier sentiment from Market Square Arena in Indianapolis (Florida State) and St. Louis Arena (UCLA) on one extreme to Freedom Hall in Louisville (Kentucky) and Madison Square Garden (St. John's, plus Columbia and Manhattan) on the other.

The other four games away from home have been "pure" road games, all in the Big Ten, which leaves only five of those to go.

"We need a home game," Knight said before the Illinois game. The Hoosiers get one Monday night, their biggest yet. It's against Purdue, and it's for, among other things, the Big Ten lead.

Benson's wrist injury clouds a happy IU day

His own fouling limited May to 21 minutes and 18 points at Michigan State Monday, but fate dealt him a few even-up minutes Saturday.

Partly by accident, May threw in three field goals in a 100-second span late in a runaway game to finish with 27 points. The accidental part was that Abernethy was sitting at the scorer's table waiting to replace May when those last three field goals were scored.

"When they finally buzzed the buzzer, it woke me up," deadpanned Abernethy.

That was with 1:44 left in the game, May's third foul the play that terminated his time on-stage, more than two minutes after Knight tried to take him out.

Abernethy took advantage of his mop-up time to score one more field goal that gave him his season high of 17 points . . . and qualified him for a needle. "When you're out there with us scrubs," Wisman told Abernethy, "coach doesn't mean for you to do the shooting. You're just supposed to be the stabilizer."

Things were light for the Hoosiers Saturday.

There was one anxious note injected by a first-half spill Benson took after laying in a fast-break basket. Benson landed on his left wrist, causing a sprain that was confirmed to be nothing worse by x-rays back at Bloomington Hospital Saturday night.

Benson removed any doubt about his availability for Monday's Purdue game by playing the last half with the wrist heavily taped and scoring half his 16 points, two on another fast-break basket that saw him take the lead pass too far downcourt for a normal layup, so he improvised and twisted in a shot, left-handed.

Benson beat the Illini downcourt for three fast-break baskets, partial penalty for an Illinois offense that kept the man Benson guarded, Washington or Ken Ferdinand, well out on the court. "They keep you out there, you'll keep getting layups," a friend told Benson. "Yeah," he said wryly, "no rebounds, but more layups."

He finished with 9 rebounds, 8 of them on defense. Only May, with 10, had more as IU had solid control of the boards, 39-29.

Abernethy also noted another Benson contribution that helped Abernethy to a 6-for-6 shooting performance in the first half. "Bennie dropped off a couple of great passes," Abernethy said.

Knight explained Abernethy's 15 first-half points as a simple matter of "taking advantage of whatever is there."

"I wasn't being played tightly," Abernethy said. "It didn't seem to be a conscious sag. I just was open and Bennie and Bobby got me the ball.

"I was glad to see our defense and offense sorta go together this time. We've had some games where we made mistakes either on offense or defense, but this time we put the two together pretty well."

Crews, who made a couple of exceptional passes

Kent Benson checks his teeth as Bob Wilkerson looks in

that led to easy shots inside the Illinois defense, indicated he felt a good Hoosier performance coming on. "We had been practicing pretty hard," he said. "Then Coach gave us yesterday off, and it seemed to work out pretty well. I thought we really thought about the game a lot and got ready for it."

Crews said he expected a slower-paced game from the Illini. "We expected them to be very patient," he said. "I think our defense early forced them into more of a scramble situation than they wanted."

IU offense or defense best? Illini vote split

Illinois' basketball players had a tough time deciding whether the Indiana offense or the Hoosier defense impressed them more.

The maze of blocks Hoosiers set for each other made some of the most notable impressions.

"When they picked people, they were *picked*," said Otho Tucker, a three-year starter considered Illinois' best defensive player.

"It's like going through a tightly-grown forest, through a lot of tall trees," Washington said.

Tucker called the Indiana maneuvering "really pretty slow. In 15 or 20 seconds, though, they can have you jammed down in so tight you're running into their players and your own . . . and pretty soon, somebody pops out for a 15-foot shot."

"They take their time," Matthews agreed, "and they set good picks and keep running their offense until they get somebody open. They don't take bad shots. Every time they shoot, they're wide open . . . except for Scott May. He'll shoot *over* people. He can do it and get away with it."

Tucker had the initial duty on May, and he said, "I was really impressed with his quickness. He's a good shooter, and he really gets up and follows through.

"But the big thing is his quickness and the way he works to get his shot."

Ferdinand shared defensive duty on Benson, and Ferdinand got Benson's day started shockingly by blocking his first shot.

"He's a big fellow," Ferdinand said. "He surprised me with his hook shot from 5 to 10 feet out. I expected him to turn around and shoot the jump shot, which is what I blocked the first time he tried it. But after he started using the hook, he had me guessing."

Washington called Benson "real mobile. When he was going downcourt on the fast break, he kinda surprised me the way he was flying."

Then there was the Hoosier defense.

"They just keep putting the pressure on you all the time," Williams said. "They start when you take the ball out of bounds, and they never let up."

Indiana 71, Purdue 67

Indiana is alone atop the Big Ten basketball standings today, but the way the Hoosiers got there has Purdue looking eagerly toward Feb. 16 and the rematch of the two archrivals at the Boilermakers' Mackey Arena.

IU coach Bob Knight was blunt about his team's 71-67 squeeze-through Monday night before 17,405 at Assembly Hall.

"Without any question, Purdue played better and harder than we did," Knight said. "They beat us everywhere but in the final score. I'm not happy about it."

The game between the league's co-leaders swung to the Hoosiers partly because Scott May, IU's only effective scorer in the second half, got a good bounce when he missed a free throw with 23 seconds left and IU ahead, 67-65.

May's miss bounded high into the air, arching over Purdue rebounders in the inside spots allotted to defensive players. IU's Bobby Wilkerson used all of his 6-7 frame, long arms and springy legs to pick off the rebound and save possession for IU.

With 18 seconds left, Jim Crews sank both halves of a one-and-one, the clincher in IU's 25th straight Big Ten victory.

A basket by Purdue guard Jerry Sichting at 0:02 and two free throws by Wilkerson just ahead of the buzzer completed the scoring. What would have happened had May's miss bounced into Purdue hands, no one knows . . . but Knight suspects.

"I can't recall one single time when our defense stopped them in the second half," he said, terming the Wilkerson rebound "the key break of the game, not really the key 'play' of the game. That wasn't so much a play as the ball just happened to be there."

Purdue spent the entire game in a zone defense until IU's possession game forced the Boilermakers out of it at the end. Indiana came close to shooting the Boilermakers out of it a few times in the first half, but the Hoosiers couldn't get the plucky young Purdues convinced.

Tom Abernethy's three-point play with only 57 seconds gone in the game gave IU a 5-2 lead, and the Hoosiers expanded it quickly — to 10-4, then 14-6.

There was no shortage of open shots against the zone, and Indiana hit enough of them to move up 10 (34-24) on May's jump shot with 5:04 left in the half.

The Hoosiers scored only two of the next six times they had the ball, so Purdue left at halftime down just 44-35. Knight had seen enough by then to be uneasy. "There were a couple of times we were just on the verge of getting the lead up to 15," he said. "If we had, it might have been a different

ball game the second half, but they didn't permit us to get there.

"And they pretty much dominated the second half."

Purdue wasn't quite so overpowering the second half as Knight's memory recalled. But the Boilermakers did sting the Hoosiers for consistent scores to edge back into the game.

The IU lead was down to 55-52 when Knight took a time out and demanded some inside scoring. Center Kent Benson responded with a field goal 11 seconds after the time out and ripped a pass to Abernethy for an open jump shot the next time the Hoosiers had the ball.

The shot missed, and so did one by Crews from a gap in the Purdue zone — part of an 0-for-4 night on those by Crews, usually one of the Hoosiers' best marksmen.

And suddenly, the Hoosier lead was gone. Tom

Back-to-back, Bob Wilkerson and Purdue's Wayne Walls

Scheffler's tip-in popped Purdue ahead, 58-57, the first time the Hoosiers had trailed in the second half of a (1) Big Ten or (2) home game this year.

Abernethy fought his way to two offensive rebounds to get the basket that returned IU to the lead, but guard Eugene Parker countered to put Purdue up again, 60-59, with 9:28 left.

May worked into the Purdue defense for a short jump shot and a 61-60 Hoosier lead at 9:05 . . . and the see-sawing stopped right there.

Purdue had the ball five times and couldn't change the deficit, and neither could Indiana until Benson swatted in a rebound at 6:30 for a 63-60 Hoosier lead.

Kyle Macy's jump shot at 2:10 trimmed IU's lead to 67-65, and the Hoosiers were content to stop scoring there if they could keep the basketball.

To that point, Purdue had been charged with only two fouls the last half, leaving IU with four to go before being required to shoot a free throw. The Boilermakers whacked away at 1:47, 1:21, 0:40 and 0:29. Each time, IU got the ball out of bounds again and worked the ball into play against Purdue pressure.

"We had to keep getting the ball in-bounds, and that can be tricky," Knight said. "That may be the best thing we did in the whole ball game."

The Hoosiers had to do it one last time after Sichting's basket at 0:02 and a quick Purdue time out. Abernethy lofted a pass to Wilkerson in mid-court to beat the Boilermaker press for the last, clinching time.

May scored 32 points despite 4-for-9 free-throw shooting that cost him a net of 6 points. Abernethy had 13 points and Wilkerson 10, along with 8 assists and 4 steals.

Benson, who denied his sore left wrist had anything to do with an off night on open shots, didn't get many of those (8 shots altogether, counting 2 tips) and finished with just 8 points, his lowest league total. He had his best rebound night so far in Big Ten play with 12, but the teams finished even on the boards.

Parker had 14 points, Walter Jordan 13, Macy 11 and Scheffler 10 for Purdue, which left town 4-1 in the league and 9-5 overall.

Indiana, 6-0 in Big Ten play and 15-0 overall, won its fifth in a row over Purdue.

IU's top tipper, Bob Wilkerson, out-taps Tom Scheffler

INDIANA 71							
	M	FG	FT	R	A	PF	TP
May, f	40	14-21	4- 9	4	2	4	32
Abernethy, f	40	6-13	1- 1	5	2	3	13
Benson, c	40	3- 8	2- 3	12	0	3	8
Buckner, g	12	1- 3	0- 1	4	2	3	2
Wilkerson, g	40	4- 9	2- 2	9	8	2	10
Radford	25	2- 7	0- 0	1	1	2	4
Crews	13	0- 4	2- 2	0	2	2	2
Team				7			
Totals		30-65	11-18	42	17	19	71

PURDUE 67							
	M	FG	FT	R	A	PF	TP
Jordan, f	37	6-13	1- 3	7	4	3	13
Walls, f	32	3- 8	0- 2	5	0	2	6
Scheffler, c	20	5- 8	0- 0	5	0	2	10
Parker, g	37	7-13	0- 1	3	3	2	14
Macy, g	27	4- 8	3- 4	2	1	3	11
Sichting	18	4- 5	0- 0	1	0	2	8
White	19	1- 2	1- 4	3	0	1	3
Thomas	7	0- 3	2- 4	2	0	0	2
Steele	2	0- 0	0- 0	1	0	0	0
McCarter	1	0- 1	0- 0	0	0	1	0
Team				13			
Totals		30-61	7-18	42	8	16	67

SCORE BY HALVES

Purdue 35   32 — 67
Indiana 44   27 — 71
  Errors: Purdue 16, Indiana 13
  Technical fouls: Purdue bench 2

	FG	Pct.	FT	Pct.
Purdue	30-61	.492	7-18	.389
Indiana	30-65	.462	11-18	.611

  Officials: Richard Weiler, George Solomon and Phil Robinson
  Attendance: 17,405 (capacity)

Hard times continue for struggling Buckner

Knight all but confirmed the obvious Monday night: Buckner, a four-year starter struggling to get his game together the last few weeks, may be replaced in the Hoosiers' starting lineup.

Buckner played only 12 minutes while the four other starters went all 40 in IU's scramble past Purdue. Quick fouls contributed to his early exit, as they have in each of the Hoosiers' Big Ten games.

Indiana's problems with Purdue hardly started and ended with its co-captain's troubles. IU had only glimpses of smoothness whatever the combination Monday, and Knight clearly is looking.

"Yeah, there's a definite chance we will start somebody else," Knight said. "I think we have to reassess a lot of things.

"What we are in need of is a catalytic personality out there, and I don't think that was available to us in this game.

"We'll see what happens the next couple of days in practice."

Knight clearly wasn't focusing on one player or one position in his displeasure with the route the Hoosiers took to the victory that boosted them into sole possession of first place in the Big Ten.

"Sure, it's a disappointment when we work like hell — and by 'we' I mean these players — to get to a point where we play like we did Saturday (at Illinois) and then fall off the next time out," Knight said. "We can't be up one game and down in the valley the very next time.

"Ours was a very lethargic team. We have to be discouraged about things we didn't do.

"I thought Purdue shot well and we obviously didn't. Their guards completely outplayed our guards in the ball game. I don't think it was even close."

'Naturally get fired up against No. 1'—Parker

Sichting split time with starting guards Parker and Macy and played a role in the spunky second-half comeback that gave the Hoosiers a traumatic time. His biggest problem in the game was physical. At 6-1, he was at a distinct disadvantage on defense, having to guard 6-7 Wilkerson or 6-5 Crews.

"Wilkerson has long arms and he is quick," Sichting said, laughing. "He's too tall to be playing guard, really. He's the only one we couldn't match up man-to-man because he is so tall."

The Purdue comeback came, Sichting said, because "I think we were a little more patient on offense the second half. Plus, their defense . . . maybe they got tired. I'll say it this way — maybe we just adjusted a little bit to their defense."

Parker agreed that Purdue came in mentally ready.

"You naturally get fired up against the No. 1 team," he said.

"I knew from previous years that Indiana puts a lot of pressure on the ball, but they leave a lot of openings. I tried to beat their guards and then maybe pass off. The second half I tried to be patient and take the opening when I had it.

"We weren't surprised that we stayed with them. The second half we just wanted to come out and execute. We knew we made some mistakes the first half, and we wanted to correct that. Indiana got some early steals because they put us where they wanted us."

Parker, 6-1, played in an unusual spot — on the baseline — in Purdue's first-half 1-3-1 zone. "It's a sound idea by coach (Fred) Schaus," he said. "I'm on the baseline because I can get out to cover the wings quicker than anyone else. I tried to get to May if he was in my area."

May seemed unruffled. He got 19 of his 32 points in the first half. The Boilermakers went with a 2-3 zone most of the second half, and he went 6-for-10.

"May is just super," Schaus said. "Indiana has two great offensive threats in May and Benson. We didn't want to give up that many open shots to May, but we couldn't shut them both off."

Benson wound up with only eight shots. He hit three, two of them tip-ins.

Schaus refrained from claiming, indeed denied the very existence of, a moral victory. "But I was still very pleased with the way we played," he admitted. "I was very pleased with our poise."

Jerry Sichting protects the ball as Quinn Buckner dives

Indiana 85, Minnesota 76

Top-ranked Indiana played the fall guy in a Minnesota dream for 20 minutes Saturday, then awakened the Gophers to reality with some overwhelming second-half play that produced an 85-76 Hoosier victory.

The Big Ten regional network peeked into an ambush scene complete with determined players and 14,130 fans. The two groups took turns inspiring each other in a first half that closed with Minnesota leading, 45-40.

It was the first time the Hoosiers have trailed at halftime in two years — 50 games. The way they responded at the start of the second half didn't encourage repetition of the effrontery.

Indiana ripped Minnesota's 2-3 zone defense with 8-for-8 shooting the first eight times it had the ball after halftime. The Hoosiers added three steals during the stretch, and the net result was a sudden 56-49 lead. After seven minutes, the lead was 64-53, and Minnesota never again worked up a real run at the Hoosiers.

"I felt the start of the second half was as enjoyable a segment of basketball as we have played all year," Hoosier coach Bob Knight said. "And it was as important a five-minute period as we've had all season. We had to have it."

There were plenty of victory keys for the Hoosiers — among them the scoring of Tom Abernethy, the defense of Bob Wilkerson and the guard play of sophomore Jim Wisman, a new starter.

Abernethy led the Hoosiers in scoring for the first time in his 94-game collegiate career, and he included some big baskets in his 10-for-13 shooting and 22-point total.

Scott May, who had 21 points, got the Hoosiers rolling with jump shots the first two Indiana possessions of the second half, and Wilkerson scored the next two Hoosier goals. Wilkerson's second one, which provided Indiana's first lead (48-47, with 18:16 to go), was a combination effort with May — Wilkerson deflecting a pass, then May completing the interception and lofting a pass to Wilkerson for a layup.

Then it was Abernethy's turn to find a tender spot in the Gopher zone. The 6-7 senior popped to the top of the foul circle for three quick jump shots that put the daylight in the Hoosier lead.

"When the jump shots started going for people like Abernethy in particular, we were in trouble," Minnesota coach Jim Dutcher said. "They can attack so many ways. They just rotated their big men out and shot over our guards."

Wilkerson's defensive contribution was humanizing Minnesota forward Ray Williams.

Williams was the main reason Indiana fell behind. The 6-2 New Yorker, an all-American at San Jacinto, Cal., junior college a year ago, introduced himself to IU with 22 first-half points —

most of them from amazing distance. "I don't know whether I've ever seen anyone shoot better than he did the first half," Knight said. Williams was 9-for-12 with May the hapless chaser.

Wilkerson inherited the job the second half and permitted Williams only two field goals in the period when Indiana amassed the 64-53 lead. "Wilkerson and Abernethy played extremely well the second half — Wilkerson on defense and Abernethy on offense," Knight said.

Wisman had his IU-career high of 12 points as all five Hoosier starters made double figures. Included was a 16-point day that made junior Kent Benson the 17th IU player to score 1,000 points. He has 1,003.

Wisman was credited with a 5-for-5 shooting day, though his first try of the afternoon missed. Nothing else he tried did — including two straight 18-foot jump shots he delivered when Minnesota had its lead up to 24-16 in the first half and appeared to have a chance to break away.

Minnesota was left to wonder what more it needed for victory. The Gophers shot .615 (to Indiana's .619) and outrebounded IU in a game where there weren't many rebounds, 26-24.

INDIANA 85

	M	FG	FT	R	A	PF	TP
May, f	36	10-23	1- 2	4	3	5	21
Abernethy, f	40	10-13	2- 3	5	2	3	22
Benson, c	40	7-10	2- 3	9	2	3	16
Wisman, g	40	5- 5	2- 2	1	7	0	12
Wilkerson, g	32	7-10	0- 0	3	9	4	14
Buckner	8	0- 2	0- 1	0	2	3	0
Radford	1	0- 0	0- 0	0	0	0	0
Crews	3	0- 0	0- 0	0	0	0	0
Team				2			
Totals		39-63	7-11	24	25	18	85

MINNESOTA 76

	M	FG	FT	R	A	PF	TP
Winey, f	36	5- 8	1- 2	4	0	4	11
Williams, f	40	14-21	6- 6	5	7	4	34
Thompson, c	40	6-12	5- 6	13	2	4	17
Lockhart, g	40	5- 7	0- 0	5	5	0	10
Saunders, g	38	2- 3	0- 0	3	0	3	4
Johnson	4	0- 0	0- 0	0	0	0	0
Jones	2	0- 1	0- 0	1	0	1	0
Team				0			
Totals		32-52	12-14	26	14	16	76

SCORE BY HALVES

Indiana	40	45	— 85
Minnesota	45	31	— 76

Errors: Indiana 11, Minnesota 18

	FG	Pct.	FT	Pct.
Indiana	39-63	.619	7-11	.636
Minnesota	32-52	.615	12-14	.857

Officials: Art White, Gary Muncy and Carel Cosby
Attendance: 14,130

Williams finished 14-for-21 for 34 points, the highest total against Indiana since South Carolina's Kevin Joyce put on a memorable artillery show of his own with 41 points in 1972.

Gopher center Mike Thompson, playing under a court order that temporarily set aside an NCAA suspension for selling complimentary tickets, provided the Gopher rebound edge with 13 by himself, and he scored 17 points.

20th one the happiest of birthdays for Wisman

Wisman celebrated his 20th birthday the perfect way, scoring in double figures for the first time as a collegian and playing all 40 minutes in an Indiana victory over Minnesota.

The birthday part didn't intrude into Wisman's thinking as he prepared for the game — the second one he has started at IU. "The last time they told me I was going to start (against Northwestern three weeks ago), I was really nervous," he said. "This time, I decided it was kinda silly to get all worked up. It worked to my disadvantage."

Wisman didn't feel particularly comfortable in the opening minutes, as Minnesota shot away to a 12-4 lead with an attack that included a couple of fast-break layups. "I felt responsible for those," he said. "Even if it's not one of our men scoring, we guards have to stop the fast breaks."

Meanwhile, IU's offense was sputtering, too — "maybe because the other guys weren't used to having me in there," Wisman said.

But Wisman paid his dues with a couple of momentum-checking jump shots after Minnesota had reclaimed an eight-point edge (24-16), and he kept going to total 12 points — including a game-sealing one-and-one conversion with 1:23 to go and IU stalling with a 79-72 lead.

Wisman enjoyed the start but he admitted to thoughts of the man he replaced in the Hoosier lineup: senior Quinn Buckner. "Quinn has had some physical problems," Wisman said, "but he really showed a lot of character all week. He really helped me prepare for this game — he showed me a lot of little things — and he was helping me and encouraging me all through the game.

"He's a real leader. He's had so many super games and he's gonna have so many more. It's a privilege to be on a team with him."

Saturday was a special day, too, for regular starters Benson and Abernethy.

Benson's 1,000th point came on a special basket. He and Minnesota's Thompson had a dandy duel going offensively and defensively when Benson challenged the jumping and shot-blocking skills of Thompson with a turn-around shot into

Bob Knight and Jim Wisman — Talking time

the Gopher's face — with IU ahead, 64-57, and Minnesota trying to get a comeback going with 11:46 to play.

Benson hit the 12-foot jump shot and picked up Thompson's third foul, too, for a three-point play. "I just went up and took the shot," Benson said. "It was right there.

"Thompson is quick. He's an excellent jumper and good shooter."

Abernethy scored in the 20s for the first time as a Hoosier with 22, the first time the senior ever led IU in scoring. He hit three straight jump shots in the second-half sprint that changed a 45-40 Gopher lead to 56-49, Indiana.

But even before the hot stretch, Abernethy said he "felt pretty confident" about ultimate victory — although Minnesota was shooting almost 70 per cent and had its biggest crowd of the year roaring. "There have been games where we were ahead at the half when I've felt less confident," Abernethy said. "I really didn't see much we were doing real bad that first half. It wasn't so much that I didn't expect them to keep shooting so well. It wasn't anything about *them*; I thought *we* could do better.

"The first half, we weren't really moving well against their zone. We were making useless cuts. We made a good adjustment at the half and the shots were there. The ones I had were just 15-foot shots that anybody can make."

Tip opening second half Knight's first good clue

It didn't take long in the second half for Knight to be pleased by what he saw Saturday.

The opening tip was enough.

Knight had used Benson for the center jump with Thompson opening the game — a switch from Wilkerson, who has handled the job the last two years.

"Bobby had not been timing his jump real well," Knight explained. But Thompson out-jumped Benson at the beginning of the game, and, with IU trailing, 45-40, at halftime, Knight went back to Wilkerson to start the second half. Wilkerson delivered the ball with a perfectly timed leap that got him above Thompson, an outstanding jumper himself.

"That in itself was a hell of a play," Knight said. "If they get it and score, we're down seven."

The jumper was one of several switches Knight made at halftime, some of them intentionally delayed that long though Minnesota's first-half success strained his patience on holding back.

Knight also switched defensive assignments for Wilkerson and May, moving Wilkerson onto the Gophers' scorching scorer, Williams. Wilkerson cooled him from a 22-point half to 10 and May did a solid job on guard Osborne Lockhart in the half when the Hoosiers reversed the game's flow.

The other moves were on offense — maneuvers in ball direction that cleaved open holes in the middle for jump shots by Abernethy and May.

"Sometimes you try to just get through the first half and then make your adjustments," Knight said. "The best time to make them is at the half."

Nothing done in the Hoosier dressing room was predicated on the probability that Williams and Minnesota couldn't continue their astounding 70 per cent outside shooting. "You have no guarantee they're not going to shoot 70 per cent the second half," Knight said.

"On offense, we were doing a lot of moving but not really finding the openings. We tried to put our people where they could get shots."

"But we're not a tremendously high-scoring basketball team. Our offense produced enough points the first half to get the job done; 40 points is a lot to score against a zone. But we were having so much trouble on defense."

Knight was asked how he had tried to counter Thompson's rebounding. "So many of their shots were going in the first half, his rebounding was inconsequential," Knight said. "There were other things we couldn't get controlled."

The phrasing was similar to some used by Dutcher in explaining why the Gophers ran successfully at the start of the game and couldn't in the second half.

"You can't run unless they miss a shot," he said. "The second half, they weren't missing.

"They have tremendous balance. They can

Gopher hotshot Ray Williams fires over Kent Benson

75

attack so many ways. Had they not hit as well to start the second half (8-for-8), it might have been different.

"That's why they're No. 1, I guess. They make those big baskets. They were good shots. They were all squared to the basket."

Dutcher was a better prophet than he intended to be.

"I told our ball club at the half the game would be won in the first five minutes of the second half," he said, adding with a grin: "And it was, only unfortunately for us it was Indiana that won it.

"I can't fault our play. We played pretty hard. I didn't think we moved the ball very well starting the second half, but that's about the only thing I can criticize.

"Most teams are over-cautious against Indiana. We decided if we got a broken-floor situation on a break, we were going to take the shot."

But once the Hoosiers corralled the fast break and started getting points of their own, the team dictating the terms had changed.

With 13:10 to go and Indiana around the Gophers (60-53) and moving out, Dutcher called

---

"I still think they're No. 1, but I don't think they're as overpowering as they were last year. I said at the time that was the best college team I'd ever seen. When Scott May was in there, you couldn't find a weakness."

— Jim Dutcher
Minnesota coach

---

time out and switched from the zone defense he had used the entire game to a man-to-man.

"The thing you have to do when zoning is have good movement with the hands up and rebound the misses," he said. "They didn't have any misses."

Then, after Thompson scored for Minnesota at 4:51 to cut IU's lead to 79-70 and IU got the ball back after an exchange of misses, Knight put the Hoosiers in a control game — no surprise to Dutcher.

"They play that better than anybody," he said. "When they get into a critical situation, they're not going to make errors. They're too experienced and too poised."

The greatest Hoosier poise, though, came in the first half, when the pressure was immense. Every Gopher shot seemed to be going in, and the Gopher crowd got caught up in the upset bid, loudly. "I've never heard an arena that loud, anywhere," Knight said. "Not even up here a few years ago when they had 18,000 people in the stands.

"Our kids did show some poise. This was a tough one to win."

Thompson remembers a personal warning

Thompson remembered the scene well: halftime, his team ahead of No. 1-ranked Indiana, 45-40, and his sitting in the dressing room, head down, concentrating on the situation.

"I remember thinking to myself, 'If we don't come out and play well at the start of the second half, we'll lose,'" Thompson said after Indiana's comeback victory was posted.

Elsewhere in the Gopher dressing room at half-time, Williams was having no negative thoughts of any kind.

Williams, whose Gopher high going into Saturday's game was 27 points, had 22 by halftime — a dandy little shooting showpiece he laid before the regional Big Ten television audience.

He got those points going head-to-head against May, IU's all-round all-American. "He's a tough cat," May said. "I gave him a little room out there on the floor because I didn't think he'd take shots that long. I've never guarded anybody who shot from that far out the way he did." Williams was 9-for-12 that half.

The second half, Wilkerson switched on to Williams and gave him nothing. Williams scored five more field goals, but Wilkerson also swiped the ball from him a few times (Wilkerson finished with four official steals and Williams was charged with eight turnovers).

"I made him come out to the top of the key to get the ball," Wilkerson said. "A couple of times, I knew he was going to flash to the ball, so I kinda trailed him across and then came to the side for the steal."

"Wilkerson played me a lot closer than May," Williams said. "He fronted me real good. It was hard for a guard to get the ball to me."

Williams said he felt a good game coming on — for him and the Gophers. "I knew everybody was ready to play," he said. "I was really up for the game.

"I wasn't worrying about Indiana being No. 1 or anything. I was just really ready.

"It was a good feeling. Before the games, I would get a little nervous — not really nervous but wondering how our team was going to do. But this time, every time I went up to shoot, I felt confident."

Williams's 34-point game was the biggest point total IU has allowed in Big Ten play in four years. Like Thompson, he wasn't surprised at the way Indiana came out the second half.

"We knew they had to do something because we were playing so well," he said. "Part of it was our defense. We came out flat-footed. They had one particular pattern on us and kept making it work."

Indiana 88, Iowa 73

Indiana matched the Big Ten record for consecutive conference victories Monday night by putting together one of the showpieces of its three-season, 27-game streak.

Iowa was the latest victim, the Hawkeyes making an all-out run at IU before 13,395 in their packed, 49-year-old Fieldhouse only to lose much as Minnesota did Saturday — to overpowering second-half play that gave Indiana an 88-73 victory.

Thus, Bob Knight's Hoosiers came home today with a 17-0 record that includes 8-0 in the Big Ten, where Michigan's 76-75 upset at Illinois cleaved open a sudden two-game Hoosier lead.

Knight liked the whole weekend. "We took a hell of a shot from Minnesota Saturday and the same from Iowa in this one," he said. "I don't think I've ever taken a team on a road trip and been more pleased with the results."

The Hawkeyes couldn't have asked for much better offensive play — especially from guard Scott Thompson, who took up where Minnesota's Ray Williams left off Saturday in bedeviling Indiana with uncanny outside shooting.

Thompson, whose 21 first-half points kept Iowa close (Indiana led, 43-39), finished with 28 points on 13-for-20 shooting, and the whole Iowa team shot .557.

But Indiana passed the offensive heroics around a little more liberally and shot over .600 for the second time in the weekend and only the ninth time in Hoosier history. Five of those have come this year — the latest one .615 on 40-for-65.

Bobby Wilkerson, so often a defensive blotter for the Hoosiers while others did the team's blazing, was the man whom Thompson was victimizing with long-range bombing in the first half.

But Wilkerson, meanwhile, was keeping Indiana alive on offense with his best shooting night as a collegian — ultimately, 10-for-12 for 21 points, topping the 18 he had against Michigan last year as his career high.

Wilkerson kept stepping into open spots in Iowa's zone defense as he fired in five shots in the first 6½ minutes for a 15-12 Hoosier lead, then three more in a row a few minutes later for a 28-23 Hoosier edge with 7:48 to go in the half.

However, Thompson swished 8 straight shots to move Iowa into a 35-32 lead 4½ minutes before halftime, when the spotlight shifted to IU's Scott May and Quinn Buckner.

Buckner popped off the Hoosier bench with 4:24 to go in the half, and seconds later Knight switched him on to Thompson. Thompson didn't get another shot the rest of the half.

And May, who hit his first two shots and then drew five blanks, got back on target with 9 points

in the last four minutes of the half to boost Indiana into its 4-point lead.

"I thought we were very fortunate the way things had gone to be four ahead at the half," Knight said. "Then what put us in really good position was scoring the first couple of baskets in the second half."

Kent Benson and May delivered those as Iowa slid into a 47-39 hole. The Hawkeyes got within four one more time (47-43) but never got any closer.

"I felt absolutely certain we were going to come out that second half and play our best ball of the game," Iowa coach Lute Olson said. "But we didn't, and Indiana's defense had a lot to do with that."

In the middle of the second half, the Hoosiers

INDIANA 88

	M	FG	FT	R	A	PF	TP
May, f	37	15-22	2- 4	8	4	2	32
Abernethy, f	32	2- 6	0- 0	5	4	2	4
Benson, c	37	5-11	3- 4	9	4	3	13
Wisman, g	17	1- 3	0- 0	1	3	2	2
Wilkerson, g	37	10-12	1- 1	0	3	3	21
Valavicius	8	2- 3	1- 1	3	2	1	5
Buckner	22	5- 7	1- 1	2	6	2	11
Radford	2	0- 0	0- 0	0	0	0	0
Haymore	2	0- 0	0- 0	0	0	0	0
Bender	2	0- 0	0- 0	0	0	0	0
Crews	2	0- 1	0- 0	0	0	0	0
Roberson	1	0- 0	0- 0	1	0	0	0
Eells	1	0- 0	0- 0	0	0	0	0
Team				4			
Totals		40-65	8-11	33	26	15	88

IOWA 73

	M	FG	FT	R	A	PF	TP
Frost, f	39	10-16	0- 4	5	6	3	20
King, f	38	5-11	0- 0	6	2	4	10
Haberecht, c	27	2- 6	2- 2	5	1	3	6
Thompson, g	36	13-20	2- 3	3	2	1	28
Wulfsberg, g	30	2- 3	0- 0	2	6	1	4
Mayfield	7	0- 1	0- 0	3	0	1	0
Peth	15	2- 3	1- 2	0	1	1	5
Gatens	4	0- 0	0- 0	0	1	2	0
Mays	4	0- 1	0- 0	0	0	0	0
Team				4			
Totals		34-61	5-11	28	17	16	73

SCORE BY HALVES

Indiana	43	45 — 88
Iowa	39	34 — 73

Errors: Indiana 13, Iowa 18

	FG	Pct.	FT	Pct.
Indiana	40-65	.615	8-11	.727
Iowa	34-61	.557	5-11	.455

Officials: Charles Fouty, Jim Bain and Mike Mathis

Attendance: 13,395 (capacity)

applied the back-breaker with brilliantly efficient play at both ends.

It was 58-52 with 11:17 to go when Buckner hit a jump shot that touched off a string of 10 straight times when possession of the basketball by Indiana meant at least 2 points.

The Hoosiers did it patiently, artistically, chillingly, and Iowa couldn't come close to keeping up.

May finished with 32 points, matching his 1976 Big Ten high (against Purdue), and he hit 15 of 22 shots to do it. But Wilkerson's 21 bothered Olson more.

"We gambled on Wilkerson," Olson said "and all of a sudden he's the greatest shooter in the world. With them, you've gotta gamble somewhere."

"Wilkerson was the guy who really got us going," Knight said. "The second half, May did a very good job offensively. Sometimes you overlook his scoring because he's hitting 12 to 14-foot shots, not 20-footers."

'A lot of pride involved,' Knight says as 'Q' stars

Some clouds parted for Buckner Monday night, and the Indiana University basketball picture — never exactly gloomy in this 17-0 year — brightened a little more.

Buckner, a reserve for only the fourth time in his four-year, 105-game Indiana career, had some notable success on defense and offense as the Hoosiers whipped Iowa.

But Knight saw something more in the Buckner performance. "When you talk about his play in this game, you start with the fact that here's a kid who didn't start but came back and did a hell of a job," Knight said.

"He's started 15 straight games this year before this weekend and Lord only knows how many in a row before that. There's a lot of pride involved. But he just comes in and plays well. To me, above everything else, his attitude was the thing that was impressive."

Buckner was inserted when Indiana was struggling to get Iowa's Thompson off a scoring binge that produced 21 points in the game's first 16½ minutes.

The co-captain the Hoosiers call "Q" managed to cool Thompson, but at the same time, Buckner was gaining some confidence in his own ability to go at top speed again after stamina problems in recent games.

"I was a little worried about it," he said, "and I think I was playing like it for a little bit. But once I got going, I was glad my wind was still there. The longer I played, the better I felt for a long while there, and that was a real relief to me."

His strategy for playing Thompson came out simply and emphatically: "Don't let him get the ball," Buckner said. "That's all I was trying to do."

Thompson agreed: "I think Buckner's instructions were to come in and not let me get the ball," he said. "I just wasn't getting it at all.

"When Wilkerson was on me, I think he was helping out a little more on our other guys. We had five guys moving, and when he had to help out on somebody else, I was getting a pass.

"But Buckner was stuck on me. I think Buckner's a tremendous defensive player. I've always thought that."

Wilkerson didn't enter the game anticipating the openings he found in the Iowa zone.

"They were playing Scott, and Wisman just started the ball toward him and reversed it to me and it was open every time."

Wilkerson hit his first five shots, missed two, then drilled his last five for an IU career-high 21 points. "When they're going in like that," he grinned, "you do look for your shot a little more."

IU pep band — a lively, colorful part of Assembly Hall pageantry

Indiana 114, Wisconsin 61

The Big Ten record for consecutive basketball victories is solely owned by Indiana now, after a 114-61 wipeout of Wisconsin Saturday.

The new recordholders aren't exactly breathless about their feat. Exasperated was a better word for Scott May, the leader again Saturday with a 30-point show in 25 minutes of playing time, when a questioner refused to believe May and his teammates were as blase as they claimed to be about breaking Ohio State's 14-year-old record for consecutive Big Ten victories.

"It's halfway through the *season*, man," May said. "We can't be thinking about records. We've got the rest of the season to go."

The rest of it — nine league games and perhaps some extras, if present trends continue — looked a little merrier to IU's archcritic, coach Bob Knight, Saturday.

Even in sailing along unbeaten, Knight said, "I think in some phases of play we were somewhat sporadic. I hope we can see a characteristic emerging where we are as tough as we can be defensively. I don't think we have been until the last three games.

"If we can continue, it will be a real good defensive team."

Wisconsin coach John Powless summed up the Hoosiers he ran into Saturday with only one word: "Awesome."

"They're just awesome. We used kind of a funny little defense there at the start and thought we were giving them some trouble with it. They don't score for three minutes, and they only have 12 after six minutes.

"But we only have 4 ourselves. They didn't let us do anything."

Indiana did get away to its slowest offensive start of the year, missing the first five shots and staying on zero until May drilled a jump shot at 17:01 of the first half.

But the Hoosier defense hadn't tarried on takeoff at all. The only shots Wisconsin was getting were hurried outside flings by the Badger guards, and it took more than 11 minutes before one of those hit the mark.

By then, Indiana was gone.

Bob Wilkerson, who came out of Minnesota and Iowa last weekend with his shootin' hand hot, started the Hoosiers in that direction by swishing a couple of shots over the Badgers' 1-3-1 zone.

That got the 17,587 in residence properly stirred for some emotional peaks that were to follow.

Wilkerson delivered one by stealing the ball in midcourt and dashing in for a layup that rolled off the front of the rim — just in time for 6-11 Kent Benson to bang it into the hole and touch off bedlam.

Seconds later, Brian Colbert of Wisconsin worked free from Hoosier Quinn Buckner only to

Scott May burns the Badgers for a bucket

INDIANA 114

	M	FG	FT	R	A	PF	TP
May, f	25	13-20	4- 5	4	2	0	30
Abernethy, f	20	1- 6	2- 2	5	2	3	4
Benson, c	23	10-15	3- 5	9	1	2	23
Buckner, g	17	3- 4	1- 1	3	9	2	7
Wilkerson, g	21	7-11	0- 0	3	3	3	14
Wisman	18	0- 1	2- 3	0	3	3	2
Radford	20	5- 9	4- 4	9	5	3	14
Valavicius	18	5- 5	2- 3	4	0	2	12
Crews	6	0- 0	0- 0	0	2	0	0
Bender	13	1- 3	0- 0	2	2	5	2
Roberson	4	1- 1	0- 0	1	0	1	2
Haymore	10	1- 4	0- 0	5	1	2	2
Eells	5	0- 3	2- 3	2	0	0	2
Team				5			
Totals		47-82	20-26	52	30	26	114

WISCONSIN 61

	M	FG	FT	R	A	PF	TP
Koehler, f	31	3-11	5- 7	2	0	5	11
Pearson, f	21	4- 5	0- 0	1	0	2	8
Johnson, c	22	1- 3	2- 4	4	1	4	4
JSmith, g	22	0- 4	1- 4	5	5	2	1
Colbert, g	34	6-19	2- 3	3·	4	4	14
Falk	14	1- 6	0- 0	3	0	1	2
Rudd	24	4- 6	3- 3	8	0	5	11
BSmith	23	2- 6	2- 3	1	1	0	6
Brey	9	1- 2	0- 0	1	0	1	2
Anderson	4	0- 1	0- 1	0	0	0	0
Faurote	3	0- 0	0- 0	2	0	0	0
Newburg	2	0- 0	2- 2	0	0	0	2
Team				10			
Totals		22-63	17-27	40	11	24	61

SCORE BY HALVES

Wisconsin . . . . 30 31 — 61
Indiana. . . . . 62 52 — 114

Errors: Wisconsin 34, Indiana 20

Technical fouls: Wisconsin coach Powless; Indiana coach Knight 2

	FG	Pct.	FT	Pct.
Wisconsin	22-63	.349	17-27	.630
Indiana	47-82	.573	20-26	.769

Officials: Orlando Palesse, Ed Maracich and Ken Kulick

Attendance: 17,587 (capacity)

Co-captain Quinn Buckner, cheerleaders lead the way on the start of another gala night at Assembly Hall

run into Tom Abernethy, who smashed Colbert's shot back in his face.

Buckner said thanks for the assist by delivering one of his own at the other end, pulling one whole three-man side of the Badger zone around him and flipping a behind-the-back pass to Abernethy, alone in the corner. His jump shot from there opened 14-4 daylight for the Hoosiers, and Wisconsin never got that close again.

The Hoosiers kept the score doubled on Wisconsin the rest of the half, although Knight started substituting early.

By halftime, 11 Hoosiers had played and 9 scored ... and the Indiana lead was massive, 62-30.

The Hoosiers may have gone on from there adequately, anyway. But when Knight thought he saw Wisconsin forward Dale Koehler shove and an official peering across the floor viewed it as a Buckner foul, the Hoosier coach let the caller know of his disagreement (cost: one technical foul) and mentioned the oversight to another of the three-man officiating team, too (cost: a second technical).

There may have been a return on the investment: new Hoosier interest.

Of the next eight times Wisconsin had the basketball, the Badgers lost it seven without getting a shot as suddenly renewed Hoosier zeal flashed all over the court.

It was 80-39 with more than 13 minutes remaining when Knight started pulling his regulars for the last time.

That didn't check the momentum. The reserves were as challenging on defense as the starters, and the lead kept growing.

Wayne Radford had such a frolic under the basket that — at 6-3 in a game involving 16 men taller than that — he shared rebounding honors with Benson with 9. And, it was Radford who delivered the Hoosiers' 100th point with 4:58 to go.

Rich Valavicius, who joined Radford and three starters in double figures, got the 114th point with a basket at 0:46. That was the one that broke the Assembly Hall scoring record, set in a 113-60 season-opening victory over Tennessee Tech last year. Indeed, it was a record for any of the Hoosiers' four basketball homes.

The 53-point margin tied IU's record for a Big Ten game, set in a 102-49 victory over Iowa last year.

But the item of history with the greatest import was the one dismissed so cavalierly by May.

This was Indiana's 28th straight Big Ten triumph, pushing into second place the 27-game conference string that Ohio State put together in Knight's playing days, 1960-62.

It also was the Hoosiers' 28th straight home-court victory and 48th in a row in regular-season play. Ohio State had 47 of those in a row in that 1960-62 stretch.

Besides May's 30 points (achieved with 13-for-20 shooting), Indiana got 23 from Benson (in 23 minutes), 14 from Wilkerson and Radford and 12 from Valavicius. The Hoosiers continued to shoot well, finishing at .573 with Wisconsin confined to .349 — Colbert leading Badger scorers with 14 points.

Indiana also had a 52-40 rebounding edge in finishing its first lap around the conference with a 9-0 league mark and 18-0 overall.

IU passes the buck
with all sorts of streaks

The Ohio State machine of the early 1960s — classy, poised, talented and almost always victorious — is offered by most basketball historians as the model of its age.

Knight had a player's-eye view of that team, through its three-year run of Big Ten victories that spanned 27 games, just as he's had a coach's eye-view of the 28 straight victories his Indiana team has strung in erasing the Buckeye record.

He's not convinced things have changed a whole lot in the intervening 14 years — in players' attitudes or skills.

"I saw films the other night on TV of George Mikan's (DePaul) teams in the 1940s," Knight said. "Basketball 10 years later was totally different. The style was completely different.

"But I don't think there is any great difference between the way the game was being played 21 or 22 seasons ago and the way it is now.

"I think there are a lot more good players now ... more good teams. But the good players are essentially the same.

"For example, there's never been a better player in the Big Ten than Lucas (Jerry, the leader of those Ohio State teams from 1960-61)."

A listener suggested today's shooters are better.

"Lucas shot over 60 per cent three straight years," Knight countered. "As a team, that team shot about 50 per cent. They were shooting the ball pretty well."

He headed off to another conversation, and a bystander suggested: "I think what he's trying to say is that it would be a hell of a game between that Ohio State team and this Indiana team."

"Naw," another said. "Some of those Ohio State guys are old fossils now."

Maybe a little gray at the temples but hardly fossilized, Knight recalled his days as a Buckeye and suggested he "probably got a lot more enjoyment" out of the original streak than the current one — because "you're not worried about 115 different things as a player." But, on reflection, he wasn't sure there was any real difference at all.

"As much as I can remember, I honestly don't think we paid any attention to that streak," he said. "And I don't think these kids are paying any attention to it now.

"Somebody asked Buckner after the Iowa game what his reaction was to tying the record, and he said, 'What record?' I think that's probably the attitude they all have."

The emphasis Saturday was not on streaks but on playing well at home — usually the least of concerns but one Knight mentioned and the Hoosiers took to heart after disappointing themselves in some earlier home games.

"We had a real good weekend on the road last weekend," May said. "But we really had only played well at home in our tournament. I don't know why. Maybe we relaxed a little. Maybe we figured our fans would help us get ready. But you can't play that way."

"We've been on kind of an up-and-down syndrome at home," Buckner said, "We haven't played well for our fans. As much as anything, we wanted to play a good game in front of them."

Knight was one of those fans Saturday, happy with every one of the 13 Hoosiers who got into the game.

"I thought they all played well and played hard," he said. "I thought our reserves played very well.

"Valavicius did well today, and he came in early in the Iowa game and gave us a three-point play when things were very tough. He's a tough, hard-nosed kid who weighs 215 and doesn't look it. And I thought Radford played very well.

"I thought our guard play defensively was very good, and that's really important to us."

That was primarily a reference to Wilkerson ("his shooting has come along — he's a very big asset to our offense") and Buckner ("I thought he played consistently better today").

Wilkerson continued a newfound role as a zone-breaker by hitting 7 of 11 shots — after going 7-for-10 and 10-for-12 in two games last weekend.

"I've got a lot more confidence," he said. "When I go up, I look to score. He (Knight) didn't tell me to shoot more or anything like that. I took it upon myself to look for shots."

Buckner noted that Wilkerson's success has altered the look of zones the Hoosiers are encountering. "You've got to play your guys where the other guys are putting it in the hole," he said. "And right now Bobby is doing it outside and Bennie is doing it inside. And, of course, Scott is getting them everywhere.

"I'm probably as confident in Scott as an offensive player as I think he is," Buckner said with a grin.

Rich Valavicius — 14 for rookie

'Maybe a little bit more than awesome' — Powless

Koehler, averaging 20.5 points and 10.3 rebounds in Big Ten play, scored only 11 points and had just 2 rebounds as Indiana shredded the Badgers. He scored just one field goal against Indiana's first team.

Frustrated? "No, not really," he said. "I played here last year. I expected it."

Not even Koehler, inured as he said he had become to Indiana's dominance at home, expected anything like Saturday's final 53-point margin. "Probably not that, no, but it doesn't make much difference whether it's 30 or 50," said Koehler, allowing himself another low-pitched laugh. "I expected 20 — at least 20."

Wisconsin coach John Powless, Bill Smith chat

The No. 1-ranked Hoosiers had that with 6½ minutes left in the first half, and the lead never dipped below 20 again. It only built, and Wisconsin kept adding to it with flocks of turnovers (34 in all and 6 in a row in one 2½-minute stretch in the second half) and 35 per cent shooting.

Koehler said he expected such defense, too.

"They take us out of our offense," Koehler said. "We can't do what we want. They're always helping out. You make a move and there's two guys on you. They can afford to do it — they have talent."

Powless said the Badgers had practiced in anticipation of enormous pressure, and they still wilted.

"What we practiced against and anticipated was the relentless defense we saw," Powless said. "Indiana took the second guard to double us up, and we had to pull a man away from the basket just to get a release pass to keep possession of the ball."

It wasn't just defense that thwarted Wisconsin early and often, said Powless. Wisconsin never mounted an offensive threat, and Indiana was unstoppable on the boards.

Indiana outrebounded Wisconsin, 28-12, in the first half and 52-40 for the game. Benson had only 9 of those rebounds, but Powless said Benson was the hub of that domination. "He intimidated us out there," Powless said. "He's a big key."

The biggest? "May's not too bad a key," said Powless, breaking into a smile.

May scored 30 points and Benson 23 despite playing little more than half the game. "May and Benson just ripped us apart the first half," Powless said. The pair combined for the 32 points that stood as IU's halftime margin as Powless scrambled for words. "We talked, to attempt to play as hard as we can," Powless said. "Our thoughts had to be geared toward Monday night — Michigan."

Powless said he will remember Indiana from Saturday. "Maybe a little more than awesome," he said. "Would that describe them accurately?"

Sophomore Mark Haymore has a front-row seat . . . and then some

Indiana 72, Michigan 67

Indiana was a beaten giant disappearing over a cliff when Kent Benson grabbed a final branch and swung the Hoosiers back to life Saturday.

Their 72-67 overtime victory over Michigan was the way history will remember the nationally-televised Big Ten basketball thriller, but not Johnny Orr. The Michigan coach thought victory was snatched from him five minutes earlier, when officials counted Benson's last-second rebound shot that tied the game, 60-60.

Officials were left with a couple of judgments to make with the crowd roaring, the buzzer sounding and Benson's shot through the goal. Was the ball:

- Through the rim before the buzzer?
- A tip or a controlled shot?

They count the same under normal circumstances, but they're totally different in the rule book. A shot can be in the air at the buzzer and count if it goes through; a tip must be in.

Official Bob Burson ruled Benson's basket came on a controlled shot, one that TV films showed was altered in its path by Michigan defender Phil Hubbard's block, which introduced another possible ruling: goaltending. It ain't the easiest game to officiate.

Nor play.

Nor coach.

Nor even watch. Saturday's game strained everybody.

It was a game that Indiana, a 16-point favorite on Jimmy the Greek's unemotional chalkboard, never led until the overtime.

In the Hoosier dressing room hangs the score of Indiana's last loss (92-90 to Kentucky in the 1975 Mideast Regional), along with a note: "Our defense was responsible for this." Offense was the culprit in this near-miss.

Indiana's defense kept the quick, good-shooting Wolverines under sufficient control to have the game in Hoosier hands early.

But an Indiana team that was No. 2 in the country in shooting with a .540 average going into the game spared the nets and wore out the rims with its worst start of the year: 4-for-20.

Even after that, the Hoosiers trailed only 12-9, because the Indiana defense had coaxed seven Michigan errors, five through steals or interceptions. It was not dissimilar to the openings IU had exploited for a 16-2 beginning in its 80-74 victory at Michigan Jan. 10, except in the conversion of chances.

Each Hoosier starter missed his first shot. Quinn Buckner, Bob Wilkerson and Tom Abernethy got away to a combined 0-for-13 start, and each new Hoosier problem seemed to infuse Michigan with a shot of belief.

Michigan's defensive strategy was bared by then: man-to-man defense after each Wolverine score, zone after each failure to score, and a full-court press after free-throw conversions.

The last one leaped up to bite Hoosier sophomore guard Jim Wisman, inserted in Buckner's place for the outside shooting skills he flashed in helping the Hoosiers whip a Minnesota zone three weeks before.

Wisman never got a chance to try a shot over the zone. Twice in 10 seconds, his attempts to pass the ball in-bounds misfired against the Michigan press, and Bob Wilkerson threw away a third in the stretch. Wolverine guards Rickey Green and Steve Grote converted two into baskets and the third pass sailed out of bounds. The sequence jumped the Michigan lead to 25-18 and brought Buckner back.

But Hoosier shooting problems weren't cured by halftime, which ended with Michigan a 39-29 leader and Indiana in the worst shape it has been in at the half in 73 games — since a 29-18 deficit against Oregon State in a 1973 game that never got much better and was lost by the biggest margin a Bob Knight team has been beaten at IU (61-48).

The Hoosiers didn't bolt away in the second half the way they did the only other time they have trailed at halftime in the last two years (at Minnesota, when they hit their first eight shots to change a 45-40 deficit into 56-49 command).

Scott May and Benson, virtually all of the Indiana offense up to then, delivered two field goals each to pull the Hoosiers within 41-37 with 3½ minutes gone in the second half.

But Michigan steadied to push its lead back to eight, and it was still there (55-47) after Green's basket with 9:35 to play.

By then, the hero of the Hoosier comeback had emerged — sophomore Wayne Radford, who entered the game with 12:52 to play and the Michigan lead at eight.

Michigan's Britt is surrounded by Wilkerson, May, Radford

Radford hit two shots in a row, missed one on a rebound flurry, then hit another — followed by a jump shot by freshman Rich Valavicius that cut the Wolverine edge to 55-52.

A crucial blocking-or-charging call on Green's drive into Valavicius went Michigan's way with 5:27 to go, and Michigan bled it for three points on a free throw by Green and a key rebound and free throws by Hubbard.

Radford rallied IU, though, with two baskets wrapped around his defensive rebound to make it 58-56 heading into the final three minutes.

Green hit two free throws with 2:27 to go to widen the edge to 60-56, and Michigan had that lead and the ball when Hubbard was called for traveling with 0:33 left.

Buckner swished a jump shot at 0:22 to halve the deficit, and with 14 seconds left, Grote had a chance to put things away for Michigan with a one-and-one free throw. It rolled across the rim and out, and May grabbed it and dribbled to midcourt before calling time out with 10 seconds to go.

"We wanted to split May and Benson and try to get the ball to one of them," Knight said. May got a pass at the side but had no opening and threw back to Buckner, whose try from the area where he had hit seconds before dipped in and out.

Jim Crews, inserted at the last Hoosier time out

as a possible outside shooter, contributed instead a rebound and an off-balance throw from the left baseline — the miss that Benson converted into a field goal.

Michigan didn't wilt in overtime. The Wolverines jumped out to 64-60 and 67-64 leads, but on the way, they lost Grote and Hubbard on fouls.

Again, the Hoosiers needed some impetus from Radford. He converted disaster into asset by following a Hoosier turnover with a quick steal from Michigan guard Dave Baxter, Radford spinning to hit a layup at 2:07 to cut the Michigan lead to 67-66.

Green tried to offset it with a driving shot that fell short, and at 1:26, May sank the jump shot that, after 43½ frustrating minutes, gave Indiana its first lead.

The Hoosiers had to play lots of defense to keep it. Michigan got three shots — Benson smothering one of Green's and intimidating another — and still had possession when Baxter, crowded by Radford, dropped a pass-in out of bounds at 0:39.

The Hoosiers clinched things with one-and-one conversions by Benson at 0:32 and Radford at 0:12.

Radford finished with 16 points, his career high, and, on a day when IU shooting was at its sourest, he was 6-for-7. "I wouldn't say one guy beat us," Orr said. "Benson and May helped a little."

May outscored Radford and everyone else with 27 and Benson also topped him with 21, plus a season-high 15 rebounds. But both took lots more shots as the Hoosiers hit .370 with Radford . . . or .324 without him.

Green had 23 points, Grote 16, Hubbard 12 (plus 15 rebounds) and Wayman Britt 10 for Michigan, which fell three defeats behind IU in the Big Ten race at 8-3 to Indiana's 10-0. Hoosier winning streaks are now at 29 (Big Ten and home) and 49 (regular-season games). There's no extra credit for overtimes.

INDIANA 72

	M	FG	FT	R	A	PF	TP
May, f	45	11-30	5- 7	6	2	4	27
Abernethy, f	29	0- 4	0- 0	5	1	2	0
Benson, c	45	9-17	3- 4	15	0	2	21
Buckner, g	39	1-10	0- 0	2	7	5	2
Wilkerson, g	28	1- 8	0- 0	6	7	3	2
Wisman	2	0- 0	0- 0	0	1	1	0
Valavicius	23	2- 4	0- 0	3	1	2	4
Radford	24	6- 7	4- 4	5	0	2	16
Crews	1	0- 1	0- 0	1	0	0	0
Team				5			
Totals		30-81	12-15	48	19	21	72

MICHIGAN 67

	M	FG	FT	R	A	PF	TP
Britt, f	45	3- 7	4- 4	4	3	2	10
Robinson, f	40	2- 6	2- 2	6	2	2	6
Hubbard, c	38	4-14	4- 4	15	1	5	12
Green, g	45	9-19	5- 8	3	4	2	23
Grote, g	37	6-10	4- 5	5	2	5	16
Hardy	5	0- 0	0- 1	2	0	0	0
Baxter	4	0- 0	0- 0	0	0	1	0
Bergen	7	0- 0	0- 0	1	0	1	0
Team				6			
Totals		24-56	19-24	42	12	18	67

SCORE BY PERIODS

Michigan . . . . 39 21   7 — 67
Indiana . . . . 29 31 12 — 72
Errors: Michigan 28, Indiana 21

	FG	Pct.	FT	Pct.
Michigan	24-56	.429	19-24	.826
Indiana	30-81	.370	12-15	.800

Officials: Bob Burson, Ray Doran and Fred Jaspers
Attendance: 17,743 (capacity)

Scott May — Scored go-ahead goal in overtime on 27-point day

The virtues (?) of defeat without paying the fees

The beauty of Saturday's victory, from Indiana's view, was that Hoosier poise held when plans were going blooey all around.

The last 33 seconds of regulation time will do for an example.

Indiana had the ball and a 60-56 problem. The Hoosier intent, as voiced by Buckner, who was directing the offense, was: Get the ball to May for a jump shot. "We've got the best scorer in America," Buckner said. "I wanted to get it to him or Val (Valavicius, likely to be open on the side opposite May, if, as IU presumed, Michigan's defense was sagged around Benson)."

Neither option worked, so Buckner fired himself and hit his only field goal of a frustrating day.

Step two called for a time out immediately after the basket to set up defense. Michigan got the ball back in play before the Hoosiers could get one called.

With 14 seconds left, Grote was fouled. "Did you foul him intentionally?" Knight was asked. "We didn't foul anybody intentionally," he said. Particularly not Grote, a tough and competitive former high school quarterback who has been at his best against IU in three varsity years . . . and was 4-for-4 at the free-throw line Saturday when he was fouled. "I said when he was going up to shoot

he might be the worst guy we could have fouled," Knight recalled.

Between foul and free throw, Knight took a time out — to make Grote sweat, maybe? "No," Knight said firmly. "I think that's bush league. We called time out to set up exactly what we wanted to do."

Grote missed, and May followed intent perfectly by grabbing the rebound and dribbling to center court before calling time. Ten seconds left.

Plans were drawn to go to May or Benson, preferably . . . or for whatever came open first with time so short. Buckner was the shooter, after May was checked. "It looked like it was going in," he said.

But it didn't, and Crews, inserted as a possible outside shooter, turned rebounder with a lunging effort that put the ball back on the board where Benson could deliver the tying basket. Planning is one thing; the military credo is that success comes from something more: "I&A." For improvise and adjust.

"If you were to pick one single play that made it possible for us to win," Knight said, "it might be Jimmy Crews's. He kept the ball alive. If he doesn't do that, or if he brings the ball down and dribbles out, Benson in no way has a chance to get the basket."

Knight credited Michigan with "45 minutes of really good basketball. We played 25.

"The first half, we were a step behind in thinking and in performance. And, instead of settling things down, we were going to hurry things up and get four points a shot or something.

"The second half was an entirely different ball game. And yet it's to Michigan's credit that we were playing very well and they just held in and held in and held in. Michigan is a hell of a basketball team, and the Michigan coaches have done a great job with their kids.

"I think Michigan was a better team and a tougher team today than at Ann Arbor (in Indiana's 80-74 victory Jan. 10). We got ahead of them pretty well a couple of times in that game. Today, there was a little bit of doubt." Robert is not a stranger to understatement.

Knight was reluctant to deny Michigan credit for contributing to Indiana's sub-par shooting (.370 for the day, .295 in the first half).

"What I would say about this is that we got 25 more shots, which should be enough of a cushion. And the first half, we had 14 more shots and 2 less baskets.

"At the same time, I've got to be really proud of our players for coming back like they did. And we got two really good performances from two young kids in Valavicius and Radford."

And there was a little bit of luck in there, too. Marquette coach Al McGuire keeps saying the Hoosiers need to lose one to shed pressure and improve its chance to win the national championship. Independent Marquette doesn't have to worry about such, but Indiana's first concern is widening its league lead. The Hoosiers got that and got humbled a bit, too. Who needs defeat?

IU's Wayne Radford, Steve Grote tangle

Sub Radford as super as Laz at his best

Former Indiana star John Laskowski was a shining memory Saturday afternoon, thanks to Radford, and Knight was ready to soften the blow for Laskowski as the ex-"Super-Sub" was upstaged at his specialty.

"I don't think he (Laskowski) would be upset if I said it, but I don't think any other player has come off the bench and done more in a single game than Wayne did for us today," said Knight. "He made every play that was available to him and his shooting was a decisive factor in the second half."

Radford had 16 second-half points, 6 in the overtime.

"Sometimes I haven't been mentally ready like I should when I go into the game," Radford said. "After the first half I was ready. He (Knight) just told us to start playing harder."

Radford was in the game for nearly four minutes late in the first half, but he didn't score as Indiana fell 10 behind. When he came back in the second half, he said, "Coach told me that if I got open to take the shots and not pass them up," Radford recalled.

"A lot of times in the past I might have passed the shots up, thinking maybe I was out too far. But not when he told me that (to take the open shots). They were sagging on Kent and Scott and it left the baseline and a little of the outside open."

Radford occupied those spaces and popped in one after another from the 12- to 20-foot range.

"You always look for the man with the hot hand," Buckner said. "You try to isolate him more to take advantage of it."

But Radford wasn't all that pleased with his total game in spite of what Knight said and delivered personally in post-game congratulations.

"Maybe I played well offensively," Radford said, "but not defensively. I let my man drive the baseline when I shouldn't have."

Shot-rebound-whatever, Hoosiers say it was in

Buckner, whose shot triggered all at the end of regulation time Saturday, and Benson, whose field goal ended it, didn't get caught up in the technicalities of basketball rules.

But both agreed with referee Burson that Benson's shot-rebound-whatever made it to the goal on time to save IU.

Burson ruled Benson's rebound goal a controlled shot. "I thought I did control it," Benson said. "I had both hands on it."

NBC-TV replays indicated Michigan's Hubbard got a hand on the ball after Benson, accidentally helping it into the goal. "I don't know about that," Benson said. "I know he was up there."

"I heard the buzzer," Buckner said. "There was no doubt the shot was up there. I'd say it was on the rim."

Besides giving the Hoosiers a reprieve that they cashed in during the overtime, the goal gave Benson two of the most bizarre — and most timely — rebound baskets in IU's recent basketball history.

The 6-11 junior also tied IU's other overtime game this year with a tip-in — his shoulder-high flick of a missed shot in the IU-Kentucky game tying things at 64-64 with nine seconds left. IU moved out in that overtime more authoritatively than against Michigan, putting Kentucky away, 77-68.

Benson, who was 16-for-18 in IU's January victory over Michigan at Ann Arbor, was the focal point for the Wolverines' defensive effort, including only their second trial of a zone defense this year. The first was a six-minute stretch in the other Indiana game.

"Every place I went, somebody was on me," Benson said. "The first half, we found ourselves in a hole, and the hole kept getting deeper and deeper.

"The second half, we kept hammering away and finally got to a place where we could do something. We knew we couldn't get panicky. Finally the ball started going in. The overtime gave us some breathing room."

Orr's version: 'Just like shot at Illinois'

Officials, Hoosiers and anything else to the contrary, Orr thought (1) Benson tipped in the winning shot and (2) it shouldn't have counted. "We lost a game the same way at Illinois," said Orr. "The ball wasn't in the basket.

"It's a judgment thing, you know. At Illinois, we tipped the ball in like that, and the referee said we didn't have control of the tip. Today when he tipped it in, the referee said he had control of the tip.

"At Illinois they said you have to catch it and then shoot it and have control of it," Orr said. "It's the identical thing to me, and we lost both games."

Orr bemoaned other Wolverine opportunities. "We had it in control," Orr said. "We had the same thing last year against UCLA (in the NCAA tournament). They didn't do anything to make us lose the game. It was the same thing tonight, we had the game in control. All we had to do was hit the free throw (Grote's, with 14 seconds left).

"If we didn't have to, we wouldn't shoot it. That's part of the game. That's why it's exciting."

'Learn press offense, Jimmy,' or get order in

Rickey Green and Rich Valavicius await a call

Wisman's first-half problems with Michigan's press led to his being literally jerked from the lineup, Knight grabbing the front of his shirt in getting a quick time out called and Buckner reinserted.

The scene moved coast-to-coast in pictures on both major wire services and a furore mushroomed, eased in part because the principals gave the incident a light side.

Wisman, to whom Knight apologized after the game, made it clear he wasn't offended. He said his mother watched the game on TV, "and I think she wishes she had been there to grab me.

"I screwed up. I just kind of panicked. Coach Knight doesn't put that kind of pressure on you.

He said he didn't mean to grab my shirt. It didn't bother me a bit, but the way people reacted did."

A better picture might have come later in the game when Knight objected to a call, started to make his objection when the ball was out of bounds and suddenly found himself 10 feet downcourt from his seat as play resumed — subject to an automatic technical foul under Big Ten policies. He solved the problem by plopping down on the lap of a reserve — eventual hero Radford, by coincidence. Looked a little silly for a few crisis-passing seconds, but the technical was avoided.

The intra-club mood over the issue was bared in practice Sunday. During work against a press, Knight called to Wisman: "Jimmy, either you're going to have to learn our press offense or get a tear-away jersey." Few things break up Hoosier practices, but that line did.

A happy day for Rich Valavicius, Tom Abernethy, Scott Eells

Indiana 85, Michigan State 70

"There are times," Kent Benson says, "when you go out there and feel like the world is yours.

"Other times, it's a struggle."

The world has seldom been more Benson-owned than it was Monday night, when his 38 points led Indiana to an 85-70 victory over Michigan State — another big step for the Hoosiers toward a possible fourth straight Big Ten basketball championship.

"I'd just like to borrow him for one quarter," Michigan State coach Gus Ganakas said. "He plays like he's in the NBA . . . and they let him play like he is."

The officiating tolerance Ganakas implied wasn't nearly so obvious to the 17,681 Hoosier loyalists in the Assembly Hall stands as the way the Big Red's "Big Red" was eating Spartans alive in the middle to keep Indiana safely out of catching range for the game's last 23 minutes.

Benson's big night stands as second-high for a Hoosier at Assembly Hall — Steve Downing's 41 against Illinois in 1973 a record that withstood assault by Michigan State's Terry Furlow as well as Benson Monday.

Furlow — firing freely, particularly in the last half when Indiana appeared uncatchable — totaled 40 points. The previous high by a Hoosier opponent at the Hall was 34 by Iowa's Kevin Kunnert in 1972. Kunnert's team didn't win, either.

But Benson was the deciding factor in this game, the high for his IU career and the first really "hot" game he has enjoyed at Assembly Hall. His previous high of 33 points came in last year's NCAA Regional game against Kentucky and was matched this year at Michigan. If Bennie doesn't make anything else, in Michigan he ought to be all-state.

Hoosier coach Bob Knight said Benson "did a good job of moving to get the ball. And (Rich) Valavicius, (Tom) Abernethy and (Scott) May screened well for him."

There was a hint early in the game that Benson was headed for more of a struggle than a glory day. He was the first Hoosier pulled by Knight, Abernethy — bumped from the starting lineup for the first time this year as sophomore Wayne Radford moved in — coming in with the game only 3½ minutes old to give Benson a 3-minute stretch on the bench, complete with counseling.

"The first half, he was coming out too far on the floor," Knight said. "We wanted to use him as much as we could, because he's a little bit stronger than their post people."

Indiana actually passed Michigan State with Benson on the sidelines — the score 11-8 for Michigan State when he departed and 16-15 for Indiana when he returned.

And his presence on the court didn't drastically change things for a while. Furlow, collecting free throws faster than field goals, rallied the Spartans

to a 26-22 lead before Benson contributed eight points to a surge that put Indiana in strong shape at halftime — up 46-37.

When Benson drilled his first four shots of the second half, the Indiana lead was 56-43 and Spartan organization was disappearing faster than their victory chance.

Furlow, who had 22 first-half points, threatened for a time to make the Hoosier crowd choke on its challenging chant that rang out every time Furlow touched the basketball: "Shoot! Shoot!" Terry obliged 'em every time he could, launching 30 shots in all and hitting 13 in his fifth 40-point game this year — a total topped in Knight's five Hoosier years by only South Carolina guard Kevin Joyce's 41-point explosion against IU in December, 1972.

"Furlow is probably the best shooter we've

INDIANA 85

	M	FG	FT	R	A	PF	TP
May, f	37	9-15	4- 4	6	0	3	22
Radford, f	21	4- 6	1- 4	2	3	4	9
Benson, c	34	16-26	6- 8	12	3	1	38
Buckner, g	18	0- 5	1- 4	2	5	3	1
Wilkerson, g	14	3- 8	0- 0	2	1	3	6
Abernethy	21	3- 7	0- 0	5	2	3	6
Valavicius	20	1- 2	0- 0	3	0	4	2
Wisman	24	0- 1	1- 2	1	6	1	1
Crews	3	0- 2	0- 0	0	1	0	0
Roberson	3	0- 1	0- 0	1	0	1	0
Bender	2	0- 0	0- 0	1	0	0	0
Eells	1	0- 0	0- 0	0	0	0	0
Haymore	1	0- 1	0- 0	1	0	0	0
Team				7			
Totals		36-74	13-23	43	19	25	85

MICHIGAN STATE 70

	M	FG	FT	R	A	PF	TP
Furlow, f	39	13-30	14-18	9	2	3	40
Wilson, f	35	1- 3	5- 6	2	1	4	7
Kelser, c	21	3- 5	2- 4	6	0	5	8
White, g	28	1- 2	0- 0	3	3	5	2
Chapman, g	26	2- 6	2- 2	3	0	5	6
Rivers	11	0- 0	0- 0	4	0	0	0
Riewald	15	1- 2	1- 2	4	0	1	3
Wiley	9	1- 3	0- 1	1	0	0	2
Vandenbussche	2	0- 0	0- 0	0	0	0	0
Webb	8	0- 1	0- 0	0	0	2	0
Nash	5	1- 2	0- 0	3	0	0	2
Team				10			
Totals		23-54	24-33	45	6	25	70

SCORE BY HALVES

Michigan State	37	33 — 70
Indiana.	46	39 — 85

Errors: Michigan State 17, Indiana 11

	FG	Pct.	FT	Pct.
Michigan State	23-54	.426	24-33	.727
Indiana	36-74	.486	13-23	.565

Officials: Art White, Gary Muncy and Carel Cosby
Attendance: 17,681 (capacity)

faced since I've been here," Knight said. "But one guy taking that many shots (36, counting six two-shot fouls he drew on other attempts), isn't going to beat you very many times."

Ganakas seemed to agree. "We went one-on-one too much the second half," he said. "I didn't like that. By then, though, the game was pretty well decided."

Indiana's 10-6 push opening the second half — eight of the points on Benson field goals — put the Hoosiers in firm command.

Greg Kelser, the 6-6 freshman who guarded Benson, fouled out at 7:48, Benson scoring 10 points after that before Knight pulled him to a standing ovation at 1:40. "I was trying not to let him get the ball," Kelser said. "But with his experience and his muscles, it's hard to, especially when he wants it. He's a big one."

"Benson actually destroyed us," said Ganakas. "It looked like we were playing a mountain — a big, graceful Himalaya."

Benson also led both teams with 12 rebounds (Kelser, the conference leader, had 6 for Michigan State), but the Spartans for the second time this year outrebounded IU, this time, 55-53.

May, with 22, was Indiana's only other double-figure scorer. Furlow was the only one for Michigan State.

'They will be beaten,' MSU's Furlow says

Radford became the seventh Indiana player to start a game this season, and Knight indicated he might continue to juggle the opening combination down the stretch of this 20-0 season.

"I think we'll have to adjust to certain things as we go along game-by-game," Knight said.

"For example, a guy like Jimmy Wisman moves the ball very well from one side to the other, and he's probably the most conscious of getting the ball to Benson."

Knight said he made up his mind to start Radford (in Abernethy's spot) Saturday. When the word came at a team meeting Sunday morning, "I didn't show any emotion," Radford said. "But I kinda felt nervous at first — starting before seniors.

"I felt it a little in our pre-game meeting and when they announced the lineup in pre-game, but once the tip went up, I was all right."

The game started with a look diametrically opposite from Saturday's Michigan game, when defense held the Hoosiers together through some shaky offensive minutes.

This time, the Hoosiers scored the first five times they got shots away, but they still trailed, 13-10, because they couldn't stop Michigan State.

Indiana efficiency began a bit later — the Hoosiers playing the last 13½ minutes of the half without a turnover. It may have been their longest error-free period of the year.

Valavicius, whose growing playing time reflects a similar trend in Knight's confidence in him, played most of that stretch. He wound up playing 20 minutes though scoring only two points.

Kent Benson powers in two of 38 as Tanya Webb watches

"Valavicius has played really well lately," Knight said. "He works at screening, he works on the boards, and doesn't make mistakes.

"Radford really did a good job the first half (when he scored nine points). And I thought Benson played extremely well on both boards."

Knight referred to Benson's "good job of moving to get the ball." Unlike shooting, an apparent variable, why would movement vary from game to game?

"I've never really been able to answer that question," Benson said. "I would have to say it's in the frame of mind.

"This game we just went out and tried to do the things the coach told us to do. It was more a matter of everybody going out and playing to win. I know I just tried to play as hard as I possibly could. This is what we have to do every time we play now."

The Hoosiers got inspiration for such effort with a candid post-game critique by Furlow. "We just couldn't put too many things together," Furlow said. "That was obvious. They were a better team.

"But they will be beaten. I don't think there's any team in the conference that can beat them. I think when they get outside the conference, they'll lose.

"There's only a few things they can do — go to Scott May or Benson. You cut off those two and what have you got?"

At Minnesota, "you" had Abernethy and Wisman scoring . . . at Iowa, Bob Wilkerson . . . in Saturday's key game with Michigan, Radford.

Indiana 58, Illinois 48

Jim Crews took his turn in Indiana's wild-card hero's role Saturday, and the Hoosiers — none too gingerly, assertively nor impressively — took another winning step toward a fourth Big Ten championship.

Illinois fell, 58-48, at Assembly Hall, where 17,759 spectators joined Indiana coach Bob Knight in mystification about the Hoosiers' tendency to refute basketball's legends about a home-court advantage — whether they're playing at home or away.

Illinois led the Hoosiers at halftime, 27-26, and took the issue into the last minute before Indiana put things away with four free throws by Crews and a game-closing layup by Kent Benson.

The Hoosiers hit five of their first seven shots, three of those by Quinn Buckner, to jump ahead of Illinois, 10-6, before the game was five minutes old.

But life became a struggle for Indiana about then, eased temporarily by a seven-point spurt in 45 seconds facilitated by an unusual five-point sequence.

That stretch came just after Illinois had moved ahead, 16-15, on a jump shot by Audie Matthews with 9:12 left in the half.

Jim Wisman arched in a shot from straight out front over Illinois' 2-3 zone defense, and with the shot in the air, Illinois' Otho Tucker fouled Benson in rebound jockeying. Indiana got the ball out of bounds and freshman Rich Valavicius converted a rebound into a three-point play that opened a quick 20-16 lead.

After a Tucker miss, Benson got free for his only field goal of the half to complete the seven-point run and give Indiana a 22-16 lead.

It was 26-18 after a one-and-one conversion by Scott May at 6:04 of the half. "That was the point where we had a chance to take control of the game and didn't," said Knight.

Indeed, things shifted so totally in the opposite direction that Indiana didn't score again in the half, a dismaying six minutes in which the Hoosiers missed six shots, committed three turnovers and combined all frustrations by losing a Wisman basket because Benson was called for a screening foul far from the shot. And it was his third, dictating his removal at 2:04 of the half.

Still, it took two steals by the littlest man on the court, 5-10 freshman Larry Lubin, to let Illinois slip around Indiana in the last minute of the half.

Lubin cashed one in himself after coming up with a loose ball at mid-court, then swiped the ball away after an IU offensive rebound and got a pass to Audie Matthews for a fast break that paid off in two free throws and a one-point Illini lead, the third time in the last four Saturdays Indiana has gone to the dressing room at halftime behind.

The fourth time also came Saturday.

Knight sent the Hoosiers back to the court after a relatively short halftime session, then — about three minutes before the break ended — interrupted their shooting to send them back to the locker room for some additional thoughts. Quick ones. Doesn't take long to say, "Wake up."

"He was just really upset that we weren't ready to play any better," senior forward Tom Abernethy said. The unprecedented double-session helped "maybe a little bit," he said. "But the way it turned out, we still had to fight for our lives."

It was 38-36 when Crews came on to replace Bob Wilkerson with 12:36 to go . . . and 42-40 when Crews scored over the Illini zone to start a spurt that boomed the Hoosiers ahead, 48-40, with 9:44 to go.

From there on, Indiana played it conservatively, but Illinois didn't leave its zone until 4:07 remained and Indiana's lead was 52-48.

Up to then, Indiana had gone 14-for-14 at the free-throw line, but three one-and-one misses made Hoosier life anxious in the closing minutes.

At last, Crews converted a couple of free throws at 1:00 and followed with two more at 0:28 to put the Illini away — the 31st straight victim of the Hoosiers in Big Ten play and at home and their 51st in a row in regular-season games.

After going 10-for-33 the first half (.303 — or .192 after the first five minutes), Indiana managed to squeeze out a .400 shooting day — to .564 for the patient Illini.

Indiana's edge came in other places: far better free-throw shooting (.818 for the team that hitherto ranked last in the Big Ten in that category, to .364 for Illinois), a 31-24 rebounding lead, and a none-too-pretty four-turnover margin (18 to Illinois' 22).

Jim Crews — Last-minute hero

90

INDIANA 58

	M	FG	FT	R	A	PF	TP
May, f	26	2- 9	2- 2	2	1	4	6
Abernethy, f	29	2- 6	2- 2	6	2	2	6
Benson, c	38	4-11	9-11	9	0	3	17
Buckner, g	33	5-10	0- 2	3	2	1	10
Radford, g	9	1- 2	0- 0	1	2	2	2
Valavicius	24	2- 5	1- 1	4	0	0	5
Wilkerson	18	1- 2	0- 0	2	4	1	2
Wisman	10	1- 3	0- 0	0	1	3	2
Crews	13	2- 2	4- 4	1	0	0	8
Team				3			
Totals		20-50	18-22	31	12	16	85

ILLINOIS 48

	M	FG	FT	R	A	PF	TP
Adams, f	39	4-10	0- 0	3	1	4	8
Matthews, f	39	3- 7	4- 6	4	1	3	10
Washington, c	32	4- 6	0- 0	5	1	3	8
Tucker, g	36	6-10	0- 4	5	0	3	12
Leighty, g	29	2- 2	0- 0	2	3	4	4
Ferdinand	6	1- 1	0- 0	2	0	1	2
Lubin	18	2- 3	0- 1	0	5	4	4
Team				3			
Totals		22-39	4-11	24	11	22	48

SCORE BY HALVES

Illinois	27	21 — 48
Indiana	26	32 — 58

Errors: Illinois 22, Indiana 18
Technical foul: Illinois bench

	FG	Pct.	FT	Pct.
Illinois	22-39	.564	4-11	.364
Indiana	20-50	.400	18-22	.818

Officials: Orlando Palesse, Ed Maracich and Ken Kulick

Attendance: 17,759 (capacity)

'Can't be ready to play,' frustrated Knight says

"We haven't played as well at home as we have on the road," Knight said . . . and professed no idea why.

"We've got a lot of people who have played a lot of basketball games and haven't lost very many. How much that affects them, I don't know.

"We're into a situation where it seems that playing at home we've had a tendency to relax and not be as sharp and aggressive as we have been on the road."

Losing has not been commonplace since Knight and the current seniors got together. The four-season record is 97-12, a chance to be the first class in IU or Big Ten history ever to be in on 100 victories beckoning out there.

Already, Indiana has become the first Big Ten team ever to win more than 20 games for four years in a row, so there is an acquaintance with success.

But Abernethy, one of those seniors who has been around for the fun, hardly sounds victory-glutted. Saturday's problem was not Illinois' zone defense, Abernethy said. "Not that their zone wasn't good," he said. "But it was more our lack of good play than anything they were doing.

"It was a matter of us not having ourselves ready to play. Somehow, all 13 of us have got to find a way to get ourselves ready — we've just gotta be ready to play, or we're in trouble.

"The teams that are going to be the better teams are going to be ready *every* time. If we play to our potential, we can shut a team out. We know that; we've done it."

Knight subscribed to the "ready-to-play" problem.

"At the half, our front line (Abernethy, May and Benson) had taken 16 shots and hit 2," Knight said.

"You just can't be ready to play and have that happen. I don't know what the reason was, but that's a pretty pitiful performance." The three combined for 60 points in the first IU-Illinois game.

"I thought Jimmy Crews (who came off the bench to score 8 of Indiana's last 16 points, including 4 game-clinching free throws in the last minute) played extremely well in this ball game," Knight said. "From a positive side, I would mention Crews and Buckner, in that order.

"Crews really gave us a lot of things. He got a crucial rebound, he passed for a bucket, he made a steal, he hit a couple shots and he made all those free throws.

"And Buckner got a couple of big rebounds and steals and shot a lot better."

Illinois shot .564 for the day, partly because the Illini cashed in 10 layups. A couple came on steals, one on a drive. The rest were products of a patient, spread offense that occasionally caught the Hoosiers with back-door cuts.

Those weren't free. The "patience" meants lots of ballhandling, and the Hoosiers spirited the ball away from Illinois 22 times on turnovers, 12 of them outright steals.

"We made some defensive mistakes that let them have four buckets in the first 10 minutes (on layups)," Knight said. "But our defense, with the exception of the cuts we gave up, was all right. We had some lapses occasionally, but it was all right most of the game.

"But we seemed just a little bit short and a little bit behind all day."

Part of the problem, the unrecognized part, he implied, was Illinois.

"If I've said it once, I've said it a hundred times this season, and nobody seems to listen," Knight said. "Every team in this league has good players. People just seem to be amazed every time we have a close game."

It was a "McDonald's game," the first of the season where the opponent scored under 50 and qualified all ticketholders for a free 'burger, French fries and Coke at the hamburger chain's Bloomington outlets.

But that didn't assuage Knight. While the 'burgers were being dished out, the Hoosiers were back at the Hall for an 8 p.m. chat.

Indiana 74, Purdue 71

Scott May left Purdue last year with a broken arm. Monday, he left behind 14,000 broken hearts.

May drilled Purdue for 20 last-half points, including two clinching free throws with two seconds left, as Indiana jerked an upset out of Boilermaker hands and won, 74-71, before a noisy full house (14,123) at Mackey Arena.

They came early for this one, not upset-hopeful but confident, expectant, bold and boisterous. Almost an hour before game time, cheers were bouncing around the steadily-filling arena.

And there was a time when it appeared they might get even more than just a victory — a blowout in the air when Purdue recovered from a 10-4 opening jolt to dash out to a 27-16 lead.

Quinn Buckner was gone with three fouls by then; May went out with three just minutes later.

But the people who steadied the Hoosiers came off the bench to do it — 19-time starter Bob Wilkerson, plus Jim Wisman, Wayne Radford and Rich Valavicius.

They did the scoring as IU outscored Purdue, 9-2, at one stretch, and they got the Hoosiers to the dressing room down only 39-35.

"Those guys kept us in the ball game where we could at least get something going the second half," IU coach Bob Knight said.

What the Hoosiers got going were forwards May and Tom Abernethy, dormant scorers of late but the sudden focal point of an altered IU offense. The Purdue zone defense that sagged around center Kent Benson in the teams' first meeting and enshrouded him again Monday edged out with him as Benson began operating a bit farther from the basket.

The shift stretched the zone and left holes along the baseline that May and Abernethy exploited for 31 of the Hoosiers' 39 second-half points . . . while Benson, a decoy, tried only one shot.

Indiana had fallen behind, 41-35, on Walter Jordan's rebound basket to open the second half.

But Abernethy, who had only one field goal in the first half, hit three in a row to tie the game at 18:05, Wilkerson slipping him a quick-break pass to beat the Purdue defense downcourt on the tying basket.

May broke the tie with a jump shot at 17:42, and Wilkerson got out ahead of the Boilermaker defense for a fast-break basket that made it 45-41. Purdue never caught up again.

But, neither did the Boilermakers stay down when Indiana appeared to land a knockout punch with a gorgeous flurry that jumped the lead to 58-48 with 11:25 left.

The showpiece of that stretch was a two-man fast break by May and Wilkerson — the two exchanging four passes without a dribble to spring May for a layup and drive Purdue coach Fred Schaus to a time out.

The Boilermakers, led by sophomores Eugene Parker and Jordan, nipped away to cut the lead to 70-68 with 4:10 left, when Indiana went into a stall.

The Hoosiers ran it well, burning off three minutes before Jerry Sichting fouled Wilkerson with 1:17 left.

Wilkerson hit one free throw to put the lead at 71-68. With 50 seconds to go, after Purdue had missed three shots but desperately retrieved the ball each time, 6-10 center Tom Scheffler drove straight at the basket for a close-in try.

Benson leaped high to slap it down — "a big play that really hurt us," Schaus said.

Radford fielded the rebound. and at 0:42, Wilkerson again hit one free throw and missed one (72-68). Parker's miss was fielded by Benson, and Wilkerson went to the line again at 0:19 . . . and missed.

INDIANA 74

	M	FG	FT	R	A	PF	TP
May, f	34	10-17	6- 6	7	3	3	26
Abernethy, f	32	6- 9	1- 2	6	0	1	13
Benson, c	39	5- 9	0- 0	11	0	4	10
Buckner, g	15	1- 6	0- 0	1	3	4	2
Crews, g	10	1- 3	0- 0	1	1	0	2
Wilkerson	30	4- 6	2- 5	2	7	2	10
Wisman	10	2- 4	0- 0	2	2	1	4
Valavicius	9	1- 5	0- 0	1	1	0	2
Radford	21	2- 7	1- 2	3	2	2	5
Team				5			
Totals		32-66	10-15	39	19	17	74

PURDUE 71

	M	FG	FT	R	A	PF	TP
Jordan, f	31	7-11	0- 1	9	1	5	14
Walls, f	29	3- 9	2- 2	11	0	0	8
Scheffler, c	37	4- 7	5- 7	13	0	2	13
Parker, g	36	9-19	5- 6	1	3	3	23
Macy, g	28	4-10	3- 4	0	3	2	11
Thomas	20	0- 1	0- 0	1	1	1	0
Sichting	16	1- 5	0- 0	0	0	1	2
White	3	0- 0	0- 0	0	0	2	0
Team				4			
Totals		28-62	15-20	39	8	16	71

SCORE BY HALVES

Indiana. . . . . 35 39 — 74
Purdue. . . . . 39 32 — 71
Errors: Indiana 11, Purdue 12

	FG	Pct.	FT	Pct.
Indiana	32-66	.485	10-15	.667
Purdue	28-62	.452	15-20	.750

Officials: Jerry Menz, Bob Showalter and Bob Brodbeck

Attendance: 14,123 (capacity)

Fred Schaus and Eugene Parker, Bob Knight and Wayne Radford in courtside chats

At 0:10, Purdue freshman Kyle Macy hit a free throw, missed the second, and Parker, with the 6-7 pair of May and Wilkerson pinning him deep in the corner with hands high, nevertheless swished a jump shot that made it 72-71 as Purdue took time out with four seconds left.

Abernethy took the ball out of bounds for IU to the left of the Purdue basket. "Radford, Wilkerson and I lined up near the foul line," May said. "They screened my man and I just broke for the ball."

"It was the old physics principle — action is better than reaction," Knight said. "All he had to do (once he caught the pass) was stand there and hold it or get fouled."

May had both of his arms clamped around the ball when Macy fouled him at 0:02. "I felt really confident I was going to make them," May said flatly, but with a grin he added: "Deep down inside, I was hoping I was gonna make them, too."

May finished with 26 points, after getting only 6 against Illinois Saturday and 6 the first half of this one. "May is a pro shooter," Schaus said. "He makes the tough shots even with a good pressure defense on him."

Abernethy had 13 points, Benson and Wilkerson 10 each — Benson adding 11 rebounds as the teams tied on the boards, 39-39.

Parker's 23 points led Purdue, while Jordan had 14, Scheffler 13 (plus a game-high 13 rebounds) and Macy 11 in the Boilermakers' sixth straight loss to IU.

IU 'sacrificed Benson' and forwards scored

May, of all Hoosiers, could have been forgiven some *deja vu* in his first return to the arena where an odd accident last year snapped a bone in his left arm and removed him, for all practicality, from Indiana's national tournament picture.

But his 1975 problems weren't on his mind, he said.

"I don't know if it was building into a mental thing," he said. "But I had been playing terrible and I knew I had to come out of it.

"I really had a bad game against Illinois and I had a bad first half tonight. I knew I had to come out of it, and I'm just hoping I did."

May scored 32 points against a Purdue zone in the teams' first meeting. "This time they were maybe a little more conscious of me and Bennie," he said. "At times, it was kinda like a match-up zone."

With the shots that in the first game were open to him at the edge of the foul circle no longer there, May moved to the baseline and Abernethy dropped into a low post area, with Benson taking the zone out on the floor a bit.

"We sacrificed Benson the second half," Knight said. "But what he did do (by moving out) was open things up for our forwards. So they finished with 16 buckets, and I thought Benson did a good job toward the end on the defensive board.

"There was a point in the second half when I

didn't think Benson had even touched the ball in our offense yet. We just worked around him."

"May and Abernethy hurt us in the second half," Schaus said. "You can close off a couple of places, but not everywhere.

Abernethy said the Hoosiers were "in pretty good spirits" at halftime though down, 39-35.

"It could have been worse," he said. "We had some good shots but they weren't dropping. The guys we had in at the end of the half with Bennie (Wilkerson, Radford, Wisman and Valavicius) all did a great job keeping us in the game."

"Indiana has some good players on that bench, some high school all-Americans that you haven't seen much," Schaus said. "But you'll see them next year."

"I thought Wilkerson played extremely well, particularly coming off the bench," Knight said of the 6-7 senior who usually starts but backed up Jim Crews at the start of this one.

"We started Jimmy because we were trying to get as much offensive power as we could. But it's to the credit of the Purdue defense that they didn't let Jimmy get his shot."

Wilkerson inherited a tough defensive job — Parker, "a tremendously fine offensive player," Knight described him, and the hottest guard in the Big Ten the last three weeks. He scored 23 points, but he was 9-for-19.

"Their defense maybe forced us to take some shots we didn't want to take," Parker said. "But we didn't take advantage of the foul situation in the first half. We got a little lax, maybe.

"I really wanted this game bad."

Knight sensed that about all the Boilermakers. He made a quick post-game visit to the glum Purdue dressing room and "just told them I thought they played very well. This was the kind of game that typifies Big Ten basketball. A hell of a crowd ... two teams playing awfully hard. The competition between these schools has been really something."

Penders: IU can be had, but may not allow it

Bloomington, Indiana, March 5, 1976

Columbia coach Tom Penders proved himself a bright — and merry — young man when he took his painfully light brigade charging into battle against IU in Madison Square Garden in December.

Penders dropped lots of one-liners before and after his 106-63 battering, and he has some more in this month's *Sport* magazine, in an article entitled: "Psst . . . want to know how to beat Indiana?"

Penders didn't treat his outmanned assignment as a lark. He tried some things, including the first box-and-one defense (four-man zone, one man assigned to Scott May) that IU ran into this year. It was also the last one; proved a bit too vulnerable to Kent Benson in the middle.

But, Penders points out:

• "In the final seven minutes and 50 seconds, the critical period when most games are decided, we outscored Indiana, 19-16.

• "Despite the fact that our tallest man was only 6-8, we permitted Benson only three rebounds. And we outrebounded Indiana, 35-33.

• "We held May to 12 points, or less than half his average going into our game.

• "By selecting our shots wisely, we penetrated the supposedly invincible Indiana defense to the extent of making 63 per cent of our shots.

"It is almost impossible to believe that, with all these terrific things we achieved, Indiana still managed to edge us out — by 43 points."

Gotta like a guy like that.

Penders carries on in that manner through most of an entertaining three-page article. But he did enlarge on his nominal theme with some comments and some compliments.

"I am serious about one thing: I honestly believe Indiana *can* be beaten," Penders said. "But I doubt if the Hoosiers will allow it to happen.

"For one thing, I have tremendous respect for Bobby Knight's coaching ability, and that respect is matched by my respect for his players.

"The Indiana team has class. They handle themselves like champions. I hope some of that rubbed off on my young kids; I hope we'll be a better team for having played Indiana.

"The only team I've *seen* that I could imagine beating Indiana would be Princeton. That's not just an Ivy League prejudice. Princeton has the sort of disciplined, patterned offense — a lot of picks and back-door plays — that *could* penetrate the Indiana defense. *Could.*

But Penders' lines really spice the story.

Penders described Wilkerson as "a 6-7 guard who doesn't play like a 6-7 guard . . . he plays more like a 6-10 guard, and he moves faster than Calvin Murphy." He calls Buckner "simply the most dominant floor leader I have ever seen.

"On defense, they completely shed their individuality; they blend, they merge, they melt into a unit. I swear they sneak five extra guys on the court. I am positive I have seen 20 arms all wearing Indiana uniforms and all waving on defense.

"Bobby Knight stresses defense, and he has got to be the greatest teacher that ever lived. Or else Buckner, May, Benson, Abernethy and Wilkerson are the best students.

"In the first five minutes, we didn't score a single point. I was seriously wondering how it would feel to be the coach of the first modern collegiate basketball team to be shut out.

"They never did really let up, which is a credit to the Indiana players and the coaching staff. Those kids don't look at the clock or at the scoreboard. They play hard every minute."

Indiana 76, Minnesota 64

Tom Abernethy and Jim Crews were instant replays, painful ones, for Minnesota Saturday as Indiana turned back another Gopher upset attempt, 76-64, at Assembly Hall.

The Gophers had a 39-38 halftime lead, the fourth time in five Saturdays that had happened. And the Hoosiers were still struggling to change things when IU coach Bob Knight, making his sixth substitution of the afternoon, sent in Crews, with 11:55 to go and the score tied 50-50.

It was Crews who untied it by stealing a pass in the middle of the Minnesota offense and driving downcourt to ram in an uncontested layup.

A jump shot by Kent Benson, a scoring voice virtually silenced by the sagging Gophers Saturday, and a three-point play by Abernethy shot the Hoosiers ahead suddenly, 57-50.

And, unlike a couple of earlier leads, this one was maintained judiciously.

Minnesota never again got it under five, and the Gophers made only one menacing move — with just less than four minutes left when a full-court press coaxed a Hoosier turnover as the lead dipped quickly from 67-54 to 67-58.

It was checked there, a couple of later errors against the press serving only to lower the margin that once reached 16.

Abernethy, who hit his college high with 22 points in IU's Jan. 24 victory over Minnesota and then ran into a slump that got him dropped from the starting lineup for a game, recognized the Gophers perfectly. He scored 22 again and did enough other things to qualify with Crews for some Knight praise on a day that left him generally underwhelmed.

"From the beginning to the end, we got outstanding play from Tommy," Knight said, "and I'm talking about everything he did. He got some key buckets, he played the boards, he made the passes and he blocked some shots.

"And Jimmy Crews came in and did about everything he could do. Off the top of my head, I can think of some interceptions, some rebounds, some passes and some shots he made."

Knight also had no problems recalling two points in the game where he figured the Hoosiers might have asserted the same sort of control they did after the burst that put them up, 57-50.

One came early, when the Hoosiers jumped out on Minnesota, 15-9, and pushed Gopher coach Jim Dutcher into a time out. The man must have persuasive talents. Minnesota bounced out to score 12 straight points, in only two minutes and 20 seconds.

It was 29-29 when Indiana fell back again on five straight free throws by Gopher shooter Ray Williams — on one trip downcourt.

It started when Williams drove for the basket, missed his shot, but collided with IU defender Scott May, who was attempting to block the path and draw a charge — foul No. 3 on May, officials said, and technical No. 1 on Knight, who disagreed.

Williams went swish, swish, swish; Minnesota got the ball back, and Williams was fouled again. Two more swishes.

By halftime, the man had 12 of those in a row, but he also had a throbbing right ankle. Williams crumpled and left the game with 1:26 to go in the half, Indiana down at the time, 39-33.

"That was the ball game," Dutcher said.

Indiana capitalized on his absence by freeing Abernethy for a couple of baskets that cut the halftime gap to one.

When Williams remained out and IU opened the second half by jumping ahead, 46-41, command seemed asserted. "Then we gave up a three-point play (by Osborne Lockhart)," Knight said,

INDIANA 76

	M	FG	FT	R	A	PF	TP
May, f	36	9-20	0- 1	10	3	4	18
Abernethy, f	40	9-16	4- 8	10	0	2	22
Benson, c	39	3- 6	0- 0	6	7	4	6
Buckner, g	15	4- 6	1- 2	2	2	4	9
Wilkerson, g	21	3- 8	0- 0	4	1	2	6
Wisman	17	2- 5	0- 0	1	2	0	4
Radford	19	3- 4	1- 2	1	2	3	7
Valavicius	1	0- 0	0- 0	1	0	0	0
Crews	12	1- 1	2- 2	1	3	0	4
Team				5			
Totals		34-66	8-15	41	20	19	76

MINNESOTA 64

	M	FG	FT	R	A	PF	TP
Winey, f	24	1- 4	0- 0	4	1	2	2
Williams, f	31	3-10	12-12	2	4	2	18
Thompson, c	39	5-10	7- 8	7	1	4	17
Lockhart, g	37	9-19	1- 1	3	0	1	19
Saunders, g	40	2- 3	0- 0	5	1	3	4
Korkowski	31	0- 2	0- 0	1	0	3	0
Johnson	11	2- 3	0- 0	1	0	4	4
Team				5			
Totals		22-51	20-21	28	7	19	64

SCORE BY HALVES

Minnesota	39	25 — 64
Indiana	38	38 — 76

Errors: Minnesota 17, Indiana 14
Technical fouls: Indiana bench 2

	FG	Pct.	FT	Pct.
Minnesota	22-51	.431	20-21	.952
Indiana	34-66	.515	8-15	.533

Officials: Phil Robinson, George Solomon and Rich Weiler
Attendance: 17,718 (capacity)

Jim Wisman looks for a call and the ball

the memory troubling. "We just aren't mentally alert a lot of times."

It was 48-48 when Williams re-entered with 12:26 left. That move didn't generate nearly the charge that Knight's switch to Crews did 28 seconds later. Williams managed only two points the rest of the way; Crews had four, plus three assists, two steals and a rebound.

May, with 18 points, was the only Hoosier in double figures besides Abernethy, and the two forwards also had 10 rebounds each as Indiana was dominant there, 41-28.

Thompson, the league's leading rebounder, spent lots of time outside normal center positioning — the neutralizing scheming of both Dutcher and Knight. So Thompson wound up with only seven rebounds and Benson six. Thompson's 17-6 point edge came largely on free throws (he was 7-for-8, Benson 0-for-0).

Lockhart, who scored four straight field goals in Minnesota's 12-point run, led the Gophers with 19.

Indiana got its shooting eye back with .515 marksmanship against the Gopher defense, a zone all the way until Dutcher knew Hoosier ball control was coming and went to a man-to-man with 4:58 to go and Indiana ahead, 67-54.

Be happy to be down at half, Bee advises

If the membership in basketball's Hall of Fame were only six or eight names long, Clair Bee would be among 'em.

And Clair — "Mr. Bee" to Knight, who reveres the coaching legend from the East and had him as his guest at a regular-season game Saturday for the first time in Knight's five years at Indiana — was one who felt right at home when Knight and the Hoosiers "treated" him to the joy of being behind at halftime.

"I never did have any question about which was the better team," Bee said, eyes a-twinkle as he approached a theory.

"I never tried to be ahead at the half. You could look back through my scorebooks and unless the team we were playing was just outclassed, we would normally be behind at the half."

Explain, please?

"Then I knew they'd listen," he said, smiling.

So, at the half, he thought Indiana would win?

"I thought they'd listen." Second smile.

Knight, who wasn't born yet when Bee was well into the winningest career (lifetime percentage: .827) a college coach ever had, was neither so enamored with his halftime plight nor so sure his message was getting through as Bee was.

Exasperation showed clearly in Knight's voice when he said: "I don't think we're playing very well."

He pinpointed times in the game when Indiana led 15-9 and 46-41 as missed opportunities to take control of the game. "Both of those times, we had a chance to do something, and we had breakdowns," he said. "Defensive breakdowns.

"As a result, we let some pretty good efforts go by the wayside. We had a good defensive effort on Williams to start the game (Wilkerson on him), and we get a 15-9 lead, and all of a sudden, we quit concentrating.

"Drilling isn't the answer. We can drill the next 24 hours and we can't *make* anybody concentrate."

Dutcher was happy with his team's defense, against Benson, anyway. "Thompson has played Benson very well every game they've played," he said. "He's big enough to get in Benson's vision, and he makes it difficult to play."

Benson scored just six points, shooting only six times, but he had seven assists. "They played good defense," said Benson. "They stopped things up in the middle, but it left the passes open to them underneath."

"It's pretty obvious they were concerned with Bennie," Abernethy said. "When they are, it opens things up inside for the rest of us."

Dutcher ducked all requested comparisons, but his players didn't.

"Personally, I think Marquette would beat Indiana," said Thompson, who starred in December when Minnesota dealt the No. 2-ranked Warriors their only defeat. "The only thing Indiana has over them is its bench. But as for the first five players, Marquette's are better."

Ray Williams — Down, then out

Indiana 101, Iowa 81

The blowout returned to Indiana basketball Monday night, just in time for a royal occasion.

Quinn Buckner, playing in his 100th college victory, led the way as the unbeaten Hoosiers overwhelmed Iowa, 101-81, to guarantee at least a tie for their fourth straight Big Ten championship.

To 17,691 at Assembly Hall, the means was even more significant than the historic end on this night. The electricity, the pizazz, the fun was back.

It may be valid to ask where it had gone, considering IU's perfect record — which is basically what first-time Hoosier-watcher Clair Bee, with a Hall of Famer's perceptiveness, did in pointing something out to coach Bob Knight Saturday.

"We've been talking about how we can't do this and we don't do that," Knight said. "I saw it mentioned in a local paper how often we've been behind at the half lately. But it seems like we're always ahead at the end. We've all gotten into a bit of a rut, thinking in negative terms.

"What we talked to the kids about yesterday and before this game was what we can do.

"I feel very proud of these kids. They've done some things that no other team in the history of the Big Ten has done. They've had to play a lot of good basketball in a tough conference."

They played quite a bit of it Monday night in destroying an Iowa team that was 18-6 with a five-game winning streak entering the game.

The Hawkeyes led once, at 5-4. Appropriately, Buckner swung the lead back to IU for the last time with a jump shot at 16:55.

It was his second field goal. He missed his next two tries, then bombed in seven in a row as Indiana exploded away to a 49-36 halftime lead.

When Kent Benson and Scott May hit a couple of field goals each and Bob Wilkerson added one opening the second half, the lead jumped to 59-38 and the rout was on.

The lead peaked out at 81-48 with 9:30 left. By then, Buckner had come out to a prolonged standing ovation, a gala pep band rendition of "The Mighty Quinn" and a Knight hug on the sidelines.

All starters were gone with 6:24 to go, the Hoosier lead at 85-57. Indiana reserves permitted Iowa a margin-shrinking 11-point run but managed their own positive note with a rousing finish — a three-point play by freshman Scott Eells, a steal and layup by Eells, and a steal and layup by Wayne Radford all coming in the last 29 seconds to boost Indiana over the 100 mark for the fourth time this year.

Indiana's 44 field goals included some dazzling plays. Roommates May and Buckner got things going with assists to each other in the first minute.

In the game's fourth minute, Wilkerson sailed an "Alley Oop" pass over Iowa's zone defense and Benson's timing and touch were perfect on a leap, catch and soft deposit into the goal.

The seventh and eighth minutes were nightmares for the Hawkeyes, harassed into turnovers on five straight trips downcourt while IU's lead jumped to 19-9.

Wilkerson's penetration inside the Iowa zone and slick pass to Tom Abernethy for a layup made it 25-17 at the 10-minute mark.

And, in a 57-second stretch just after that, Buckner drilled a jump shot, fooled the Hawks with a change-of-pace that freed him for a driving layup, then swished another jump shot to make it 31-17.

Knight pulled Buckner for a breather when embattled Iowa coach Lute Olson took a time out, but life got no better for Olson.

When play resumed, IU sophomore Wayne

INDIANA 101

	M	FG	FT	R	A	PF	TP
May, f	24	6-15	2- 2	6	6	4	14
Abernethy, f	31	5- 7	2- 2	6	1	4	12
Benson, c	23	7-11	1- 1	9	0	4	15
Buckner, g	26	12-19	0- 0	0	8	1	24
Wilkerson, g	29	7-10	0- 1	6	6	3	14
Radford	12	2- 3	3- 4	2	1	2	7
Crews	7	0- 3	2- 2	0	0	1	2
Wisman	14	1- 3	2- 2	1	4	5	4
Valavicius	19	2- 5	0- 0	6	0	4	4
Bender	6	0- 1	0- 1	0	1	0	0
Haymore	4	0- 0	0- 0	0	0	2	0
Roberson	3	0- 0	0- 0	0	0	0	0
Eells	3	2- 2	1- 1	1	0	1	5
Team				5			

IOWA 81

	M	FG	FT	R	A	PF	TP
King, f	·35	9-14	2- 2	3	0	4	20
Frost, f	36	6- 9	4-10	9	2	1	16
Haberecht, c	24	0- 1	0- 0	0	0	2	0
Thompson, g	35	8-13	6- 6	7	1	1	22
Wulfsberg, g	20	1- 2	4- 4	0	4	3	6
Peth	23	2- 6	9-11	2-	4	3	13
Gatens	9	1- 3	0- 0	2	0	1	2
Mays	10	1- 4	0- 0	0	2	1	2
Mayfield	3	0- 0	0- 1	0	0	1	0
Hairston	3	0- 0	0- 0	0	0	0	0
Magnusson	2	0- 0	0- 0	0	0	1	0
Team				6			
Totals		28-52	25-34	29	12	18	81
Totals		44-79	13-16	42	27	31	101

SCORE BY HALVES

Iowa........................	36	45 — 81
Indiana.....................	49	52 — 101

Errors: Iowa 23, Indiana 19
Technical fouls: Iowa coach Olson 2

	FG	Pct.	FT	Pct.
Iowa	28-52	.538	25-34	.735
Indiana	44-79	.557	13-16	.813

Officials: Jim Bain, Malcolm Hemphill and Rollo Vallem
Attendance: 17,691 (capacity)

Quinn Buckner — Head and shoulders above the rest on big night

and Notre Dame). Benson scored 15 points, May and Wilkerson 14 each and Abernethy 12.

Iowa's three top shooters — Scott Thompson, Bruce King and Dan Frost — were 23-for-36 (.644), so accuracy wasn't the Hawkeye problem. However, 10 of their 23 field goals came after the 71-42 margin was opened, 5 of them after the last Hoosier starter was out.

Thompson totaled 22 points, King 20 and Frost 16.

Buckner's order: 'Don't foul, or don't slow down'

Knight and Assembly Hall's 17,000 can look at the same game and see things differently. F'r instance: Monday night, when the thing Knight liked best about Buckner's play was his defense.

It wasn't that the man didn't notice or enjoy Buckner's 12-for-19 shooting, a signal that the Hoosier co-captain may be entering the home-stretch of the season in the grand style he achieved last year.

"But I've just felt the shooting would come," he said. "The thing I liked best about his play tonight was that he stayed out of foul trouble. He didn't get called for those reaching-in fouls. His personal discipline as a defensive player was maybe the best since he's been here."

"What he didn't say," Buckner filled in, grinning, "was what was said *before*.

"The first time I reached out and got a foul I was supposed to start running for the door and just keep running.

"I felt in pretty good shape tonight, but I didn't feel *that* good."

"He doesn't need to score to contribute," Knight said. "He can do a lot of things for us. But he's not going to contribute when he gets two or three chintzy fouls early in the game and has to come out."

His shooting clearly caught Iowa with its defense down.

"He surprised me," said Iowa guard Cal Wulfsberg. "I think he surprised 17,000 in the Assembly Hall."

"Buckner hasn't been hitting all year, and he comes out bombing 'em," said Olson. "I'm sure our defense had something to do with it, but those were 18-to-20 foot jump shots, and if he isn't the man to give them to, who is?"

"They did give me the shot," Buckner verified, smiling, "and I did take it."

"We've been talking with him about his shooting over a period of time now," Knight said. "We didn't use a magic wand.

"The strongest word for the situation is he persevered. Now he's got the thing in a groove and hopefully he'll keep it."

Radford stripped the ball away from Iowa's Dick Peth in mid-court and was headed for a layup when Olson — the *coach* — cut him off.

His device was a dash onto the court in protest of the Radford steal — a foul in Olson's eyes. Official Jim Bain had a technical foul called before Radford could get to the basket, so Radford lost the layup and a little skin above his eye, too, absorbing a cut that forced him to the sidelines for repairs on the play.

IU got its lost points back; by the time Olson was through with the playing floor, a second technical foul had been called and Jim Crews sank both free throws.

The spectacular plays didn't stop with halftime. May's steal and feed to Buckner for a fast-break layup at 15:19 turned the crowd on. When two more Buckner baskets opened a 71-42 lead with 13:40 to go, the crowd that had suffered with him celebrated for him — the inferno of noise ignited by the Buckner foray raging on unchecked, feeding on its own intensity, while the poor Iowans tried to concentrate on their own offense.

Buckner finished 12-for-19 with 24 points, way over his previous season high (16 against UCLA

Lute Olson — A smile that's not really a smile,

a white 'flag' that's not a surrender

The parallel suggested to Buckner was with his IU-record 13-for-14 game at Wisconsin last year, one that seemed to get him on track for what proved to be a strong finish to his junior season.

"Oh, I don't know," he said. "My whole game felt better than the Wisconsin game. I shot well, but I seem to remember I had a lot of defensive trouble that night."

A similarity, though, was that in each case, he felt confident the shots would start dropping although he was coming in from a relative off-game.

"Even the Purdue game," he said, "I felt I was right on the basket, but the ball wasn't going in.

"For the last four or five weeks, I've been trying to get the arch out of my shot — shoot straight at the basket."

"Quinn played an outstanding game," said May, usually the top Hoosier scorer. "I was happy to see him have a game like that."

Buckner's jump shots didn't excite May nearly so much as his driving layup with 8:42 to go in the first half. "That was a great play," May said. "When I saw that, I said to myself, 'He's back.' "

Buckner's night also included eight assists, giving him a 40-point contribution in 26 playing minutes. Two assists against Minnesota Saturday had boosted his career total to 501, making him the first Hoosier officially to go over 1,000 points as a scorer and a passer.

And there was the historic matter of playing in his 100th winning game at IU.

"I'm sure a lot of others have won 100 — haven't they?" Buckner said.

Quite a few, but no others for a while . . . like about 25 years. A quick NCAA check turned up Paul Unruh of Bradley as the last, and he was an all-America on Bradley's 1950 NCAA runnerup team.

Seniors Buckner, Abernethy and Crews also are the first three ever to play on four Big Ten champion basketball teams. Abernethy officially played in 92 of those 100 victories over the last four years, Crews in 91.

"It was really a good night in a lot of respects," Knight said. "We got the ball downcourt well, we boarded well — I just thought we played really well.

"We tried to emphasize two key areas — anticipation on defense and concentration on offense. I think we accomplished a lot of it, and I've gotta be pretty pleased."

The night was full of interesting statistics. 'Twas brought to Knight's attention, for example, that the three-year record of the Ohio State teams he played on — usually considered the premier Big Ten powerhouses of all time — was 78-6.

And, that Monday night's victory made the three-year record of the current Hoosiers 78-6. Your reaction, sir?

"Well," he said, grinning, "I would have rather been 84-0 . . . "

Indiana 96, Wisconsin 67

It was first-place Indiana against last-place Wisconsin Thursday night, but Hoosier all-American Scott May admitted he was specially inspired.

"When you're playing for the *championship,* you've gotta put out," May said.

So Indiana has the clear-cut Big Ten basketball championship, delivered with a 96-67 rout of the Badgers and a career-high 41 points by May.

Wisconsin came into the game with the longest losing streak in its basketball history, 13 games. But the Badgers were as fired up as May. It was Senior Night, the last home game for five Wisconsin seniors and for resigned coach John Powless, who reflected before the game:

"The crowd always gives the seniors a nice hand and gets everybody ready. I don't think we've lost one of these (a home finale) since I've been here."

It had been five years, anyway, and the biggest Badger crowd in a good while, 9,343, was there to do its noisy part.

The inspiration didn't just work with seniors. Sophomore forward Bill Pearson admitted he was "super-inspired," and he played like it with 14 first-half rebounds.

Pearson and sophomore guard Brian Colbert did the scoring as Wisconsin gave the Hoosiers their worst game-opening treatment of the year — 6-0 after 75 seconds, 8-2 with three minutes gone.

But after the Hoosiers had missed their first six shots, Quinn Buckner hit a jump shot, May scored a rebound basket and May slipped away on a fast break for a three-point play that gave Indiana the lead, never to be given back.

Pearson's second rebound basket had Wisconsin still within 21-18 with nine minutes to go in the half. But Indiana scored seven points in a row, the first five by May, to take a 28-18 lead, and the pullaway had begun.

By halftime, May had 19 points and 13 rebounds and Indiana's lead was 39-26.

"We were getting the ball inside (against Wisconsin's zone defense) the first half," IU coach Bob Knight said, "but we missed a lot of good shots so we weren't really accomplishing anything.

"We seemed to get stronger the second half."

May, 9-for-10 from the field the last half, personally outscored Wisconsin, 7-2, in the opening four minutes as the Hoosier lead jumped to 48-28.

"Maybe they just got tired," IU forward Tom Abernethy said. "They really were playing hard at the start of the game."

May did most of his sniping from the wings and the baseline. As the Badger zone stretched to counter him, Hoosier passing took on a sheen. Abernethy, 0-for-5 the first half, was 5-for-6 the second, helped chiefly by Bob Wilkerson's passing and an effective inside screening game.

At times, the Hoosiers seemed to be putting on a clinic. "They have two different styles," Powless said. "They can show great patience on offense and

also run with the ball effectively. The cheap ones they get off the break kill you."

It was 88-62 with 2:30 left when May and Abernethy, the last Hoosier regulars on the floor, came out to a loud ovation.

May posted career highs for both points (33 against UCLA was his previous peak) and rebounds (he had 18; his previous high was 17 against Iowa last year).

His point total was the highest by a Hoosier since Steve Downing had 41 against Illinois in 1973. The two now share eighth on the IU list for scoring in a Big Ten game.

Abernethy was the only other Hoosier to make double figures, scoring 12.

Captain Dale Koehler, one of the departing

INDIANA 96							
	M	FG	FT	R	A	PF	TP
May, f	37	16-26	9-10	18	1	1	41
Abernethy, f	33	5-11	2- 3	6	2	1	12
Benson, c	23	2- 5	2- 4	9	3	4	6
Buckner, g	19	3- 8	0- 0	3	2	4	6
Wilkerson, g	33	2- 7	1- 2	12	7	4	5
Wisman	11	1- 5	0- 0	1	2	1	2
Valavicius	13	3- 4	0- 0	5	0	4	6
Radford	12	1- 2	3- 5	3	2	1	5
Crews	10	3- 3	1- 2	0	2	0	7
Bender	3	0- 0	0- 0	1	0	1	0
Eells	2	0- 0	0- 0	2	0	0	0
Roberson	2	1- 1	0- 0	1	0	0	2
Haymore	2	2- 3	0- 0	1	0	1	4
Team				5			
Totals		39-75	18-26	67	21	22	96

WISCONSIN 67							
	M	FG	FT	R	A	PF	TP
Koehler, f	39	5-23	7- 9	12	3	4	17
Pearson, f	25	3-11	0- 2	16	1	5	6
Johnson, c	32	4-13	0- 1	6	0	5	8
Colbert, g	38	8-17	0- 2	4	3	4	16
JSmith, g	30	3-12	0- 0	4	5	2	6
Paterick	10	2- 6	2- 2	0	0	0	6
Brey	10	0- 1	0- 0	1	1	1	0
Rudd	11	4- 6	0- 0	2	0	0	8
Falk	2	0- 0	0- 0	0	0	0	0
BSmith	2	0- 0	0- 0	0	0	0	0
Piacenza	2	0- 1	0- 1	0	0	0	0
Team				1			
Totals		29-90	9-17	46	13	21	67

SCORE BY HALVES

Indiana 39   57 — 96
Wisconsin 26   41 — 67
　Errors: Indiana 15, Wisconsin 11
　Technical fouls: Wisconsin 2 (bench, Johnson)

	FG	Pct.	FT	Pct.
Indiana	39-75	.520	18-26	.692
Wisconsin	29-90	.322	9-17	.529

　Officials: Jerry Menz, Bob Brodbeck and Bob Showalter
　Attendance: 9,343

seniors, led Wisconsin with 17 points, and Colbert had 16.

For the second time all year (the first was in their 80-74 victory at Michigan Jan. 10), the Hoosiers had more turnovers than their opponent (15-11 Thursday).

But Indiana offset that with a 67-46 rebound margin — the highest rebound total for a Big Ten team this year — and with .520 shooting to Wisconsin's chilly .322.

Now three games up on Michigan with two to go, the Hoosiers are assured of their second clearcut Big Ten championship in a row, third in four years (Michigan interrupted the string by sharing the championship with IU in 1974) and sixth in history to go with six co-championships.

'Gotta be comparable to all-time greats'

The goals left for Indiana's basketball Hoosiers the rest of the regular season are mainly esoteric ones, now that what Knight called "our primary objective when the season started," the Big Ten championship, is assured.

There was no celebration of the feat last Saturday when IU clinched at least a share of a fourth straight Big Ten title.

"We weren't particularly interested in tying for anything," Knight said. "Winning the thing outright was kind of our objective in coming up here.

"Now we're just interested in finishing up without slipping off. The kids will have to work at that and so will we as coaches."

There's a notable bit of history beckoning if the Hoosiers can get by Northwestern and Ohio State and complete a second straight 18-game sweep against Big Ten opposition.

In the 70-year history of the conference, no team has ever gone unbeaten in the league two straight years. Closest to it was Wisconsin — 12-0, 11-1 and 12-0 from 1912 through '14. Then, Ohio State — 13-1, 14-0, 13-1 from 1960 through '62.

Indeed, Indiana last year was only the 11th team in league history to make it through the conference schedule unbeaten, and just the fifth since 1930. Others in the "modern era" besides the 1975 Hoosiers and 1961 Buckeyes were Purdue, 1930, 10-0; Illinois, 1943, 12-0, and Iowa, 1970, 14-0.

Then there's the matter of back-to-back unbeaten seasons, over the full schedule. Indiana (29-0, 1974-75) and Ohio State (24-0, 1960-61) are the only Big Ten teams in the last 56 years to get through the schedule unbeaten.

And nationally, in the 38 years that the NCAA has conducted a championship tournament, the only team that entered the tourney two years in a row with an unbeaten record was UCLA's 1971-72 and 1972-73 group, led by Bill Walton. One team, in all college basketball.

"They've gotta be comparable to the all-time great teams in collegiate basketball," Powless said of the Hoosiers.

"I think I have a valid basis for saying that because of having been with the team that set the NCAA record before UCLA came along."

Powless speaks of his days as freshman coach under Ed Jucker at the University of Cincinnati, when the Bearcats won the 1961 and '62 NCAA tourneys and appeared to have the 1963 meet won as well before Loyola of Chicago stormed out of a deep hole and won in overtime. Two titles and a runnerup finish represented the closest anyone came to three NCAA championships in a row until UCLA began its ridiculous string of seven straight titles in 1967.

During those three golden years (1961-63), Cincinnati was 78-6 . . . as was Ohio State from 1960-62 . . . and as was Indiana from 1974-76 until Thursday night, when the Hoosiers won their 79th game.

That makes Indiana, with its current seniors as the nucleus, the recordholder among Big Ten teams for victories in one year (31 last year), two (56, this year and last), three (79) and four (101).

High, there!

"They're a great team. I caught a little flak in Sports Illustrated for saying I considered them one of the all-time great teams — I guess because of the margin they beat us by. I don't care a whole lot about what they say. The margin could have been 15 and I'd have still said they were awesome." — John Powless
Wisconsin coach

two weeks ago, effective at the end of the season, surfaced again in Knight's post-game remarks.

"The thing that hurt Wisconsin in this game is the thing that has plagued them all year: they're not a real good shooting team," he said. "It's too bad, because if they were, they'd be a good basketball team, because they play hard, they go to the boards well and they fight like hell."

Powless looked at a statistics sheet as he mused: "The first half we get 46 shots and we just don't put it in the hole.

"But at least our guys were able to walk off with a little bit of pride tonight." In his last Madison appearance, so was their coach.

Throw in five (118) and six (135) as well. It's been a pretty successful era.

Powless ducked a question popular in his home state: Who would win between No. 1-ranked Indiana and No. 2-ranked Marquette, each of which beat his Badgers twice? But, he clearly likes the Hoosiers' chances to represent the Big Ten well against anybody because "when they haven't had a great flowing game, they still have found a way to win. Bobby has always found a way."

The normal "flow" at center was interrupted Thursday night by Wisconsin's zone defense that surrounded Benson.

"We primarily wanted to keep the ball outside," Powless said. "And when May had the ball, we used basically man-to-man principles to make him give the ball up."

Ya win some and ya lose some. Benson had only five shots and six points. May had a career-high 41 points.

Benson's low-production night and a thigh injury Buckner picked up in the first half were Hoosier ripples. (Buckner came back to play a while in the second half with the thigh bandaged. "It was a little stiff," he said, adding with a grin: "But I *will* be ready to play Monday.")

Knight again was happy with the production of his reserves. "Our bench has really helped us all year," Knight said, singling out "Jimmy Crews, Wayne Radford and Rich Valavicius in the first half, especially" for mention.

"These guys have been playing all year in pressure situations," Knight said. "We had a bench last year with a lot more experience — John Laskowski (the Chicago Bulls' rookie starter who sat on the bench Thursday night as the guest of Knight, who spurned all temptations to wave "Super-Sub" in, civilian suit and all), Tommy Abernethy and Jimmy Crews. But the players we have been using off the bench this year have experience now. Our bench has become a source of strength."

Knight and Powless have been warm friends during Knight's five Big Ten seasons — a fact he mentioned in telling a Madison basketball boosters group Thursday noon that "you should feel privileged to have had a man of the caliber of John Powless as your basketball coach."

Some of the feeling for the man who resigned

Pearson impressed by May shot choice

A year ago, Wisconsin was giving Indiana a tough early fight at Assembly Hall, and the Badgers appeared to stand off a Hoosier scoring try when rookie Bill Pearson pulled down a defensive rebound.

When Pearson took a second to look for a man to throw the ball to, though, May wheeled behind him, popped the ball up in the air and out of the surprised Pearson's grasp and converted the thievery into a basket that got Indiana rolling toward a 35-point victory.

Pearson holds no ill feelings. May ranks high on his admiration list, a standing bolstered by the Hoosier senior's 41-point contribution to Indiana's Big Ten title-clinching victory at Wisconsin Thursday night.

"They have good shot selection, don't they?" Pearson said of the Hoosiers before focusing on Thursday's standout.

"May really impressed me," he said. "If he doesn't have a shot, he doesn't press it. He just takes the good ones."

Powless rigged his zone defense to give extra attention to May. "Even when they take the ball away from him, you know they're going to come back to him," Powless said. "He's got the best range of any of their players. Hell, he may be the best player in the United States."

Bob Knight — Press-ing matters

Indiana 76, Northwestern 63

Indiana had the look of a sleek machine on a check-out run most of the way Monday night as the Hoosiers raced along unbeaten with a 76-63 victory at Northwestern.

That left one lap to go — against Ohio State Saturday at Assembly Hall — to send the already-crowned Big Ten champions into NCAA play with their second straight undefeated regular season.

The Hoosiers had a few pings and sputters in the second half — ironically, when Northwestern junked the zone defense that all opponents have been using against IU and went to a man-to-man.

Whether shock at finally seeing a non-zone had anything to do with the Hoosier problems, IU coach Bob Knight wasn't sure. "It kinda hurt us," he said of the Wildcats' man-to-man.

"I thought the first half we played real good — I thought we were ready," said Hoosier forward Scott May, the game's scoring leader with 25 points. "We just lost it in the second half. Maybe that did do something to us."

"Could've been," senior guard Quinn Buckner said. "But our offense against a man-to-man *should* be able to handle it."

The tone of all three was more clinical than worrisome. This was a game the Hoosiers took charge of in the opening minutes and never let open up to Northwestern ambition.

May and Buckner got the Hoosiers ahead with first-minute baskets, and May's jump shot at 17:56 broke a 4-4 tie and popped the Hoosiers ahead for good.

Guard Tim Teasley's outside sniping kept Northwestern close, 18-16, before May contributed half the points in a 12-4 Hoosier spurt that put the Wildcats down, 30-20.

Billy McKinney, Northwestern's standout junior scorer who matched the Wildcat career point record (1,368, Jim Burns, 1967-69) later in his 20-point game, got his first field goal at 6:53 after being harassed into an 0-for-5 start by his bedeviling friend, Bob Wilkerson.

But Indiana got that one back with a dazzler for the sellout crowd of 7,098, about a third of them Indiana backers.

Buckner ran down a rebound in the deep, left corner at Indiana's defensive end. Almost teetering out of bounds, he saved the possession with a behind-the-back flip to May, then hurried downcourt for a fast-break feed from May — the role reversal carried off perfectly at both ends.

May's seventh and eighth field goals of a 17-point first half came in the final minute to boost Indiana's lead at the break to 45-29.

Things never really got sticky in the second half. "I thought we got off to the kind of start we wanted," Knight admitted. "If there was any let-up it was in the second half, not the first, and that's a hell of a lot better for me."

Kent Benson, one man who showed no adjustment problems at all in being sprung from the swarm normally around him in a zone, kept Northwestern from making much of a move by dominating the game for a five-minute mid-half stretch.

Three straight times, Benson ripped Northwestern misses off the Hoosiers' defensive board — the sort of rebounds that resound in mind and memory.

Indiana didn't get a point after any of those, the score stuck on 53-37. But when McKinney broke the stalemate with a jump shot for Northwestern, Benson hit a free throw and then ripped in three classic hook shots in a three-minute show that shot Indiana's lead up to 63-43.

The edging for the exits and clearing of the bench began seconds later.

INDIANA 76

	M	FG	FT	R	A	PF	TP
May, f	37	12-23	1- 4	7	2	4	25
Abernethy, f	31	2- 5	4- 4	5	2	1	8
Benson, c	39	5- 9	7-11	14	2	2	17
Buckner, g	22	5- 9	0- 4	7	3	4	10
Wilkerson, g	32	3- 8	0- 0	4	13	3	6
Crews	6	1- 2	0- 0	1	2	1	2
Radford	13	2- 3	1- 3	5	1	1	5
Valavicius	8	0- 2	0- 0	0	0	1	0
Wisman	6	0- 1	3- 5	1	1	1	3
Bender	3	0- 0	0- 0	1	0	0	0
Roberson	1	0- 0	0- 0	0	0	1	0
Haymore	1	0- 0	0- 0	0	0	0	0
Eells	1	0- 2	0- 0	1	0	0	0
Team				1			
Totals		30-64	16-31	47	26	19	76

NORTHWESTERN 63

	M	FG	FT	R	A	PF	TP
Svete, f	34	3- 6	0- 0	6	2	2	6
Allen, f	15	0- 2	0- 0	1	1	2	0
Wallace, c	34	3- 3	1- 4	11	1	3	7
McKinney, g	35	7-19	6- 6	4	5	0	20
Teasley, g	35	10-23	0- 0	5	5	4	20
Hildebrand	13	0- 2	0- 1	2	1	4	0
Boesen	18	3- 8	2- 3	5	0	4	8
Klaas	15	1- 1	0- 0	1	1	1	2
Wall	1	0- 0	0- 0	1	0	1	0
Team				8			
Totals		27-64	9-14	41	16	21	63

SCORE BY HALVES

Indiana.	45	31 —	76
Northwestern.	29	34 —	63

Errors: Indiana 17, Northwestern 17
Technical fouls: Northwestern bench 3

	FG	Pct.	FT	Pct.
Indiana	30-64	.469	16-29	.516
Northwestern	27-64	.422	9-14	.643

Officials: Orlando Palesse, Ed Maracich and Ken Kulick

Attendance: 7,098 (capacity)

Benson finished with 17 points and 14 rebounds, his most productive game since his 38-point explosion against Michigan State Feb. 9.

Both he and May could have helped themselves to fatter totals. Benson missed 4 of 11 free throws, and May missed 3 of 4, including a one-and-one chance. As a team, the Hoosiers missed 12 free throws the last half alone, a problem more responsible than either Hoosier sloppiness or Northwestern defense for their fall-off in point production.

Still, Indiana led by 19 with two minutes to go. Northwestern scored the game's last six points to pare the margin but scare no one.

"In this game," Knight said, "I was concerned about the fact that we had won the conference championship last Thursday and there might be some relaxation. And I really don't think there was.

"I was really pleased with the first half. We were up 16 on the road, and I think Northwestern was ready to play."

The Hoosiers got good overall results from their starters. Besides the scoring of May and Benson, the guards chipped in 16 points (10 by Buckner) and 16 assists (13 by Wilkerson, one below his team high for the season). Tom Abernethy, the fifth starter, had 8 points and 5 rebounds.

Indiana shot a sub-par .469 and matched Northwestern in turnovers (17 each). But the Hoosiers did have firm control of the boards, whipping the Wildcats, 46-28, in actual rebounds.

Hoosiers get Wallace vote: 'They're No. 1'

Northwestern center James Wallace felt qualified and willing to serve as a ratifier for what the pollsters have been saying about Indiana all year long.

"They're No. 1," Wallace said. "We played Marquette, Washington and Oregon State . . . and they're No. 1."

Wallace stuck to his own position, center, to define Hoosier strength.

"Benson fits into the framework of their game perfectly," Wallace said. "If Benson was selfish, it would be different. But he's willing to take the ball when he gets it.

"They're such a well-rounded team, everybody gets their shots, and everybody is content to look for the open man. So they don't have to shoot too much outside of 15 feet."

"They're a great ball club — a *great* ball club," Wildcat coach Tex Winter said. "It's just an amazing thing that a Big Ten team can win every game two years in a row.

"You've gotta be so much better than everybody else to do that. There are going to be nights on the road when things don't go so well.

"The only thing I would really be worried about is when they go out of the area and play somebody else and get a different-officiated game.

"But I think their chances in the tournament are excellent, and I certainly wish them luck."

Winter suggested the 1974-75 Hoosiers might

"Actually, the second-place team in the Big Ten will have an easier time than the winner. They won't have to play Marquette, or the SEC champion, and they won't have to play Notre Dame, which is creditable although they don't seem to beat anybody when they play somebody good."

— Johnny Orr
Michigan coach

have been a better team . . . but not when that group entered the NCAA tourney.

The broken arm May suffered four games before the end of the regular season last year was the difference . . . in many ways, Winter said.

"If May had been in the lineup, Indiana would have been a little better ball club than this year," he said.

"There's no doubt in my mind they would have won in a walk with him in there last year. I shouldn't say 'in a walk.' Not in a national championship tournament. But I think they would have won.

"This year they have a little more experience, and their big gain is that they've got Scott May."

"Every year's team is a little different," Knight said. "This is a team that isn't as free-wheeling and as rambunctious as a year ago. Last year's team had a tendency to feel if it got into trouble it could shoot its way out of it.

"This team has been able to stick with things and fight it out. This might be a better rebounding team, and at times it has been a better defensive team.

"We've had a little bit tougher way to go. Teams have played us very hard and very well, but I still feel these kids have done a hell of a job of getting things done."

Hoosier passing sparkled in fashioning the 45-29 first-half lead, and Wilkerson was the man with most of the credits and debits in the passing department — 13 assists, 5 turnovers. He also had the defensive duty on McKinney most of the way and performed well in that role.

Winter professed no surprise. "I thought he was sensational last year," Winter said.

"Wilkerson has improved steadily since he's been here," Knight said. "He has a more direct influence on the game than he did a year ago, when we used John Laskowski in there a lot. But Bobby has been a tough man to play against on defense, and offensively he has stepped up his scoring."

Knight also noted the play of Benson ("I thought he really rebounded well — there was a period in the second half where he really dominated things") and Buckner ("The first half he sparked us on offense and played well defensively").

104

Indiana 96, Ohio State 67

When it was all over the but the shouting, it was a long, long way from over at Assembly Hall Saturday afternoon.

It was an incongruous day, one in which the basketball game was almost like a movie co-featured on a program with stage shows before and after.

The game didn't suffer. Top-ranked Indiana became the first team ever to go through two straight Big Ten seasons unbeaten . . . the second team in all the collegiate world ever to put two unbeaten regular seasons back-to-back . . . since the NCAA has been in the business of picking a national champion, anyway, and that's 38 years worth of ever.

The Hoosiers did it with class, blasting away from Ohio State in the opening minutes and sailing to a 96-67 victory.

To be sure, that was what Saturday's 17,756 came to see: Victory No. 27, assuring a new banner to go alongside the one freshly hoisted at one end of the Hall, white letters on a red silk background proclaiming:

Indiana University
Big Ten Champions
Undefeated Season 29-0
UPI National Champions
1974-75

A couple of tiny copy changes and that one's twin can be prepared immediately. It's the other end, where banners hang commemorating NCAA championships in 1940 and 1953 and a Final Four trip in 1973, toward which further Hoosier work this year will be directed.

Thoughts of future problems obviously hadn't penetrated the concentration of the remarkable basketball players Saturday's crowd came to see for the last time on home ground.

Neither were they particularly fearful of a pratfall in their last game. "Oh, no — everybody was ready to play," junior center Kent Benson said. "You could feel that."

Coach Bob Knight's version of his pre-game instructions: "I just told them we weren't expecting them to go out and scale Mount Everest — just go out and play."

They didn't scale Mount Everest, but they must have resembled it to the poor Buckeyes, trapped by fate into facing their most formidable job without their captain and center, 6-10 Craig Taylor.

"I'm not singing the blues," said retiring Buckeye coach Fred Taylor, honored in pre-game ceremonies, "but we really had no one big enough in there. When we lost him, we lost about 14 rebounds a game."

Benson, the one non-senior in the Hoosier lineup, was so charged up about the emotional afternoon that he soared too high, sailed too far, shot not wisely and too well . . . or too darned straight, anyway. Benson was charged with Assembly Hall's

INDIANA 96

	M	FG	FT	R	A	PF	TP
May, f	26	10-18	1- 2	9	0	2	21
Abernethy, f	21	3- 7	2- 3	0	2	2	8
Benson, c	28	10-16	1- 3	11	2	2	21
Buckner, g	24	4- 7	1- 2	3	10	2	9
Wilkerson, g	18	2- 8	0- 0	4	5	1	4
Crews	14	3- 5	2- 2	0	0	1	8
Valavicius	13	3- 4	0- 1	5	0	3	6
Radford	15	4- 6	0- 1	6	1	0	8
Wisman	14	0- 2	0- 0	2	3	2	0
Haymore	5	0- 1	0- 0	4	0	2	0
Roberson	8	2- 4	3- 3	4	0	2	7
Eells	5	1- 3	0- 0	2	0	0	2
Bender	9	1- 4	0- 0	3	2	0	2
Team				2			
Totals		43-85	10-17	55	25	19	96

OHIO STATE 67

	M	FG	FT	R	A	PF	TP
Daugherty, f	28	2- 9	0- 0	1	3	0	4
Poole, f	32	4- 9	9-11	6	2	3	17
Hammond, c	31	4- 8	2- 6	12	2	3	10
Wood, g	29	6-14	1- 1	4	1	4	13
Bayless, g	22	5- 7	1- 1	1	0	3	11
Cline	20	3- 7	0- 0	4	0	3	6
Bolden	21	2- 8	0- 0	2	1	0	4
Smith	6	1- 2	0- 0	1	0	2	2
Burris	3	0- 1	0- 0	0	0	0	0
Scott	1	0- 0	0- 0	0	0	0	0
Team				7			
Totals		27-66	13-19	39	9	19	67

SCORE BY HALVES

Ohio State 23   44 — 67
Indiana 52   44 — 96

Errors: Ohio State 21, Indiana 20
Technical foul: Benson

	FG	Pct.	FT	Pct.
Ohio State	27-66	.409	13-19	.684
Indiana	43-85	.506	10-17	.588

Officials: Carel Cosby, Gary Muncy and Art White
Attendance: 17,756 (capacity)

Scott May, Buckeye Mark Bayless bump

105

Kent Benson, Fred Taylor say farewell

first stuff. Price: the two points he scored and one technical foul, his first one at IU.

It came in the first two minutes Saturday, after Tom Abernethy and Benson had converted Quinn Buckner passes into a 4-0 Hoosier lead.

Indiana got the ball back on a Buckner steal, and Bob Wilkerson drove for a layup that bounced out — straight out, just as Benson came flying along way above the rim. He caught, crammed and blushed as officials, paid to be prudish, enforced the anti-dunk rule that only the game's rulesmakers love.

The Buckeyes caught their breath with the technical and converted it into a 4-3 look on the scoreboard.

But from 9-7, the Hoosiers galloped away. They ran well; they defended well; they shot well. Suddenly, the lead was 29-11 and Knight was scanning his bench for the first removal of his starters.

It was 52-23 at halftime, and the starters came back. They jumped the lead to 69-34 and the exiting started for good. For the last time at The Hall. For the moments that the 17,756 had awaited with delicious dread as long as they had thought about Saturday and its special side.

Knight made it a six-course feast. Wilkerson left first, to a standing ovation that roared on after play had resumed.

Forty seconds later, it was Abernethy . . . then, at 10:18 with the lead 75-45, Buckner, who shook hands with Taylor on his way to a rugged welcome at the IU bench — four quick whacks by Knight while the crowd roared on a day of 9 points, 10 assists and 6 steals.

Benson left at 9:14, the applause no less for his junior status after a 21-point, 11-rebound day.

And then it was May, at 8:38 with the lead at 81-49 — 21 of those Hoosier points behind his name.

Jim Crews scored eight points before his ceremonial derricking came at 7:44.

There was a wrung-out atmosphere in the stands and on-court the rest of the way until the buzzer finally came and the seniors were back on-court for more applause, more congratulations, personal farewells.

The Hoosiers finished with a .506 shooting mark and a 55-39 rebounding edge. Freshman Fred Poole led with 17 points as the beleaguered Buckeyes ended with a 10-game losing streak, a 2-16 league record that made them last, a 6-20 overall record that was the worst in Taylor's 18 years.

The game sends Indiana into NCAA play (against St. John's at South Bend next Saturday) with a 27-0 record, its other live streaks packed away for another team and another year — 37 victories in a row in the Big Ten, 57 in a row in regular-season games, 34 in a row at Assembly Hall. And two straight years of being No. 1.

'You get attached to a group like that'

Taylor described his feeling for the first group of basketball players he recruited at Ohio State as a "love affair I had with those kids."

And Knight, one of "those kids" from Ohio State days gone by, knew the feeling from both directions, coach-to-players, player-to-coach, in one afternoon Saturday. One nice afternoon, very nice.

"Nice" isn't the sort of word common to basketball. But what went on at Assembly Hall on this Saturday stretched way beyond basketball into an area of human relations that said much about the people involved.

It was a day when a sign hung at one end of Assembly Hall saying simply: "To the coaches and team — our attitude is gratitude."

So was Knight's, who took full advantage of a scheduling coincidence that made farewell day for Taylor and for the class Knight recruited in his first full season as IU coach one and the same.

Knight clearly was gratified that Indiana University fans and administration joined him in a final-day tribute to Taylor, the dean of Big Ten coaches and seven-time winner in one of the nation's most competitive leagues.

Taylor was honored in a pre-game ceremony carried throughout the Big Ten region on the league's TV network. It was a tribute that started with IU President John Ryan, who called Taylor to the center of the floor for an expression of "our appreciation for the magnificent contribution he has made to a great sport and for the credit he has been to his profession, to his university and to the Big Ten."

Ryan gave Taylor a plaque, and IU Foundation President William Armstrong presented a chair. Knight came on to hand him a basketball signed by some Taylor friends . . . and a fishing rod from the IU team. "They know that most of what they're doing, you're responsible for," Knight said, "and I'll tell you one thing: they don't like all of it."

Fred Taylor — Chaired and cheered

Taylor has been a strident, a scowling, a combative opponent, and he noted the difference in mutual attitudes as he faced a cheering audience.

"There've been a few times over here when things weren't quite this nice," Taylor said, smiling.

A voice from the stilled stands cried out: "Just wait!"

And Taylor kept smiling: "That's what we're stalling for — we don't *want* to play."

He and his team did want to, but on this day, there was no chance. The neutralizing force they had in the middle in repeated duels with the Hoosiers over the past two years, center Craig Taylor, wasn't even in the building, laid up in a Columbus hospital. Without him, there was no real hope for a Buckeye surprise, and not many minutes into the game, the crowd clearly was waiting for the post-game program it knew was coming, when IU's seniors would get one last introduction.

Knight brought them out with the comment: "In the past four years — and I speak now as a fan — we all have been privileged to sit in this building and watch five tremendous young men perform their skills."

The five came on to perform well in a drastically different role, stepping up in alphabetical order to say thank you five different ways.

Jim Crews' opening line was a suggestion that "all you people come out next year and see Wayne Radford."

Bob Knight with Columbus pals Dick Otte (left), Fred Taylor

107

"We were kidding before he went out," Radford said later. "I didn't think he'd *say* it. I told him: 'Tell those people not to worry about next year, because *I'll* still be here.' "

There is some comfort to Hoosiers in that, and in the return of Kent Benson, IU's junior center who is a year away from soloing in such a farewell. Saturday, Benson was an impressed spectator: "I got cold chills. I hate to see those guys go."

The second straight unbeaten season was a *fait accompli* when Knight finally felt comfortable discussing it.

"As a season winds down," he said, "you're very grateful when your team has an opportunity to compete for things, and along the way has won some things that will give them lasting memories.

"Whatever the expectations were at the start of the season have been more than fulfilled over the course of the season.

"You get attached to a group like that. They have represented everybody so well in so many ways."

Knight said he and his staff will start preparations today for the Hoosiers' first-round NCAA tourney game with St. John's next Saturday at South Bend. It was a thought that almost intruded on this Saturday, when it was more fitting and proper to deal, for one graspable second before plunging back into responsibilities, with what has happened up to now.

They go into it with the congratulations and best wishes of Taylor, who told Knight: "I hope you win it all."

Taylor was as impressed with the game as with the pre-game ceremonies that he obviously appreciated. "They went after everything with such enthusiasm," he said of the Hoosiers. "It was the kind of thing you'd expect from an unbeaten team. We wanted to slow them down, but they just wiped us out. They got so many shots in close.

"You could see the way Benson started that he meant business."

After the game, Taylor went to the IU locker room to tell the Hoosiers:

"You guys are really competitive. I really enjoy watching guys who compete — my own team or another — with a great deal of enthusiasm and integrity."

It was a day of last hurrahs, for five seniors and an "enemy" coach. Winners all.

'Hard to believe it's all over' — May

May pranced in small circles like a nervous racehorse while deafening applause echoed around him in Assembly Hall Saturday afternoon.

He was one of IU's five senior basketball players brought to a center-court microphone after Saturday's victory over Ohio State, an emotional and popular last-day ritual since Knight's first of four straight Big Ten championship seasons.

In introducing May, Knight made a news announcement — May, IU's 6-7 scoring leader, was

---

"I just want to tell you people that when I came to Ohio State, I had just completed 14 years of consecutive attendance at Sunday School. And after my three years of sitting on the bench with him, I added words to my vocabulary that have done nothing but keep me in one jam after another for the last 11 years."

— Bob Knight
At banquet for Fred Taylor

---

picked by United Press International as recipient of its James L. Naismith Award as, Knight noted, "the outstanding player in the country."

It was the second such award for the man from Sandusky, Ohio, previously picked as the No. 1 college player for 1975-76 by professional general managers and scouts for *The Sporting News.*

When May finally got a chance to speak, his grin flashed repeatedly as he said:

"It's kinda hard to believe it's all over . . ."

The crowd interrupted with a protest: "It's not . . . it's not."

But May, obviously referring to the times he could step onto Assembly Hall court as a member of the IU team, continued:

"It's been a lot of fun. Thank you very much. I've appreciated it."

The other four seniors had similar thoughts:

• Abernethy — (Shutting off rolling applause with a smile). "There're five of us coming up, so you'd better be quiet or we'll be here a while. I'd like to give a special thanks to the coaching staff. You people are part of it all, and I'd just like to say thanks to all of you."

• Buckner — "I want to thank Indiana University and particularly coach Knight for giving me an opportunity to play at such a great university."

• Crews — "Thanks for coming these last four years. Keep coming out; I'm sure the success will be the same."

• Wilkerson — "I just want to say thanks to coach Knight and all the IU players, and we really appreciate all the IU fans."

May will receive the UPI award at the Atlanta, Ga., Tipoff Club's awards banquet April 4 — one day before Knight will coach and May will play in the Pizza Hut Classic at Las Vegas.

May finished with 56 votes to 54 for Notre Dame's Adrian Dantley. Benson, named to the UPI all-America first team along with May and Dantley, was third with 17 votes.

Bob Wilkerson — A last hurrah

Bob Knight to Quinn Buckner — 'Good (whack!) job'

Buckner to Tom Abernethy — A four-year clasp

A moment 17,756 awaited with delicious dread — Quinn Buckner, fellow seniors say 'Thanks'

Indiana 90, St. John's 70

The theory that it's always easier to play Indiana the second time around went the way of all myths Saturday.

It was shot down along with a good St. John's team, 90-70, as the No. 1-ranked Hoosiers switched from regular-season to NCAA tournament play without missing a beat.

It was the same St. John's team that the Hoosiers struggled to get by in December at Madison Square Garden in New York, 76-69.

The scene was Notre Dame's Athletic and Convocation Center this time — Assembly Hall North on a day when red-wearing, bellowing Hoosiers filled almost all of the 11,345 seats. They had much to bellow about, including another all-America performance by college basketball's 1975-76 player of the year, Scott May.

May, Indiana's 6-7 senior forward, scored 33 points, 19 in the first half as Indiana took a 44-37 lead.

St. John's cut it to 48-47 opening the second half, though, and the Hoosiers appeared to be struggling. IU coach Bob Knight lifted 6-11 center Kent Benson because "he was as tense as a drum — he seemed to be tight and anxious, trying to make the great play instead of just playing his game."

He was replaced with 6-3 Wayne Radford, which gave Indiana a center-less lineup and St. John's some instant match-up problems. Before the Redmen could think about the necessary switches, 6-8 sophomore George Johnson — the St. John's center — was well out on the court trying to defend against usual Hoosier forward Tom Abernethy.

Abernethy made a fake, "saw an opening to the basket, and just took it." His driving layup checked St. John's momentum, and a half-minute later, May drilled a jump shot to boost Indiana ahead, 54-49.

Benson returned, out only a minute and 27 seconds, and he got the basket that kept the Hoosiers charging — May setting it up by frisking St. John's Beaver Smith of a rebound and feeding Benson for a layup.

Benson's impact showed up again seconds later when he smothered a shot by Cecil Rellford, and Radford went all the way with the deflection, hitting a 10-foot jump shot.

In less than three minutes, Indiana jeopardy had been switched to a 58-49 position of command.

The rest of the game, 12½ minutes, "was a disaster," St. John's coach Lou Carnesecca said. "We never got back in the game."

Why?

"Because they're No. 1," Carnesecca said simply. "They deserve all the accolades they've had."

The victory, the 28th in a row for the unbeaten Hoosiers, advanced them to the Mideast Regional at Baton Rouge, La., for a Thursday night game with Southeastern Conference champion Alabama

— 79-64 winner over Atlantic Coast Conference champion North Carolina Saturday.

St. John's, which spent virtually the entire year in the nation's top 20 and bowed out 23-6, got the Hoosiers into a running game uncharacteristic of either in the early minutes. "This was a game where St. John's wasn't going to hold back anything," Knight said. "And we weren't, either. As a result, we got involved in a little bit more of a running game than either Lou or I would probably have wanted."

The wildest forays came in the opening seconds, including one stretch when the teams whipped the ball back and forth 11 times in two minutes and the score changed only from 5-4 to 7-6 — St. John's the leader at both points.

INDIANA 90

	M	FG	FT	R	A	PF	TP
May, f	38	14-23	5- 5	7	2	3	33
Abernethy, f	38	3- 5	1- 2	6	2	2	7
Benson, c	37	8-18	4- 4	13	2	3	20
Buckner, g	34	7-13	1- 2	2	3	3	15
Wilkerson, g	24	1- 5	4- 4	3	6	1	6
Radford	20	2- 2	1- 1	5	1	2	5
Wisman	2	0- 1	0- 0	0	0	0	0
Crews	1	1- 1	0- 0	2	0	0	2
Valavicius	2	0- 1	0- 0	0	0	0	0
Bender	1	0- 0	0- 0	0	0	0	0
Roberson	2	0- 1	0- 0	0	0	0	0
Haymore	1	1- 1	0- 0	1	0	0	2
Team				4			
Totals		37-71	16-18	41	16	14	90

ST. JOHN'S 70

	M	FG	FT	R	A	PF	TP
Farmer, f	21	2- 6	0- 0	3	0	2	4
Smith, f	30	2- 9	1- 2	8	1	4	5
Johnson, c	35	5-15	0- 0	7	0	2	10
Williams, g	37	10-15	0- 1	3	3	4	20
Alagia, g	34	7-13	3- 4	6	4	2	17
Rellford	22	5- 7	0- 0	2	1	4	10
Clarke	3	0- 0	0- 0	0	0	1	0
Winfree	8	1- 1	0- 0	1	0	1	2
Weadock	3	0- 0	0- 0	0	0	0	0
Menar	1	0- 0	0- 0	0	0	0	0
Calabrese	3	0- 1	0- 0	0	0	0	0
Robertson	1	1- 3	0- 0	2	0	0	2
McGuhins	1	0- 0	0- 0	0	0	0	0
McRae	1	0- 1	0- 0	1	0	0	0
Team				3			
Totals		33-71	4- 7	36	9	20	70

SCORE BY HALVES

Indiana	44	46 — 90
St. John's	37	33 — 70

Errors: Indiana 17, St. John's 20

	FG	Pct.	FT	Pct.
Indiana	37-71	.521	16-18	.889
St. John's	33-71	.464	4- 7	.571

Officials: Bob Harrold and Booker Turner
Attendance: 11,345 (capacity)

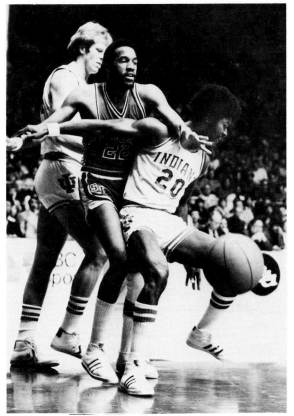
Beaver Smith caught in a Benson-Wilkerson squeeze

May's jump shot at 14:43 moved Indiana ahead, 10-9, and the Hoosiers stayed out front for a while.

They made a try at a knockout punch by pulling ahead, 21-15, on a crowd-lifting three-point play. May got the points, the reward for a tough catch of a snapping pass that Bob Wilkerson whipped through a couple of Redmen to get the ball upcourt to May, a step ahead of the pack.

St. John's rode Glen Williams' outside shooting to a comeback that caught the Hoosiers, 25-25, seven minutes ahead of the half.

Benson, 1-for-6 up to then with a succession of errors charged to him on foiled attempts to beat the St. John's defense with inside passes, broke the tie with two straight hook shots — the second set up by Abernethy's indelicate whack that kept a rebound out of St. John's hands, put it back on the board for fresh contention, and delivered it into Benson's hands. Redmen were spinning in every direction as Benson wheeled the ball quickly outside to Quinn Buckner, who jammed it just as quickly back to him cutting across the middle for his hook.

That was a third-shot basket, and next time downcourt, Indiana missed three times but kept grabbing the ball back and scored on the fourth try as May got the basket with a smooth, short hook.

That burst made it 31-25, but St. John's got it back to 31-29 and fluffed a chance to tie. Buckner removed future chances by scoring on a rebound at the Hoosier end, then stealing the ball and dashing to a three-point play that made it 36-29, the spread that stood up through halftime.

Once IU had cleaved open the 58-49 lead in the period wrapped around Benson's removal and reinsertion, the Hoosiers were off to some of their purest basketball of the year.

They went more than 10 minutes without an error. Starting with Abernethy's layup, they had the ball 16 times and scored 29 points. May delivered two three-point plays and three other baskets in the super-efficient stretch that left St. John's stretched out, 77-57.

Knight started pulling regulars at 2:15 — Buckner leaving first, to a standing ovation, and Abernethy, May and Benson coming out a few seconds behind, to individual replacements and separate ovations. Just like home.

For all his troubles, Benson finished with 20 points and a game-high 13 rebounds, while Buckner hit 7 of 13 shots and scored 15 points.

May was 14-for-23 from the field and 5-for-5 on free throws in his big game.

"May does two things," Carnesecca said.

"He knows how to get open, and he gets his shot away very fast, with great accuracy, and with great strength.

"He'll make some coach in the pros very happy. He has great intensity. And great common sense."

"I'm glad we've got him," Knight smiled. "I've talked about him a lot of times — he's a great player and a great person.

"I thought he played really within the scope of our offense. The first half, he was the main part of our offense — nothing else was going very well. But he still stayed within everything and didn't try to do it all himself."

Williams led St. John's with 20 points, but he got only two shots and two points in the first 13 minutes of the second half when Indiana was amassing its 77-57 lead. Buckner was the defender during that period, switched on to Williams at halftime.

The other St. John's guard, Frank Alagia, had 17 points and shooting success that must have been both welcome and painful to Carnesecca. Alagia was 7-for-13 in this one after going 1-for-9 when St. John's was losing a 70-67 game to Rutgers.

All the edges went to Indiana — 41-36 on rebounds, 17-20 on turnovers, .521 to .464 in shooting. And 1-0 in survivals.

"We gave it the best fight we had," said Carnesecca. "We don't have any regrets. We did about everything we wanted to this game. It simply wasn't enough.

"You saw one of the great teams in quite a few years. This Indiana team compares very favorably with the great teams at Kentucky, San Francisco with Bill Russell, the Pete Newell teams at California, UCLA in those 9 or 10 straight years. They're a great team, a great group of players.

"I think we saw them at their best. At least, I hope to God they weren't weak today.

"They're always coming at you. Great poise. Great patience.

"And they hit the boards. I'll tell you, it's going to take one hell of a team to beat them, because they just won't beat themselves."

Correction . . .

Beaver's comment or not, May 'would have been up'

Early last week, Indiana assistant coach Harold Andreas called May aside to ask if he had noticed a published comment by St. John's forward Beaver Smith.

It was immediately after St. John's had lost to Indiana, 76-69, and May had scored 29 points in the final game of the Holiday Festival at Madison Square Garden in December. "I hope we do get to play them again," Smith said, "because, personally, I know how to play Scott May now. I know his moves."

"He kinda kidded me about it," May smiled. "It helped me get ready.

"Regardless of what happened, I'd have been up for this game. But that did help."

There were other factors, too. In the closing weeks of the season, May was asked about his outlook on the NCAA tournament. IU's ticket to it, via a Big Ten championship, hadn't been nailed down at that point, so May declined to venture an outlook.

"But, I would say if it's God's will that we can play in the NCAA," he said, "it would be the biggest thrill of my life, because I don't really feel like I've played in one yet."

As a freshman, May had to sit out the season that ended with Indiana in the NCAA Final Four. The Hoosiers missed the NCAA on a playoff loss May's sophomore season, and last year, his broken arm all but eliminated him just before tourney time.

The thrill, he said Saturday, was all he expected. "Yes, it was," he said. "It's different from the regular season. In the tourney, you get only one chance. If we mess up, that's it for the year."

His 33-point game Saturday — including 14-for-23 shooting and 5-for-5 accuracy at the free throw line — indicated Smith hadn't solved quite all the moves.

"He tried to play me pretty tough (close)," May said. "But every time I'd fake, they'd go up." The result was he slipped inside the flying Redmen for a few field goals and drew fouls that produced three other three-point plays.

Buckner enjoyed the show. "I'm quite aware of what Scott can do," Buckner said, with an appreciative grin.

"Was it one of his better games?" Buckner was asked.

"Oh, I don't know," he said. "To tell the truth, I hope his better ones are yet to come."

Buckner's contributions to Saturday's victory included 15 points offensively and second-half defensive responsibilities on Williams, who had 14 points in the first half.

"I just tried to keep the ball away from him," he said. "You saw what happened when he got the ball."

Abernethy also had a defensive challenge, matched much of the game against the 6-8 Johnson, who scored 23 points in the first IU-St. John's game. Abernethy's strategy was the same as Buckner's. "He got the ball on me a couple of times and beat me to the basket," he said. "He's quick."

Abernethy may have helped May Saturday by shots he made in the first St. John's game. The Redmen visibly sagged off Abernethy in that game to concentrate on May and Benson, and Abernethy scored 10 second-half points that helped Indiana clip the Redmen.

"They were on me close this time — nothing special, but they didn't sag off," he said.

Carnesecca referred to May and Benson in post-game remarks as "two great players," but he included all the Hoosiers in wrap-up praise.

"They have a very complementary team," Carnesecca said. "They fit very well together."

Benson didn't grade himself as "great" Saturday. The 6-11 junior, named to a number of first-team all-America squads already this year, admitted he was overly excited about avenging the 23-4 beating he took from Johnson in the first game.

"I try not to let myself get like that (over-psyched)," Benson said. "But I did today."

May, Hoosiers impress Smith, Johnson, Alagia

May was voted unanimously to another all-American basketball team Saturday — this time, the St. John's "all-opponent" team.

"He just killed us," said Smith, St. John's 6-4, 200-pound senior who opened the game defending against May. "He's the best forward I've ever played against. And that includes Phil Sellers of Rutgers, Leon Douglas of Alabama, Ernie Grunfeld and Bernie King of Tennessee, and all the rest."

Little went right all afternoon for Beaver, who missed 10 minutes due to foul trouble and scored only five points, considerably short of his 14.2 average.

May also left indelible impressions on Johnson, whose first concern was Benson in the pivot.

"May is just great," laughed the 6-8 Johnson, "and shutting him down's almost impossible. Indiana does a lot of picking and screening for him. They'll pick one, two, three, sometimes four times, for him. You get a terrific beating before you even get to him. By then, you're about dead, and he's dropping in the shots — bang, bang, bang."

The player least suited by physique to take the beating Johnson described was Alagia, whose quickness and floor leadership posed a threat to Indiana all day.

"Scott and I are good friends," Alagia said, "and what he did to us out there today was no surprise. I met him a couple of years ago at a summer basketball camp (Maryland coach Lefty Driesell's).

"There were some fantastic players there — Andre McCarter of UCLA, Lenny Elmore of Maryland (now with the Indiana Pacers), Moses Malone (the Virginia high schooler who went straight to the pros), Jimmy Dan Conner of Kentucky and John Lucas of Maryland. May wasn't known that well then, but I saw him, and I said, 'Oh my God, this guy is going to be the best player in the country,' and he's sure proved it this year.

"He's a machine. If he doesn't score the first time, he scores the second or the third."

Alagia discounted any suggestion of rivalry between himself and IU's acknowledged floor general, Buckner. "Quinn was taking me down low, where his height was an advantage," said Alagia, "but otherwise I just tried to play my game. Indiana is so

Lou Carnesecca, Bob Knight shake

tough inside it's tough to penetrate, and they pound you to death on the boards."

Then Alagia offered an observation that got away from the obvious.

"They're up 15 points on us," Alagia said, "and their coach is up yelling at them to work harder, work harder, urging them on.

"And I think the players like each other, *really* like each other. You don't see any of them making faces at their teammates when someone makes a mistake. No griping. None of that.

"And they're just relentless. They never let up against you, sort of like Joe Frazier, the boxer. It's some team."

Hoosiers' attendance for 33 games 500,000

Bloomington, Indiana, March 10, 1976

It's mind-boggling to ponder the impact Indiana basketball teams have had in the four years current Hoosier seniors have been around.

In that time, Indiana basketball teams have played before more than 1.5 million people in live audiences — 779,281 in 50 home games, 780,922 in 65 away.

Saturday's game will be the seventh time in those four years IU has played in a nationally-televised game, and the Hoosiers have been on another 10 regional telecasts . . . plus regular TV coverage on their own network that spans all of Indiana plus Chicago and other spillovers into Wisconsin, Illinois, Michigan, Ohio and Kentucky.

The Hoosiers have finished No. 2 in the nation the last two years in home attendance, and they boosted their average from 16,444 last year to 16,892 this year in a likely move into first.

But the road attendance is a graphic gauge of impact, too, because the Hoosiers have rarely played before anything but a full house — the only one pulled this year at Ohio State, Michigan, Illinois and Michigan State, as well as at cavernous neutral sites like Madison Square Garden, St. Louis Arena and Market Square Arena.

The current Hoosiers could be the first IU team, and surely one of the first in college basketball history, to play before a half-million spectators in a year.

It would take a few steps down the tourney road, but the total, counting the Russian game, is 429,073. Last year's team totaled 444,326 on a schedule that included one more pre-tournament game. (Editor's post-script: The five tourney games pushed the year's total attendance to 503,598.)

The seniors' years boosted Assembly Hall's total within range of reaching the 1 million mark for IU basketball early next year. The total for five seasons is 925,407, about five games away from fan No. 1,000,000's entrance.

Indiana 74, Alabama 69

Scott May, the all-American, and Tom Abernethy, the overlooked, delivered the plays that rescued Indiana from Alabama's grasp Thursday night and sent the Hoosiers on to the final round of the NCAA's Mideast Regional tourney.

Indiana's 74-69 victory set up the meeting the nation has awaited — the No. 1-ranked Hoosiers against No. 2 Marquette, a 62-57 winner over Western Michigan in the other Thursday game before a full house of 14,150 at Louisiana State's Assembly Center.

Indiana, riding a 9-0 takeoff, led throughout the game with the quick and strong Southeastern Conference champions — until sub Keith McCord's jump shot with 3:58 to go boosted 'Bama ahead, 69-68.

The Tide never scored again. That is not to say the Alabamans died early.

May made the crucial plays that Alabama's all-American center, Leon Douglas, could not — tough luck that Douglas handled philosophically. "I think I can look past tonight to tomorrow and think this has been a good year for the team and for me." Douglas said.

He appeared the fate-tapped one when he worked IU all-American Kent Benson into foul trouble, led the comeback that caught the Hoosiers, and then, with the 69-68 score on the board, made the defensive play of the night to thwart May's first attempt at rescue.

Riding with four fouls, Douglas lived out a game-eve comment on his plan for going after the Hoosiers without eliminating himself with fouls. "I'll just have to pick out the shots I can block . . . except when we need a big play," Douglas had said.

Suddenly, the Alabama lead was imperiled by the power and grace of May on the move toward the basket. Past his own man, May swooped in for the layup that would put Indiana ahead again, but Douglas left Benson for a sweeping slap that turned May's shot aside without contact. No foul. No points.

The blocked shot gave Alabama the ball with 3:28 left, and the Tide held it until Douglas drew a two-shot foul at 2:40. He blew both free throws, but when 'Bama rebounded the second one, Douglas got another close-in shot that missed. May rebounded for the Hoosiers.

With 2:02 to go, May made perhaps his biggest shot yet at Indiana. Not really open and not particularly close in, May flashed behind a hint of a block and used the opening it offered to launch himself, turn and send a 17-foot jump shot into the goal.

That was at 2:02, good for a 70-69 lead, and Douglas made one more try to revise the Hoosier script by taking a pass near the basket, wheeling and putting it up with a powerful move. Too powerful. The shot bounced off the rim, and May was there to muscle away with another rebound, the lead preserved.

Jim Crews, Kent Benson watch 'Bama action anxiously

INDIANA 74

	M	FG	FT	R	A	PF	TP
May, f	40	9-22	7- 9	16	0	2	25
Abernethy, f	40	2- 6	4- 5	6	3	1	8
Benson, c	33	7-11	1- 2	5	3	4	15
Buckner, g	31	5- 8	2- 5	2	4	4	12
Wilkerson , g	40	6-12	2- 2	12	4	1	14
Radford	9	0- 1	0- 0	1	0	1	0
Valavicius	6	0- 0	0- 1	0	0	0	0
Wisman	1	0- 0	0- 0	0	0	0	0
Team				2			
Totals		29-60	16-24	44	14	13	74

ALABAMA 69

	M	FG	FT	R	A	PF	TP
Brown, f	25	3- 7	1- 2	5	0	4	7
King, f	25	2- 6	0- 0	6	0	5	4
Douglas, c	39	5-16	2- 6	7	3	4	12
Murray, g	38	7-11	1- 2	7	4	1	15
Dunn, g	37	7-14	2- 2	5	1	5	16
McCord	25	5- 9	1- 2	3	0	2	11
Bonds	4	1- 2	0- 0	0	0	1	2
McElveen	7	1- 4	0- 0	1	1	1	2
Team				1			
Totals		31-69	7-14	35	9	23	69

SCORE BY HALVES

Indiana	37	37 —	74
Alabama	29	40 —	69

Errors: Indiana 20, Alabama 14

	FG	Pct.	FT	Pct.
Indiana	29-60	.483	16-24	.667
Alabama	31-69	.449	7-14	.500

Officials: Irv Brown and Booker Turner
Attendance: 14,150 (capacity)

For a minute, the Hoosiers stalled, but at 0:40, Abernethy was fouled. His one-and-one chance that might have eased Hoosier anxiety plenty rattled inside the goal and bounced out, giving 'Bama a chance.

McCord wanted to go to Douglas, but the two missed connections, and the Alabama freshman wound up in a bump with Hoosier Quinn Buckner — the ball flying free in center court and McCord flying right after it. He had the ball back for an instant, but as he rolled on the floor in center court trying to get possession re-established, Abernethy came along to snatch the loose ball off the floor and start toward the Hoosier goal. At 0:14 he was fouled again — "a chance to redeem myself," he called it later.

He didn't fluff it. Swish . . . swish . . . and Indiana was affluent again, up 72-69 with 14 seconds to go. Bob Wilkerson leaped high to corral Alabama reserve Tommy Bonds' miss, and Wilkerson padded the margin with two more free throws at 0:06.

May starred on a sour shooting night. He was 9-for-22, but he totaled 25 points and grabbed 16 rebounds — the latter an impressive figure that became amazing when rebound totals for Douglas

T.R. is 'Dunn' in on a Scott May drive

and robust freshman Reginald King were posted. Together they had 13. Advantage, May.

Ironically, Abernethy was the only Hoosier who didn't make double figures. Benson, dominant himself for a seven-minute stretch in the middle of the first half when he hit six shots in a row and powered the Hoosiers to as big a lead as they had all day, 27-15, scored 15.

At halftime, Indiana led, 37-29. The lead went back to 12 (54-42), but barely two minutes later, it was a 56-52 game with Benson on the bench then with four fouls and Abernethy tending to Douglas.

May's three-point play and a driving layup by Buckner blunted the 'Bama charge, and it was 65-57 with 8:58 to go after two May free throws — Douglas' first basket against Abernethy coming just before Benson returned at 7:19.

But the Tide didn't quit, catching up (at 67-67) on T.R. Dunn's basket at 4:08 to set up the frenzy at the finish.

Douglas was "the toughest center we've had to play against," Knight said flatly. "We weren't trying to give them the outside shot, but we knew we would give up some baskets along the way trying to jam the inside.

"A key point for us was that, when Benson got four fouls (with 13:23 to go and Indiana up, 54-44), we held on pretty well. They got to us, but they didn't right then. If we hadn't been able to keep a spread with him out of the game, we would have been in serious trouble."

It was Indiana's 29th straight victory, while Alabama's season ended 23-5. The area 'Bama coach C.M. Newton made his target, rebounding, was a washout for his team, Indiana owning the boards, 44-35. But, for a change, Indiana had more turnovers (20) than the team it chased (14 for 'Bama), a shooting edge of .483 to .449 cushioning the impact for IU.

Wilkerson had 14 points (and 12 rebounds) and Buckner 12. Dunn's 16 led Alabama, guard Anthony Murray adding 15 and Douglas 12.

'May's got a little more latitude,' says Knight

Big plays glistened from the Indiana-Alabama match-up of marvelous athletes Thursday night, but none was bigger than the all-American play May delivered for the game-winning basket.

Down for the first time in the game at 69-68, Indiana got a 17-foot jump shot from May — a tough shot, in traffic, pressure thick.

"I came off a pick and that was it," May said. "I've said before if I get open, I know the ball's going to be there. Quinn and Bobby take care of that."

"If he doesn't hit that shot, then we've got to come out and pressure them and they might get an easy basket," Knight said. A fellow asked if May's shot was a "good" (i.e., high-percentage) one. "May's got a little more latitude than other guys," Knight said, smiling.

Only seconds before, May got a pick on the opposite side of the floor. As he swung to his right, he

All-Americans Kent Benson, Leon Douglas meet

saw the way open to the basket, and he drove for the goal. Douglas blocked the shot, another exceptional play under pressure.

"I knew he was coming," May said. "I didn't know whether to dump the ball off to Bennie (whom Douglas left) or go on up. I thought maybe I could get a foul on him, but, no way. No way."

So now the tourney's dream game is here: Indiana vs. Marquette, No. 1 vs. No. 2. And Marquette coach Al McGuire is ready with his psyching.

"They're No. 1 — there's no doubt in my mind," McGuire said. "But you blow sometimes. That rim becomes a teacup. I liked the way they kept their cool."

Three years ago, McGuire's Marquette team was the Mideast favorite when Indiana dumped the Warriors, 75-69, at Nashville, Tenn. McGuire raved then about Indiana's freshman guard, Buckner — "a young Oscar Robertson." He still remembers Quinn.

He noticed May above all Thursday. Benson? "Oh, yes, Benson is physically good," McGuire said, almost reverent as he added, "but May is pure talent."

"And their kid I like is the tall black kid." That's Bobby Wilkerson. Al has been peeking.

"I think it might be us who has to adjust," McGuire said of pre-IU planning. "It's usually that way. The championship team kinda looks back over its shoulder. It's the expansion team that does the reaching."

McGuire hinted advance Indiana fever bothered his team Thursday. "It's a problem the young guys can't handle," he said of the disease called peeking.

Coaches are permitted to peek; neutral coaches. Northwestern coach Tex Winter skipped the niceties of the schedule and matched the Hoosiers and Warriors mentally 2½ weeks ago.

"A quick team is the type to beat Indiana," Tex said. "Marquette has that tight zone and those quick hands.

"I really think Marquette might control the tempo of the game. I don't think Indiana's pressure defense would have that much effect on Marquette because of Marquette's quickness. But Indiana will get the ball inside on Marquette better than most people do."

Knight shut off Marquette questions abruptly in his post-game press session — before the Warriors met Western Michigan. "I haven't even seen Marquette play," said Knight, who then did.

His main thoughts before watching the Warriors were still on the Alabama game and the plays that won it over "as good as any team we've played all year."

Abernethy provided one of the biggest, scooping up a loose ball in center-court with the clock under 20 seconds and Indiana's lead one. He drew a desperation foul at 0:14 and hit the two free throws that made victory almost sure.

From the sidelines, or from in front of TV sets, there must have been thousands of Hoosiers wondering if senior Abernethy's IU life wasn't flashing in front of his eyes as he stepped back to the free throw line where, 26 seconds before, he had missed a similar chance.

"No," Abernethy said, smiling, "it wasn't like that. I just went up there trying to concentrate and get it in. The first time, I shot it a little too hard. I just wanted to soften this one." Two straight swished.

His earlier miss came after a mildly unusual Hoosier stall — guards Buckner and Wilkerson decoying under the 'Bama basket while the Hoosiers' three big front-line players (May, Abernethy and Benson) worked the ball around. "We figured those were our best match-ups for keeping the ball," Knight said, ever-confident in all-round skills . . . and free throw percentages. May, Abernethy and Benson rank 1-2-3 among the starters in that category.

It may be troublesome to Knight to realize that Winter can find challenges faster than Knight can handle them. As he focuses on Marquette, Knight could strain and hear other Winter words in the air: "I think Michigan is as good as either of them."

Michigan's still in the NCAA field, down to the elite eight now, but Wolverines are a long way down the tournament pike — two giant steps.

E-e-e-e-easy, Tex. Take it easy.

Class puts Hoosiers all by selves — Douglas

What puts Indiana in a class by itself, says Douglas, is class.

"Coach Knight is a class person, and Indiana is a class team," said Alabama's all-American center.

"Indiana is a class team because they play hard, but there's nothing dirty or anything like that," Douglas said.

The assessment did not stop with Douglas. Newton used "class" to describe the Hoosiers ("Indiana is just so sound — they have so much class. I don't know any other way to describe it"), and it popped up in comments from Dunn.

"Indiana is a tremendous ball club, every bit as good as we thought they were," Dunn said. "They have a lot of class."

What prompted the stream of accolades was Indiana's defense, a man-to-man that sagged to keep the ball away from Douglas.

"It did bother me because it was a man-to-man they were sloughing off of, instead of a zone the way most teams do," Douglas said.

"I think Indiana paid Douglas the supreme compliment," Newton said. "They took away some of their pressure defense for mid-court and on the wings so they could slough off on Douglas. We've seen this kind of thing before, but frankly we didn't expect it from Indiana.

"We haven't devised a way to get the basketball to within five or six feet of the basket with five defensive men in there.

"And it seemed there was more sloughing off without Benson than there was with him in there.

"I don't think anybody has had that kind of team success — and this is a tribute to Bobby Knight — in keeping the ball away from Leon."

The Tide never completely solved Indiana's defense, said Murray, a guard who whipped it a few times personally with his lightning-quick moves.

"I think I did all I could," he said, wearily. "We tried to play a set offense, but we couldn't get inside. The second half we went with our motion offense, and it worked a little better.

"After Benson's fourth foul, we found we could apply more pressure, and we took some gambles."

Dunn admitted that Indiana "forced us to do some things we didn't want to do," and he added: "Sometimes you get the breaks, and sometimes you don't. We didn't get any at the end."

"My reaction to the game, first of all," Newton said, "is what I told the team going in — that it was going to be a very physical game — a very aggressive game.

"We thought T.R. Dunn would be able to handle Wilkerson bringing the ball up. It tickled us, pleased us fine that he was handling the ball. But it turned out, he handled it much better than we thought he would."

Douglas said he enjoyed his all-American duel with Benson, but he denied a keen rivalry.

"After the game, I congratulated him on a great game and a great season," Douglas said.

"I think he's a good, hard-nosed, aggressive ball player. He's a lot more physical and aggressive than (Mitch) Kupchak (the North Carolina center whom Douglas totally outplayed in Alabama's first-round tourney victory last week)." This duel was a virtual standoff: 12 points and 7 rebounds for Douglas, 15 points and 5 rebounds for Benson.

Although May poured in 25 points and snapped up 16 rebounds, Douglas saw Indiana's win more as a team effort.

"I can't pinpoint one player," he said. "They had a lot of movement and cutting off picks, and it seemed like all of them were making crucial baskets."

Newton gave the experience a no-regrets valedictory. "We wanted to play the best," he said, "and we've done it."

Double-victory?

Indiana 65, Marquette 56

Indiana's unbeaten Hoosiers met one more challenge Saturday afternoon and qualified for the ultimate one in college basketball's national championship round by turning back Marquette, 65-56, for the Mideast Regional championship.

It advanced the Hoosiers to Final Four play in Philadelphia next week, where they will meet defending champion UCLA Saturday — Big Ten runnerup Michigan playing unbeaten Rutgers in the other semifinal game. The winners meet Monday night for the 1976 championship.

Indiana survived 13 minutes without Scott May Saturday but had the senior all-American at the end. The Hoosiers, winning their 30th game this year, had another thing then, too — poise. The nine-point margin came on an 8-2 Hoosier edge in the last 25 seconds, the game 57-54 and pressure-packed until then.

"It was the type of game true championship teams win," Marquette coach Al McGuire said.

It had to be won several times because the Warriors, 27-1 with a 23-game winning streak, kept clawing back. But they had no corner on tenacity, Indiana's grandest show of it coming in the first half when fouls pinned May to the bench.

Marquette went after May and Indiana with the same defense that keyed its late-season victory at Notre Dame — a four-man zone with quick, little Lloyd Walton sticking flea-like to May wherever he went, just as he had with Notre Dame all-American Adrian Dantley at South Bend.

"We figured we would see it," said Hoosier coach Bob Knight, who spent a good portion of

Tom Abernethy covers a rebound from Bo Ellis, with Scott May near

Friday's practice preparing for the defense that Indiana had met only once before — in the early minutes of the Columbia game in the Holiday Festival last December.

And it didn't work as well for Walton as it had with Dantley, the quicker May finding some openings, even with the special attention. He shot Indiana ahead in the first 20 seconds with a jump shot from behind a screen on the side.

But Indiana's feasting spot was in the middle, the rigged defense's most vulnerable spot as 6-11 all-American Kent Benson — named with May as co-winners of the regional's outstanding player award — repeatedly swept across for hook shots.

Benson hit two of those in the first two minutes and the Hoosiers hit their first five shots to jump ahead, 10-5. But trouble came quickly. On the first Indiana miss, May was called for a rebounding foul — his second personal, with co-captain Quinn Buckner already tagged with two by then, too.

The Indiana lead was 20-15 when May got by Walton but crashed into Warrior Earl Tatum after May had launched a shot, a charging foul that was No. 3 for May. Before Knight could get him out of the game (replaced by Wayne Radford), Tatum, the Marquette all-American to whom May had been assigned on defense, slipped away for a basket that cut the Hoosier edge to 20-17 with 13:23 to go in the half.

Changes were profound and fast, not all of them expectable. Indiana reacted to May's loss by jolting Marquette for eight straight points and a 30-19 lead with 9:49 to go in the half, the Hoosiers' biggest spread.

Without May in the game, Marquette reverted to a defense less vulnerable to Benson, a 1-2-2 zone pinched into the middle. Benson had five field goals and Indiana was 14-for-19 after the spurt that opened the 11-point lead.

But points came hard for every Hoosier the rest of the half as Tatum led Marquette on a 10-point run that shaved the lead to 30-29 with 5:45 still left in the half.

"There was no way I could put May back in," Knight said. "We had just made up our minds we wanted to get to the half even. Unquestionably, our play in that stretch (closing out the half) was what enabled us to stay in the game."

The Hoosiers never did lose the lead, the half closing with Indiana ahead 36-35.

Butch Lee gave Marquette its first lead with a baseline jump shot opening the second half, but Indiana freed May for three straight jump shots to reclaim command.

The Hoosiers made another try at a knockout with nine straight points that opened a 51-41 lead. McGuire drew a costly technical foul along the way when he kicked the scorer's bench in anger at a time out period.

Scott May, Quinn Buckner have a low view of activities

Without the technical, Marquette would have had the ball out of bounds, down 48-41. Instead, May hit the free throw, then the Hoosiers backed off from Marquette's zone and ran off two minutes before McGuire abandoned the zone for a man-to-man with 10½ minutes left. At 10:23, May scored to create the 51-41 lead.

But there the Hoosiers hit "kind of a dead spot," Knight noted later. Working carefully and patiently in trying to set up and take nothing but high percentage shots, Indiana had a string of five straight errors. A couple of traveling calls and some near-misses on passes that would have produced layups went into the streak, which, though costly, ran off 3½ minutes of time.

The stretch wasn't fatal because the Hoosier defense was making points come hard for Marquette, too. The Warriors made it to within 51-46 before Benson ended the dry spell with two free throws with 4:31 left, then followed with a layup on a May pass that opened a 55-46 lead, only to be cut back to 55-52 on three straight Marquette baskets.

May didn't leave it there long. With 2½ minutes left, he drove out of the right corner with the basketball and left his feet 10 feet from the basket — shooting or passing intentions unsure. Just before landing, he put up a soft shot that rolled in — "a big shot . . . a very, very big shot," McGuire said.

Freshman Bernard Toone matched it for Marquette, then stole the ball back in mid-court but slipped and traveled. Reprieved, the Hoosiers held the ball until May was fouled at 1:09, but his miss on the first of a one-and-one try returned possession to Marquette.

The Warriors worked patiently for a good shot and got it at 0:40, 6-9 forward Bo Ellis breaking free for a turn-around jump shot shot 6 feet in front of the basket. He missed, Indiana rebounded, and when play stopped at 0:25 with Tatum's fifth foul, McGuire exploded at officials with a claim that Ellis had been fouled — putting both hands into the slender junior's stomach and pushing him away with gusto to demonstrate his point.

All he won was a second technical, the key as first Tom Abernethy, Bob Wilkerson and then Abernethy again hit both halves of one-and-one chances to clinch the game. Buckner's joyous dash to an uncontested layup at 0:02 provided the deceiving final margin. Benson led the Hoosiers with 18 points, and May had 15.

The Hoosiers were thrifty with their shots, taking only 47 and hitting 27 for a .574 mark to Marquette's .379 on 25-for-66; 2 fewer field goals and 19 more shots for the less-judicious Warriors.

That was the pivotal statistic, for Marquette had edges in rebounds (34-33) and turnovers (12 to Indiana's 19). Tatum had 22 points, but guards Lee and Walton were just 5-for-27, Indiana guards Buckner, Wilkerson and Jim Crews 7-for-14.

INDIANA 65

	M	FG	FT	R	A	PF	TP
May, f	27	7-10	1- 2	3	2	3	15
Abernethy, f	40	4- 7	4- 5	5	1	2	12
Benson, c	40	8-12	2- 2	9	0	2	18
Buckner, g	40	4- 9	1- 2	8	5	2	9
Wilkerson, g	23	2- 3	2- 2	3	7	1	6
Radford	7	1- 4	0- 0	1	0	1	2
Valavicius	6	0- 0	1- 2	2	0	0	1
Crews	17	1- 2	0- 0	1	3	1	2
Team				2			
Totals		27-47	11-15	33	18	11	65

MARQUETTE 56

	M	FG	FT	R	A	PF	TP
Ellis, f	36	4- 6	1- 2	7	3	3	9
Tatum, f	36	10-15	2- 2	6	2	5	22
Whitehead, c	35	3-10	1- 2	9	0	4	7
Lee, g	31	4-18	0- 0	2	0	1	8
Walton, g	40	1- 9	0- 0	2	2	3	2
Rosenberger	8	1- 2	0- 1	1	1	2	2
Toone	8	2- 5	2- 2	4	0	0	6
Neary	6	0- 1	0- 0	2	0	0	0
Team				1			
Totals		25-66	6- 9	34	8	18	56

SCORE BY HALVES

Indiana	36	29 —	65
Marquette	35	21 —	56

Errors: Indiana 19, Marquette 12

	FG	Pct.	FT	Pct.
Indiana	27-47	.574	11-15	.733
Marquette	25-66	.379	6- 9	.667

Officials: Jack Ditty and Irv Brown
Attendance: 14,150 (capacity)

Al McGuire — No more tourneys?

Indiana jumps at chance to go to Final Four

"Unemotional" is the way those who have watched and reveled will remember the people who have put together the amazing Indiana basketball winning strings of the mid-1970s.

But that icy calm is purely surface stuff, the Hoosiers showed Saturday in a leaping, hugging celebration at the buzzer that signaled their three-year quest to get back to the NCAA Final Four at last was successful.

Buckner, the iciest of all on court, let loose with some of the best hops and whoops. "I was up there pretty good, wasn't I?" he said, mildly chagrined. "I feel pretty good."

And Knight, not much of a jumper, was caught in mid-celebration by some prying eyes, and he didn't even try to deny he was excited.

"For some of our kids, it's the last shot," he said, "and I just wanted *them* to get there. I told them afterwards nothing could have pleased me more.

"What they have done in representing our basketball team and this university the last four years has just been tremendous."

He had no one more prominently in mind than Buckner, a leader as a freshman on the last Hoosier

team to make it to the Final Four and co-captain of every Indiana club that has been trying since. "Buckner played a great basketball game," Knight said. "He had a tremendous tournament down here. Considering his leadership and his all-round play, we couldn't have asked any finer performance from the captain than we got down here."

There were contributions from every point on the floor in Indiana's victory over Marquette in one of the NCAA tournament's rare and special moments — No. 1 vs. No. 2. It doesn't happen often; only once in the last eight years (North Carolina State and UCLA, 1974 semifinals). And it's the first time in 24 years the top two teams in the final polls came from the same regional area.

The polls looked good Saturday. Two classy teams went after each other while a nation watched.

"The one whole key was our ability to hold the ball," Knight said. He meant gamelong, under pressure from the quick and clawing Marquette defenders who harassed lots of opponents in winning 27 of 28 games before Saturday. "I felt all along if we didn't throw the ball away, we would be all right.

"I was really pleased with the way our kids handled the ball against a variety of presses. I thought our guards did a real good job, and I'm including Jimmy Crews in that.

"Bobby Wilkerson hurt us on defense the first half, and I took him out for it, but when he came back in the second half, he got his head back up and played really well — and that's not easy to do after a bad start."

The game was cerebral. Both Knight and McGuire were forced to make decisions and switches as the game ran along like a river course, far from straight.

Three fouls against May in the first 6½ minutes drastically altered Hoosier planning, and even affected McGuire's, enabling him to leave the special defense tailored for May to a more orthodox one that wasn't so inviting to Benson's pivot play.

At halftime, Knight had to choose which Warrior to assign May to — anticipating whichever it was might become exceptionally active in hope of drawing his fourth foul quickly. "We didn't want to get him involved in the post play," Knight said, "so we stuck with him on Tatum and figured he would take mostly perimeter shots." Tatum did, and May never did draw No. 4, let alone a disqualifying fifth.

So, May was there with 2½ minutes left to make a spontaneous and risky play that may have won the game.

Marquette was within three points when May headed for the basket, jumped, and suddenly had a decision to make — basketball in hand, the basket about 10 feet away, and not much time for thinking.

"I was kinda looking back to the middle, looking for some type of play," May admitted. "The last thing I could do was put it up."

"I really thought Scott was going to draw a foul," said Buckner, who was moving toward the basket. "I've seen him do it so often in practice."

Benson, was open for a pass on the right side of

the floor — "but there was a man between us," Benson said. "Scott couldn't see me."

So, May shot, and the ball went in — "our big-basket play," Knight quipped. "I give a signal and Scott makes a big bucket."

Those two were May's last of a 15-point game and 40-point tournament that earned him ranking with Benson as co-winner of the regional's Outstanding Player Award.

Benson, May and Bob Wilkerson will be going to the Final Four for the first time.

"It's a great feeling," Benson beamed. A year ago, a Hoosier season was wrecked at Saturday's juncture, Kentucky stopping the Hoosiers one game short of the Final Four, 92-90. "I felt empty," Benson said, thinking back.

May's memories were even bleaker, a broken arm making him virtually useless in last year's tournament. "With a couple minutes to go in the first half," May said, "it kind of crossed my mind: 'Here I am on the bench again — just like last year.'"

"We had trouble a year ago — we blew it," Buckner said. "But that was last year. We were just trying to get there with this team."

Warriors go home with 'We're No. 2' feeling

Two technicals in the 1974 NCAA championship game against North Carolina State caused McGuire to vow never again to "take" an intentional technical. Two more Saturday, when he again sent a team against the No. 1-ranked club in the nation, left the competitive Warrior coach in low spirits, talking of a bizarre future plan.

"I personally feel I'm affecting my club in tournaments," he said. "I probably will not come to another tournament.

"Maybe I'm paranoid. I don't think I'm jinxed, but I seem to be hurting my team. If we get back in this thing again, I think I'll just stay home and let coach (Hank) Raymonds and coach (Rick) Majerus handle the team."

His first technical came for kicking the scorer's table, the second for suggesting too loudly that the officials erred in not calling a foul on Indiana when Ellis broke for a last-minute shot, the Warriors three down at the time.

Scott May, Kent Benson celebrate a regional title, Final Four berth

Both technicals were disastrous to the Warriors, and both, McGuire made it clear, were unintentional.

"It's hard after a loss not to sound bitter," he said, "and I'm trying. I told the official: 'You look at it on film (the Ellis shot). What do you make here? I'll cover it and bet you 7-1 it was a foul.'

"The first one (technical) was a very key play with Bo again, but I see it through tainted glasses. I see it Marquette's way, my way, not the officials' way or the NCAA's way.

"The technicals hurt. But who's to say? Indiana probably would have beaten us anyway. I say Indiana's a better ball club.

"I'd like to congratulate Bobby and the Indiana team. I hope they win the whole thing. They've got a great ball club, and they deserve to be in Philadelphia."

Pre-game speculating gave Indiana a muscle edge underneath, but Marquette outrebounded the Hoosiers, 34-33. The Warriors, however, paid the price in fatigue at the end, McGuire said.

"I thought it was the first time we ever were physical," he said, "but I think we were tired at the end, and you can't work at 100 per cent efficiency. Indiana plays a powerful defense. You probably saw one of the best defensive games in quite a while. It was tough at both defensive ends.

"Benson's so strong. He wears you out."

Indiana's quick start, jumping to a 16-7 lead, caused McGuire to scrap his original plan.

"I thought we were speeding it up too fast at the start," he said. "We wanted to go to Bo. We didn't think they could handle him without shoving, but it didn't work."

"The shot May hit was a big shot — very, very big," he said.

Walton's leg muscle, bruised against Western Michigan Thursday, was "not at 100 per cent," McGuire said. "He usually comes back and steals some of those times after they break the press."

McGuire singled out Whitehead for a "real fine ball game," but his fondest words were saved for Tatum:

"I've said Earl Tatum was the greatest talent I ever had. I was pleased to see him jump. It's a shame to see his year end. It's funny. His first year, Indiana beat us, too."

Tatum, however, seemed to have no regrets, convinced that college basketball's best and next-best teams met Saturday.

"Since they beat us, they're No. 1," he said. "We're gonna go back to Milwaukee now and say we're the No. 2 team. If we'd beaten 'em, we would be No. 1.

"I hope they go all the way. They're from our area, you know, and they have a hell of a coach and a great team."

The Warriors drew some second-guessing for not attempting to drive more with May on Tatum opening the second half and the Hoosier star saddled with three fouls.

"The coach told me I could do what I wanted," Tatum said, "but they were packing up the middle. There wasn't no room. I could see the big man (Benson) coming in and Abernethy came over, too. You can only go so far before the big man gets in your way.

"We weren't looking to foul anybody out, because that would have broken up our continuity on offense."

Tatum and his teammates go back to Milwaukee without the victory they hungered for — "We wanted to play this game for a long time," he said — but satisfied they took their best shot.

Ellis and Lee agreed that Marquette played as well as it could.

"We played well, and they played well," Ellis said.

"Indiana is a super basketball team. They play together so well. I think the game indicated that we played pretty well. We were able to do everything we are capable of doing."

"Yeah, we had a good shot," Lee said. "But Indiana's a great team, and you can't take anything away from 'em.

"A couple fouls, some technicals and Scott May from the corner — that's what beat us."

Kent Benson — Co-MVP at Baton Rouge

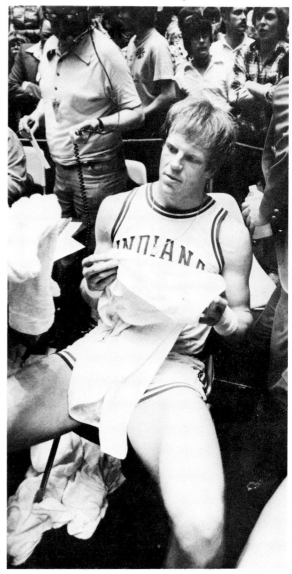

Indiana 65, UCLA 51

A merry sendoff to Philadelphia

Indiana brushed aside another giant Saturday and now has only Big Ten rival Michigan between it and a national championship to crown one of college basketball's greatest seasons.

UCLA, the sport's standard of excellence for the basketball lifetime of the unbeaten Hoosiers, fell in semifinal play Saturday afternoon at The Spectrum, 65-51.

Michigan made it an unprecedented all-Big Ten final by routing Rutgers in the other semifinal game, 86-70. So the Wolverines, losers in two tense struggles with Indiana this year, 80-74 at Ann Arbor and 74-69 in overtime at IU, will get a third shot with a season's national supremacy on the line, the Big Ten's first NCAA championship in 16 years assured.

"Michigan is the best basketball team we've played this year," said Indiana coach Bob Knight. "But I think it's great that we're playing them. I don't think there's ever been anything that says more about Big Ten basketball than our two teams going through two tough regionals and playing for the national championship."

Indiana's 31st straight victory this year was much like its first, an 84-64 whipping of UCLA on the neutral St. Louis Arena court.

Then, Indiana moved out to a 36-28 halftime lead and steadily pulled away. This time, it was 34-26 at halftime, and the Hoosiers opened a 12-point lead with the first two baskets of the second half. The lead never got below six afterward and was never wider than the final margin.

But there were more anxious moments in this one than the Hoosiers experienced in that November game that shook the college world, particularly the part of it in Los Angeles.

This time, the Hoosiers were in trouble before they broke a sweat. Knight, fearing the inside play

of UCLA's 6-11 all-American forward, Richard Washington, pulled a surprise by opening the game with his 6-11 all-American, Kent Benson, assigned to guard Washington.

It backfired quickly. Benson picked up one foul 25 feet from the basket when he played too tight on the slender Bruin, and he got a second on a rebounding play with only 92 seconds gone.

Knight took his quickest time out of the season, at 18:05 of the half, to switch Tom Abernethy onto Washington, who had five points by then with UCLA ahead, 7-2.

What followed was Abernethy's finest hour in an under-acclaimed year . . . and almost his final one. With 7:18 to go in the game and IU ahead by 10, Abernethy ran into Washington in center court away from the ball and crumpled with a bruise above his left knee.

He left the game and never returned, but the Hoosiers' orthopedist, Dr. Merrill Ritter, said he should be available for the championship game.

INDIANA 65

	M	FG	FT	R	A	PF	TP
May, f	40	5-16	4- 6	4	5	2	14
Abernethy, f	33	7- 8	0- 1	6	2	3	14
Benson, c	38	6-15	4- 6	9	0	4	16
Buckner, g	40	6-14	0- 1	3	2	3	12
Wilkerson, g	38	1- 5	3- 4	19	7	3	5
Crews	11	1- 2	2- 3	3	3	0	4
Team				4			
Totals		26-59	13-21	45	19	15	65

UCLA 51

	M	FG	FT	R	A	PF	TP
Washington, f	38	6-15	3- 4	8	3	3	15
Johnson, f	36	6-10	0- 1	6	0	2	12
Greenwood, c	26	2- 5	1- 2	10	0	2	5
Townsend, g	36	2-10	0- 0	3	2	1	4
McCarter, g	27	2- 9	0- 0	4	3	5	4
Drollinger	8	0- 3	2- 2	1	0	3	2
Holland	4	0- 2	0- 0	0	0	0	0
Spillane	8	0- 2	0- 0	1	2	0	0
Smith	10	3- 4	0- 0	0	0	3	6
Hamilton	4	0- 1	1- 2	0	0	0	1
Vroman	3	0- 0	0- 0	1	0	2	0
Lippert	1	0- 0	2- 2	0	0	0	2
Olinde	1	0- 0	0- 0	0	0	0	0
Team				1			
Totals		21-61	9-13	37	10	21	51

SCORE BY HALVES

Indiana	34	31 — 65
UCLA	26	25 — 51

Errors: Indiana 16, UCLA 14

	FG	Pct.	FT	Pct.
Indiana	26-59	.441	13-21	.619
UCLA	21-61	.344	9-13	.692

Officials: Irv Brown and Jim Bain
Attendance: 17,340 (capacity)

Hoosiers all around, Richard Washington's ready to score

Before he left, he had an immense impact. Abernethy hit 7 of 8 shots in the game and shut down Washington without a point those last 18 minutes of the first half, while Indiana was taking charge.

The Bruins last led at 19-17, but Hoosier Scott May, checked with 14 points on the day he set an IU one-season scoring record, tied the game with a jump shot at 7:41, and Benson teetered the Hoosiers ahead with two free throws at 7:26.

Baskets by Abernethy and Quinn Buckner completed an eight-point run that gave Indiana a 25-19 lead. It widened to 32-23 before closing at 34-26.

The Hoosiers didn't go bolting away in the second half; they missed their first three shots, four of the first five.

But their defense was making inside shots unavailable to the Bruins, who couldn't sink outside ones. And 6-7 Bob Wilkerson, having the best rebounding day ever by a Hoosier guard (19), shut off the boards to the Bruins.

After Abernethy limped off, UCLA managed a run at the Hoosiers. Three close-in misses by Indiana went with two baskets by Bruin sub Gavin Smith to chop the lead to 52-46 with 6:04 left.

Scott May, Richard Washington move in

Indiana reacted with extra patience. They worked the ball for a minute and 45 seconds before breaking May open for a drive to the basket. His shot missed, but he earned two free throws that he sank with 4:18 to go.

Wilkerson rebounded Jim Spillane's miss, and the Hoosiers held the ball again until Abernethy's replacement, Jim Crews, was fouled with 2:42 to go. Crews missed the shot but fielded his own long rebound, and 10 seconds later May broke under for the basket that put UCLA down by 10 and all but out.

Wilkerson made enough big plays in those last two minutes to guarantee, personally, that the lead would stand. His interception at 2:19 brought him a one-and-one free-throw chance that he exploited for two points and a 60-48 lead.

Then, with the last seconds being counted off in the Hoosier cheering section, he smashed a shot by UCLA freshman Brad Holland so deep into IU's attacking court that when Crews ran it down he had an easy, margin-fattening layup.

Benson's 16 points led the Hoosiers, while Abernethy and May had 14 each and Buckner 12. Wilkerson's day included only 5 points, but 3 of those came when he slipped inside UCLA's standout forward, Marques Johnson, for a rebound basket and free throw that opened a 45-32 edge early in the second half. He also had 7 assists to go with his mammoth rebound total that gave Indiana a solid 45-37 margin on the boards.

Forced to live or die with its outside game, UCLA died with paltry .344 shooting (to the Hoosiers' .441, also sub-par). Bruin guards were 4-for-24.

Indiana became the first team to beat UCLA twice in one season since Duke did it to UCLA on a two-game Bruin invasion of North Carolina in December, 1965.

Abernethy no instant star to Knight

Abernethy had an ice bag strapped to his bruised left knee as he stood in the center of a press group and got star treatment for his role in Indiana's victory over UCLA.

Abernethy played himself into a prominence that made the ice bag a *cause celebre* looking toward the championship game. The man whose consistent work has been consistently overlooked all year suddenly loomed as an irreplaceable gem.

But Abernethy wasn't concerned: "It's just a bruise. I'll be all right Monday."

Knight didn't see Abernethy as any sort of sudden star. "Abernethy's been a great player for us all year long," he said. "He's done a great many things for us — scoring, handling the ball, rebounding, playing defense."

But he didn't anticipate having to go to him so soon as a defensive answer to Washington. "We thought they'd put Washington in a low post early," Knight said. "He has gotten more aggressive as the year went on, and I was afraid he'd shoot over Tommy. At least at the start, we wanted Bennie there with a hand in his face."

Two quick fouls changed the assignments, but Abernethy didn't overstate his contribution. "I tried to get as much help as I could," he said. "The

Behind Buckner block, Abernethy scores

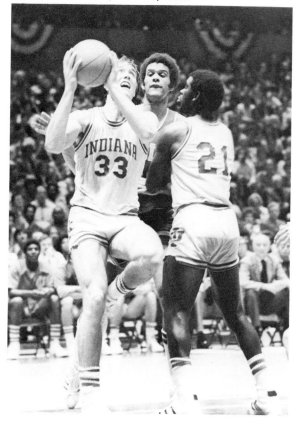

guards were coming back in well, so if he started to drive, I knew they were going to help me out."

"I felt it would be a hard game, harder than the one in St. Louis," Knight said. "We knew they were a better team now than then, but we felt we had improved, also.

"We felt we had to stay with them the first seven or eight minutes because of the emotion they brought into the game. When we did that, we felt we were in good shape."

Knight called Wilkerson's rebounding "a big key for us, as vitally important to us as it was in the Alabama game (when he had 14 rebounds).

"But then I can't say too much for Quinn Buckner's play, or Jimmy Crews's play at the end. It was a tremendous team effort, and I'm very proud of them."

Wilkerson said his route to the boards was open because "it's harder to block out a guard. I was just going to the ball and the other guys had it open for me. I knew Quinn was back when we were on offense, so I could just go to the boards."

Buckner called Wilkerson "one of our biggest attributes. We can move him any place — outside, where most people say he doesn't belong, or inside if we need him there."

Buckner admitted to some thoughts during the week of the precedent that loomed for the Hoosiers — their 24-point regular-season whipping of Kentucky that became a 92-90 regional loss in the rematch a year ago.

"Yeah, I thought about it," he said. "All you can do is learn a lesson from that kind of thing."

Knight called Saturday's game "a game between two great squads who played hard. The strong defensive pressure made it the kind of game it was."

He couldn't resist a parting aside to Greenwood, who called IU's opening victory "a practice game" and vowed "we'll win the one that counts."

"I thought it was going to be a knock-down, drag-out ball game," Knight said, adding with a grin: "David Greenwood said the game didn't count in November. I kinda thought they both counted."

Touchy moment for Tom Abernethy

'Indiana best team we've played' — Johnson

In the gloomy minutes after a rare whipping had been dealt to UCLA back on Nov. 29 in St. Louis, the Bruins' stars were their rallying points — Washington and Johnson quietly conceding an edge to Indiana at that time but warning that they expected a rematch in March in Philadelphia.

When it came Saturday, the two were left gloomy again.

"Materialwise, I don't think they have as much as we do," Johnson said. "But coach Knight takes advantage of what he has. They just went out and executed better than we did.

"Indiana is very mechanical, and I don't mean that in a derogatory way. They are very well drilled. They run their offense so well. If Scotty May was open for a second, they hit him.

"I'd say they're the best *team* we've played since I've been here.

"I'm disappointed not to go all the way, because that's the UCLA tradition. But my general reaction is that we did pretty well."

Washington said he was "surprised a little bit" when Indiana opened the game with Benson guarding him, and he had warm words for Abernethy, who took him most of the way.

"Abernethy is a good, solid defensive player — yes, I think he's as good as I've faced," Washington said. "He wouldn't let me in close enough so that I could shoot over him.

"And Indiana is such a good help team, it's hard to say any individual is a star because the whole team plays such good defense.

"They were sagging quite a bit, and I thought we could have taken better advantage of that situation. But our guards couldn't hit — it was a combination of their defense and our lack of patience on offense."

"Indiana was a great team in November, December, January and all the way through the season," Bartow said. "I think there is no doubt that we were a better team today than in November. Indiana may be a better team, too.

"They're a great team, knit together in great fashion, and that's a credit to Bobby Knight. The way they play help defense all the time makes them the toughest defensive team in the country.

"They kept the ball away from all our players who have done well all year."

Jim Crews finds a seat, full house or no full house

Indiana 86, Michigan 68

'The White House' calling, Mr. Orr

Philadelphia, March 29

The telephone rang early last Sunday morning in the John Orr residence, and when Mrs. Orr sleepily asked who it was who wanted to speak to her husband, a voice said gravely:

"The White House."

"A minute later, John's on the phone," Indiana coach Bob Knight said to a group of reporters Sunday, still gleeful over the coup. "He says, 'Who is this?' and I said, 'Jerry Ford, John,' and he said, 'Really!'

"And then I overplayed my hand.

"I told him how I just wanted to congratulate him on winning the regional and tell him how proud he had made 'M' men all over the world. I went on too long. If I had just stuck with short sentences, I think I'd have had him."

Orr picked up the dialogue then: "I told him, 'President, hell. How could any dumb bastard from Ohio State get to be President?' "

The episode says a lot about the two coaches who will be battling each other tonight for college basketball's championship in the coziest title game ever arranged.

They coach on two different wave lengths but they laugh together.

Wednesday, to get Philadelphia properly prepared for the four-team invasion coming its way, the Final Four coaches were put on a joint telephone hook-up with a roomful of eastern writers.

Orr, who may be even quicker and better with poor-mouthing than he is with one-liners, was droning on to a new audience about how little and skinny the team he was going to send against mighty Rutgers was when Knight's voice cut through:

"Aw, cut that stuff out, John. I'm tired of hearing it. You list Wayman Britt at 6-2. When I tried to recruit him, he was 6-5. If he stuck around there one more year, he'd be 5-11."

But Orr will talk.

"A guy asked me if I'm looking forward to getting at Indiana again," Orr said. "I asked him: 'Think I'm nutty?'

"That game down at Indiana, we played everything — zone, man-to-man, sometimes both at once, we were so confused. But we had them confused, too. Knight asked me once: 'What in hell are you playing?' and I said, 'Damned if I know, but we're not changing.' "

At last, at long last, Indiana got its shot at the national collegiate basketball championship Monday night and won it with class that guaranteed the 1975-76 Hoosiers ranking with the all-time greats.

The last of the disbelievers, fiery, feisty and fleet Michigan, fell by an 86-68 score in the 38th NCAA tournament's championship game.

What isn't told by that final margin — fifth biggest in tourney history — is that at halftime, the dancing in the streets was going on in Ann Arbor, not Bloomington.

Indiana, rocked by the loss of starting guard Bob Wilkerson to a head injury in the third minute of the game, trailed at halftime, 35-29.

Scott May's jump shot pulled the Hoosiers even at 39-39 with 15:55 to go, and it was still tied, 51-51, after Michigan freshman Phil Hubbard's basket with 10:15 left.

The last 10 minutes made the Hoosiers champions for the third time in history (joining IU's 1940 and '53 titlists of the late Branch McCracken), and for only the seventh time in NCAA history that a team made it all the way unbeaten. Indiana's 32-0 record matches the best ever (by North Carolina's 1957 champions).

May, college basketball's player of the year, broke the tie with a jump shot at 9:58, and the sequence that happened in the next minute helped sap Michigan's last will.

Freshman Rich Valavicius, whose high school tournament experience never got beyond the regional level, was on the floor only 14 seconds in his first college championship game when he drilled a jump shot from the top of the foul circle for Hoosier breathing room, 55-51.

Michigan tried to counter, sub Dave Baxter putting up a shot from the right side and Hubbard pulling the rebound down on the left side and putting a shot back up.

Kent Benson, a boss of the backboards the last 20 minutes, turned the shot back with a clout that sent it high in the air and deep on the court, where another of the late-game Hoosier standouts, sophomore Jim Wisman, fielded it.

Seconds later, Benson drew the fourth foul on Hubbard, and in another minute, Hubbard was gone on fouls — the 10th time he fouled out of a game this year and the third straight time in games with Indiana.

Guard Steve Grote kept Michigan close for a while after Hubbard's departure. The Wolverines trailed only 63-59 when May snapped up a loose ball under the Hoosier basket and let it slip — in the right direction, the ball looping high and almost straight up, coming down in the basket.

Before Michigan could recover, Tom Abernethy, freshened by Valavicius' three-minute relief stint, intercepted a Grote pass, and Quinn Buckner sank two free throws.

Thirty seconds later, it was Buckner who retrieved the ball on a defensive rebound and Abernethy who hit two free throws, and Indiana was suddenly atop a 69-59 margin with 4:58 left.

It grew to 73-59 with less than four minutes to go when Michigan made a final try, sparked by two quick Indiana turnovers against the Wolverine press.

Freshman Tom Staton scored all five points as Michigan cut the lead to 73-64 with 3:27 to go, and after another Hoosier turnover, it was 74-66 with 2½ minutes left.

Wisman's two free throws at 2:22, a basket by May at 2:11, and a steal and layup by Buckner at 1:47 cleaved open an 80-66 margin, and the Hoosiers were in.

Near tears himself in the emotion of victory, Hoosier coach Bob Knight pulled Buckner at 0:44 and hugged his three-year co-captain for a few long and poignant seconds.

Then came Abernethy, whose play on a bruised leg won him the greatest recognition of his Hoosier career — election to the five-man all-tourney team. Abernethy checked out to the same reception as Buckner, while time stood still with May at the free throw line.

After he hit both free throws to round out a 26-point night, May came out, dancing all the way . . .

Bob Wilkerson helpless as Rickey Green scores

Seconds later, a season is over for dazed Wilkerson

128

then Benson, named the tourney's outstanding player after a 25-point, 9-rebound final game.

The last senior, Jim Crews, came out after hitting two free throws at 0:12. Mission accomplished.

"It's been kind of a two-year quest for us," Knight said.

"These kids are very, very deserving. I know better than anybody how hard and how long they have worked for this."

Things looked shaky during the first half, when the dominant characteristic of the game was Michigan's zeal. "They outhustled us," May said frankly.

Wilkerson went out when he got in front of Michigan's Wayman Britt on a breakaway layup by Britt, who was looking away from Wilkerson when he came down after his shot. Britt's elbow caught Wilkerson in the head and knocked him out.

The game was held up for about eight minutes while treatment was given Wilkerson, who left the floor on a stretcher . . . his game, season and Hoosier career obviously ended.

Wayne Radford was Knight's first choice to replace Wilkerson — "because I thought Michigan might be doing a lot of zoning, and Radford's shooting might help us," Knight said.

The Hoosiers fell back, 18-10, before Knight took a time out at 12:09 of the half, Crews replac-

ing Radford. The next five times Indiana encountered the zone, the Hoosiers scored to scoot ahead, 23-20.

It was the end of Orr's defensive switching system — man-to-man after a Wolverine score, zone after failure to score. He junked the zone and stuck strictly with his man-to-man, benefitting the rest of the half from more aggressive defense but faltering when fouls started to accumulate and when Benson, the object of the zone, proved too much for Hubbard to handle by himself.

Just as vital were three fouls May drew on his nemesis, the super-sticky Britt, in the first four minutes of the second half, forcing him out of the game at that point with four fouls.

"We played a very good first half (Michigan shot .615)," Orr said, "but when we got into foul trouble, we couldn't keep up."

It was Indiana's third, and most convincing, victory of the year over the Wolverines, who finished No. 9 in the polls and 25-7 in the record book.

Besides the 51 points from Benson and May, Indiana got 16 (plus 8 rebounds, 4 assists and 5 steals) from Buckner and 11 points from Abernethy. Four Wolverines also scored in double figures, led by Rickey Green with 18.

The unprecedented final game match-up of two members of the same conference saw Indiana come out with an edge in every statistic. In the pressure of the championship game, the Hoosiers had their best tournament mark on turnovers, committing only 13 for the game and just one in the first 16 minutes of the second half. Michigan had 19 turnovers, and the Wolverines also were outshot (.525 to .474) and outrebounded, 36-34.

Quinn Buckner gets an arm of John Robinson

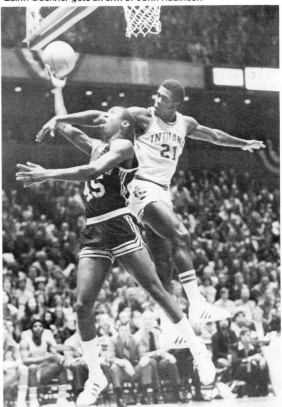

INDIANA 86

	M	FG	FT	R	A	PF	TP
May, f	39	10-17	6- 6	8	2	4	26
Abernethy, f	35	4- 8	3- 3	4	1	2	11
Benson, c	39	11-20	3- 5	9	2	3	25
Buckner, g	39	5-10	6- 9	8	4	4	16
Wilkerson, g	3	0- 1	0- 0	0	0	1	0
Radford	7	0- 1	0- 0	1	0	0	0
Crews	12	0- 1	2- 2	1	4	1	2
Wisman	21	0- 1	2- 3	1	6	4	2
Valavicius	4	1- 1	0- 0	0	0	0	2
Haymore	1	1- 1	0- 0	0	0	0	2
Bender	1	0- 0	0- 0	0	0	0	0
Team				3			
Totals		32-61	22-28	36	19	19	86

MICHIGAN 68

	M	FG	FT	R	A	PF	TP
Robinson, f	38	4- 8	0- 1	6	2	5	8
Britt, f	31	5- 6	1- 1	3	2	5	11
Hubbard, c	31	4- 8	2- 2	11	0	5	10
Green, g	39	7-16	4- 5	6	2	3	18
Grote, g	35	4- 9	4- 6	1	3	4	12
Bergen	5	0- 1	0- 0	0	0	1	0
Staton	9	2- 5	3- 4	2	0	3	7
Baxter	6	0- 2	0- 0	0	0	2	0
Thompson	2	0- 0	0- 0	0	0	0	0
Hardy	4	1- 2	0- 0	2	0	0	2
Team				3			
Totals		27-57	14-19	34	12	25	68

SCORE BY HALVES

Indiana		29	57 — 86
Michigan		35	33 — 68

	FG	Pct.	FT	Pct.
Indiana	32-61	.525	22-28	.786
Michigan	27-57	.474	14-19	.737

Errors: Indiana 13, Michigan 19
Officials: Bob Wortman and Irv Brown
Attendance: 17,540 (capacity)

Benson joins Huffman as NCAA award winner

Benson joined a notable list in winning the most outstanding player award at the NCAA championships, and he also kept alive a personal string.

He is the second Indiana player to win the NCAA award, and there has been a long time between Hoosiers. Marv Huffman, like Benson a New Castle product, won the first such honor given for leading the 1940 Indiana team to the championship.

It's the third straight IU season Benson has closed by winning the outstanding player award in a tournament.

The thought of three such awards in a row hadn't crossed his mind until it was mentioned in a question. "This means a whole lot more than last year," he said, smiling. "A *lot* more."

Last year, he was cited after his 33-point, 23-rebound game in defeat in the finals of the Mideast regional. The year before, freshman Benson was the MVP as Indiana won the Collegiate Commissioners Association tournament.

"This is a team award — we all know that," Benson said. "I wouldn't have been able to get it

Champions' reward for Bob Knight, Scott May, Quinn Buckner

without these other guys working just as hard."

Benson and May combined for 51 points, and they took over the backboards in the second half to spark Indiana's breakaway to the championship.

"It was just a matter of me going out and gathering myself the second half," Benson said. "I just went up stronger and played harder."

Benson and his Michigan match-up, Phil Hubbard, were cautioned by officials a couple of times to cool the action down. "We were getting a little physical under there," Benson admitted. "All through the Big Ten season and the tournaments, too, it was pretty physical."

Benson, May and Buckner all agreed the early-game loss of Wilkerson to a head injury affected Hoosier play.

"I think we all thought, 'Wow, Bobby's out — we've gotta go at it a little tougher,'" Buckner said. "Bobby means a lot to us. How can you find another 6-7 guard with his quickness and his agility?"

"I knew with Wilkerson out, somebody had to help Bennie on the boards," May said. "I figured it was my job." Both he and Buckner helped; they had 8 rebounds each and Benson 9 as Indiana had a slight board edge.

"I thought Michigan kinda outhustled us the first half," May said. "Everybody came out the second half just to go after it a little harder. There was no panic. We've been in that situation before."

"Michigan is a hard-nosed, tough bunch of guys," Buckner said. "We don't like to compare, but I'd have to say Michigan is as good as anybody we've played."

Wisman, who had played only a few minutes in the tourney, logged 21 minutes and got some praise from Knight for his back-court play that included six assists.

"We put him in because he moves the ball a little bit quicker," Knight said. "He did a great job of taking it from side to side."

There was poetic justice in the prominent Wisman role, because it was another Michigan game in which he was victimized a couple times by the Wolverine press.

"Oh, yeah, I recognized that press," Wisman said, smiling. "I tried to look at it from a different angle. I made some stupid mistakes the other time, and it made me really conscious this game of what I should do."

A backcourt rival, Michigan's Grote, sat in another dressing room down the hall and nominated Buckner as Indiana's MVP.

"When you do the kind of things Quinn Buckner does and hit for double figures the way he did the last month of the season, he is their best," Grote said. "I'm a guard, and I have to play him. When he goes out of the game, I'm happy."

But the difference in Monday's first and second halves, he said, was "Wisman. Indiana couldn't hit the first pass to the wing to get into its offense. Then he came in, and they started to run their game and to muscle us.

"This was World War III. They won the first two, too."

For Kent Benson, No. 1's no longer a question

Flexibility key weapon for champion Hoosiers

It's difficult to imagine more precision or detail in a game plan than Knight prepares ... nor quicker demolition of same than Knight got in the last three testing rounds of the NCAA championship tournament.

In the quarterfinals against No. 2-ranked Marquette, his two senior co-captains, Buckner and May, picked up two fouls each in the first two minutes, and May left with a third 13½ minutes before halftime.

Against UCLA, it was Benson who drew two fast fouls, causing a three-way transfer of defensive assignments among the Hoosiers' front-court players.

Monday night was scarier. There were personal concerns on the Hoosier sidelines when Wilkerson lay stretched out, unconscious, after a blow to the head in the third minute of the NCAA championship game. Knight had those, and he had to be concerned practically, too, because Wilkerson was guarding Michigan's No. 1 scorer, Green.

"You don't have time to think about a whole lot of things at a time like that," Knight said. "You just have to adjust and try to keep going."

There was considerably more of that left at halftime, when Indiana had a shaken and bewildered look and a 35-29 deficit to deal with. The faint of heart were bailing out from coast to coast.

"We weren't able to pressure as much without Bobby," Knight said. "The second half, we did put a little more pressure on their guards. We felt we were allowing them to move the ball around a little more than we should.

"Offensively, we didn't really feel too bad. We missed a lot of layups — we counted seven or eight at halftime. And that makes a hell of a lot of difference in your offense.

"But we did try to get the ball to Benson a little more the second half. I don't think we got the ball to him nearly as much as we could have in the first half."

Benson scored 15 points, May 18 and Buckner 12 in the second half — enough from those three, as things turned out, to deliver victory. All represented pleasant productivity for Knight.

It fell to Knight, during his time under press questioning, to read aloud the all-tournament announcement, and he didn't do it unembellished. He announced Benson as the press' choice for outstanding player, IU's May and Abernethy, Michigan's Green and UCLA's Marques Johnson to the other four spots.

"There should be a sixth guy, and that's Buckner," Knight said. "Benson had an outstanding tournament all the way through. The two most outstanding players in the tournament were Benson and May."

May was another who was prominent in both teams' game plans. He was renewing an old duel with Michigan's defensive standout, Britt.

"Britt is the best defensive player we've played against all year," Knight said. "We knew it would be a tough match-up — Scott's offense against his defense. But I thought May did an excellent job." He scored 26 points to lead both teams and fouled Britt out nine minutes early.

"They played a great second half," Orr said. "I don't know what more we could have done.

"We played a very good first half, and when we had to make the big shots at the end, we couldn't make them."

Rutgers' coach Tom Young noted after his team's loss to UCLA in the consolation game that "UCLA had the best talent here." The comment was relayed to Orr, who shot back: "Indiana was the best team here, we were second-best, and anyone who doesn't know that is an imbecile."

May consensus pick as player of year

Scott May completed a sweep of national basketball honors unprecedented in Indiana University basketball history, including consensus recognition as the Hoosiers' first national collegiate player of the year.

And his junior teammate, Kent Benson, gave IU another "first" — the Hoosiers' first pair of consensus all-America players in one season.

May was named by a wide variety of electorates to the player of the year award.

The first one came in March, when professional basketball general managers and scouts in balloting conducted by *The Sporting News* picked the 6-7 Indiana forward from Sandusky, Ohio.

As the weeks went by, May was named the winner of the James Naismith Award as United Press International's player of the year.

Then Associated Press's electorate also went for May, and, at the NCAA basketball finals in Philadelphia, the National Association of Basketball Coaches presented May with a handsome silver trophy as its player of the year.

Basketball Weekly named May its winner the week of the finals. And, the Citizens Savings Foundation named May and teammate Benson co-winners of its player of the year award, the first time two players from the same team had received the 71-year-old award.

May also was the leading vote-getter in all-America voting by National Basketball Association coaches — 17 of the 18 NBA coaches voting for him.

May also has made every recognized all-America team that has been picked, after becoming IU's first consensus all-America in 20

Scott May — Player of the Year

years last year. He also was the Big Ten's most valuable player as a junior.

Benson also made virtually every major all-America team and capped his junior season by being named the outstanding player at the 1976 NCAA finals. May and Benson shared the award at the Mideast Regional.

May, named the outstanding player at both holiday tournaments in which Indiana competed (the Holiday Festival at Madison Square Garden and the Indiana Classic at Assembly Hall) had his IU career high of 41 points when Indiana clinched the clear-cut Big Ten championship by winning at Wisconsin.

Benson, who finished third in UPI's player of the year picking and was the only other player besides May considered by *Basketball Weekly* for its award, had his career high of 38 in a Hoosier victory over Michigan State at Assembly Hall this year.

Senior Quinn Buckner, the first IU player to score *and* pass for more than 1,000 points, also made the Citizens Savings all-America squad.

Bedlam hits Bloomington

Sometimes madness pays.

If you stayed home late Monday night and watched the Academy Awards on TV, you know that *One Flew Over the Cuckoo's Nest*, that black comedy about life in an insane asylum, copped all the big prizes.

And if you decided to venture outside, then you know that all the inmates must have escaped.

It was bedlam in Bloomington.

Pandemonium.

They diagnose it as "Hoosier Hysteria," and happily, there's no cure.

At about 10:05 p.m. Monday, Indiana University's basketball team was writing the final glorious chapter in a storybook season with an 86-68 win over Michigan that clinched a national championship and an undefeated season.

At about 10:06 p.m., the loyal masses began pouring into the streets. The rain was pouring down, too, but frankly, Scarlett, no one gave a damn.

The last time Bloomington saw a demonstration of these proportions, it was Vietnam, not basketball, that stirred the blood.

Basketball's more fun.

The big gatherings were on Kirkwood Avenue, on Walnut Street and at Showalter Fountain in the middle of campus, but hundreds of smaller parties erupted everywhere — in homes, apartment complexes and, of course, the bars.

It all began on Kirkwood with people running up and down the sidewalks, shouting at each other, hugging, slapping hands. Then they began spilling out into the street, sharing "soul grips" and cold beer with the passing motorists. Horns were honking; freshly-tanned coeds were laughing and hanging out of car windows. Traffic began to slow, and then was forced to a complete halt as the crowd grew just like Good Ol' Topsy. By 10:30, there were at least 1,000 people on the street.

Carryout sales at Nick's Ole English Hut were "unbelievable," said one bartender. Almost all of that booze made its way out to the street, where people used it for squirting, head-dousing, and, oh yeah! drinking.

The Indiana cheerleaders would have been proud of this bunch. Chants of "We're No. 1," "Here we go, Hoosiers, here we go," and "I-N-D-I-A-N-A" filled the air. The only things noisier were the constantly exploding firecrackers and cherry bombs.

Eventually, the mob harkened to the shouts of "downtown! downtown!" The march led up Kirkwood to Walnut Street, then turned right and headed past the courthouse square before meeting hundreds of celebrants who were pouring out of the Bluebird, Barzo's Blitz and other taverns along the main drag.

Police said at least 4,000 people were out by that time, tying up all three lanes of traffic on Walnut from Fourth to Seventh Street. Drunks stood on the tops of cars, trying to lead renditions of the Indiana fight song. Four young men, just back from Florida, decided to show off their tans

A Kirkwood salute

and stripped to the buff. A four-piece brass band serenaded the crowd with *The Mighty Quinn* and *Indiana, Our Indiana*. It was Bloomington's version of a bacchanalia, complete with flowing wine and dancing satyrs.

It would be more than three hours before the fans dispersed and police got traffic moving freely again.

Meanwhile on campus, Showalter Fountain was the center of attention with at least another 2,000 students showing up there. They laughed and hugged, climbed all over Venus, and eventually pulled one of the bronze fishes right off its mounting.

After the students' splashing and thrashing had spilled most of the water out of the fountain, Delta Upsilon obligingly brought its famous old firetruck and began spraying more water everywhere — everywhere, that is, except into the fountain itself.

The same, slow-moving, cars-honking, people-cheering traffic jam was repeated in the middle of campus. A Volkswagen, its fenders scraping on the pavement from the weight of more than a dozen happy passengers riding in every conceivable location, circled the fountain again and again.

It was all in sharp contrast to the scene just a few hours before when police reported almost no one on the streets. Everyone was inside — in the Union building's trophy room, at the bars in front of giant television screens, in a thousand homes — all watching IU's biggest basketball victory ever.

And it was one of Bloomington's biggest nights, too . . . a night for celebrating, rain or no; a night when this little town may very well have been the best place in the whole wide world to be.

A welcome home to NCAA champs

Epilogue

Won 33 games ... and battle for identity

Indiana's 1975-76 basketball team became the national collegiate champion by winning 33 games — every one of them in the national spotlight.

But the most significant of all Hoosier victories may have been missed by the spotlight.

Something internal. Personal.

In January of this basketball year, Iowa coach Lute Olson said:

"I thought last year's Indiana team was the best in the country without any question at all. I thought it was the best college team at both ends of the court that I had ever seen."

It was a sincere and significant compliment,

Bob Knight — A time, a year to smile

Jim Crews

'Can mold 4 all-Americans into national champion'

Normal, Illinois, March 16, 1972

Jim Crews, a 6-4 all-state guard from University High School in Normal, Ill., today announced he will attend Indiana University next fall, and Crews's high school coach, Bob Metcalf, said:

"Indiana's got a real winner."

Jim Crews — 'A real winner'

Crews made his final decision between Indiana and Maryland after cutting the recruiting field down quickly. The ultimate reason for the decision, Crews said, "was coach Knight . . . definitely.

"I think Indiana has a bright basketball future. I could tell at the end of the year they were really on their way."

Crews scored 626 points for University, a 21-9 team, but both Metcalf and Knight talked first of Crews's ball-handling. "He's the best passer I've ever seen in high school," Knight said.

"He'll do anything he has to do to win — pass the ball or shoot the ball," Metcalf said. "He's the type who can take four all-Americans and mold them into a national champion."

Crews scored 1,424 points in his career. He set a school record of 41 points with Knight in the stands to see the "ball-handling" guard snipe in 19 of 31 shots, most of them out on the court. "Our charts showed him shooting 44 per cent for the year from beyond 24 feet," Metcalf said. "He's certainly effective against a zone or sagging defense."

JIM CREWS

	G-S	FG	Pct.	FT	Pct.	R	Avg.	Hi	A	PF-D	TP	Avg.	Hi
1972-73	28- 22	65- 132	.492	17- 25	.680	58	2.7	7	78	59- 1	147	5.3	14
1973-74	22- 9	26- 57	.456	9- 13	.692	38	1.7	5	56	21- 0	61	2.8	14
1974-75	26- 0	15- 33	.455	6- 6	1.000	13	0.5	2	20	9- 0	36	1.4	8
1975-76	31- 1	36- 78	.462	30- 35	.857	23	0.7	3	42	20- 0	100	3.2	9
Career	107- 32	142- 300	.473	62- 79	.785	132	1.2	7	196	109- 1	344	3.2	14

134

but it inevitably carried the sort of cut that became familiar to the 1975-76 Hoosiers, for Olson went on:

"Personally, I don't think they're as good as they were a year ago. They're not the outstanding shooting team that they were.

"But they're still a great basketball team."

It was a strange sort of sibling rivalry, considering so many in the group put down were so big in the team that came before.

It was a slight to Tom Abernethy, the "new" team's only new starter . . . and yet it wasn't, because implicit in it was recognition that Abernethy's availability in a seventh-man role was a major strength of the team before.

So it was a slight to Jim Crews, Wayne Radford, Jim Wisman and Rich Valavicius, the "Super-Subs" of a new year. And yet all they did was deliver when needed, miraculously so on occasion.

It was a slight to the development of the four

Scott May
'Always puts forth a sincere effort to win'

Sandusky, Ohio, May 8, 1972

Scott May, a 6-5, 210-pound forward regarded as one of the top high school athletes in Ohio this year, said in a Toledo newspaper interview that he is leaning toward IU.

Scott May — 'Leads by example'

May averaged 30.1 points per game this year, shooting 51 per cent from the field and 71 per cent from the free-throw line. He also averaged 14.2 rebounds per game.

As a junior, he averaged 25.1 points and 14.1 rebounds per game, and as a sophomore, his averages were 13 points and 10 rebounds.

Sandusky coach Gary Reynolds said May's "strongest assets are the manner in which he accepts coaching and leads by example, two athletic values often challenged in modern times. He always puts forth a sincere effort to win, on or off the court."

The *Cleveland Plain Dealer* named him "the finest citizen-athlete in the 18-year history" of the Buckeye conference.

May made the 25-man "cum laude" list of *Coach & Athlete* magazine's all-America team after making all-state at Sandusky both as a basketball forward and a football end. He was one of two players who made the magazine's 100-man all-America list in both football and basketball. Quinn Buckner of Dolton, Ill., Thornridge was the other.

May will concentrate on basketball in college. He lettered four years in the sport at Sandusky and one coach called him "the Jim McMillian" type."

SCOTT MAY

	G-S	FG	Pct.	FT	Pct.	R	Avg.	Hi	A	PF-D	TP	Avg.	Hi
1973-74	28- 27	154- 313	.492	43- 56	.768	150	5.4	11	41	95- 2	351	12.5	27
1974-75	30- 25	204- 400	.510	82-107	.766	199	6.6	17	57	66- 1	490	16.3	29
1975-76	32- 32	308- 584	.527	136-174	.782	245	7.7	18	68	95- 2	752	23.5	41
Career	90- 84	666-1297	.513	261-337	.774	594	6.6	19	166	256- 5	1593	17.7	41

starters who returned — Scott May, Quinn Buckner, Bob Wilkerson and Kent Benson. Unintended slights. Sibling slights. "Wasn't Billy the greatest you ever saw? And Jimmy, you're good, too."

There may have never been an athletic team that played so long under such demanding pressure. And did so well.

It had to prove it could stand on its own in an exhibition game before the season ever began. Not a normal exhibition game: a game that drew 17,000 people in Indianapolis and matched the new combination against a veteran Soviet Union national team still trumpeted globally as the reigning Olympic champion.

As the nation's No. 1-ranked team, it had an unprecedented challenge in its opener — No. 2 UCLA, the once and perennial champion that was a 1975 interloper only in Indiana. Indiana, a 1975-76 interloper in No. 1, to UCLA and many others conditioned to Bruin occupancy of the spot.

It was a team accused of somehow overachieving in that nationally televised test . . . of being *too* ready, *too* motivated, *too* zealous to stand up to four months of act-following.

It was a team that paid for the "not as good as they were a year ago" rap every time it went out, because the UCLA aura of invincibility was denied it. Team after team, arena after arena, bubbled with a belief that these No. 1 Hoosiers could be had, and in sports, that's being stripped of a significant asset.

Its schedule was full of teams that, indeed, did have a valid shot. And took it.

But the Hoosiers kept winning. Grindingly, sometimes. Luckily, a time or two. Impressively, on

Tom Abernethy

'Big thing about him is attitude; he'll help IU'

South Bend, Indiana, May 15, 1972
Tom Abernethy, an H-T all-state and Indiana All-Star basketball player from South Bend St. Joseph's, announced today he will attend Indiana University.

Abernethy is a 6-6, 191-pounder who set a South Bend scoring record with 648 points in leading St. Joseph's to a 22-3 record and its second straight South Bend sectional championship. He made his final selection of Indiana after considering Purdue, Iowa State and Memphis State.

IU coach Bob Knight described him as "a very, very smart player — an excellent team player. We're very happy to get him." Abernethy played at center for coach Bob Donewald at St. Joseph's, starting on teams that went 39-8. He was a teammate of IU freshman John Laskowski last year, and Donewald smiled: "Those two have made a pretty good coach out of me."

Donewald said "one of Tom's great assets is that he never tries to do the things he cannot do. A lot of players, especially stars, are not that keenly aware of their limitations.

"He can put the ball on the floor, he can get the ball to the big people, and he's an exceptional passer. He will have to work on his outside shooting, but that's partly my fault. I never let him wander away from the hole very far.

"I don't think Tom is through developing physically. His best basketball is ahead of him. The more he plays out on the floor, the more knowledgeable he's going to get, and he's going to mature a lot more physically. He'll also work hard on the areas where he needs improvement.

"The big thing about him is attitude — I feel very confident that regardless of what his role is, superstar or the last sub on the bench, he'll help Indiana University."

Tom Abernethy — 'Best ahead of him'

TOM ABERNETHY

	G-S	FG	Pct.	FT	Pct.	R	Avg.	Hi	A	PF-D	TP	Avg.	Hi
1972-73	18- 0	18- 48	.375	4- 7	.571	46	2.6	6	9	15- 0	40	2.2	12
1973-74	27- 1	62- 113	.549	36- 48	.750	100	3.7	9	19	33- 0	160	5.9	19
1974-75	32- 0	51- 97	.526	31- 54	.574	96	3.0	9	23	38- 0	133	4.2	12
1975-76	32- 31	133- 237	.561	55- 74	.743	169	5.3	10	65	63- 0	321	10.0	22
Career	109- 32	264- 495	.533	126-183	.678	411	3.8	10	116	149- 9	654	6.0	22

many an occasion, but not so many that the "beatable" tag was ever shed.

It became almost ludicrous. At a time when it was almost unanimously ranked No. 1 in the nation, it was almost unanimously ignored by "experts" predicting the outcome of the NCAA tournament. The ultimate test.

Disbelief was so obvious that a fellow who had watched it all happen and been in each of those hostile arenas commented to a colleague on the eve of the first tourney game that this Indiana team "may be the most underrated No. 1 team in history."

And even in the flush of Philadelphia, after the mastering of what generally is acknowledged to have been the toughest tournament path ever put before an NCAA champion, it may still be.

Because unappreciated is the pressure, the "prove-it" challenge that a group of players that assuredly is not the most talented team in history stood up to and whipped.

Not the most talented, but maybe the toughest, in a mental sense. It was a team that knew it could be beaten, heard it every day, but wouldn't be.

It was a team with "no bench" that withstood the loss of all-America center Kent Benson for key minutes in a regional game with strong Alabama, the loss of college player of the year Scott May for 13½ minutes in a head-on meeting with Marquette ... and, in the most testing circumstances, the shocking loss of starting guard Bob Wilkerson in the opening minutes of the championship game that it had entered with Tom Abernethy, at long last recognized as a formidable player, bothered by a leg injury.

Bob Wilkerson

'With Bobby, 5-10 guard didn't have a chance'

Anderson, Indiana, May 16, 1972

Bob Wilkerson, who came to Bloomington in March as the leader of Madison Heights' first "Final Four" basketball team, will return this fall as an Indiana University student.

Wilkerson, a "very, very quick big man" at 6-6 and 185 pounds, was a member of the H-T all-state team and he is his school's first representative on the Indiana All-Stars.

Wilkerson showed exceptional versatility, playing all three positions on offense for coach Phil Buck. "He did so many things for us," Buck said. "He led us in scoring (18.9 per game), but he really didn't have to score to be a good ball player for us.

"Probably his greatest asset was his defense, and he also led us in assists."

On defense, he normally was the point man in a 1-2-2 zone defense. "With Bobby out there," Buck laughed, "a 5-10 or 5-11 guard didn't have a chance. He was really taken out of the offense. And nobody got down in the lane area. That was no-man's-land with him out there.

"He played that spot for us for three years, and since we were always putting pressure on the ball, his job was pretty much like a man-to-man. I don't think he'll have any trouble at all making that adjustment."

He totaled 1,061 points in his 66-game career. The Pirates won 53 of those games. "He's not a great outside shooter but he's an adequate shooter," Buck said. "He broke up a couple of zones for us with his outside shooting."

Bob Wilkerson — 'Greatest asset defense'

BOB WILKERSON

	G-S	FG	Pct.	FT	Pct.	R	Avg.	Hi	A	PF-D	TP	Avg.	Hi
1973-74	28- 4	45- 112	.402	12- 22	.545	74	2.6	8	33	51- 1	102	3.6	12
1974-75	32- 32	98- 217	.452	33- 53	.623	141	4.4	14	112	80- 1	229	7.2	18
1975-76	32- 29	111- 225	.493	29- 46	.630	156	4.9	19	171	77- 0	251	7.8	21
Career	92- 65	254- 554	.458	74-121	.612	381	4.1	19	316	208- 2	589	6.4	21

It was a team that looked itself in the eye all year long and pushed a little harder.

In late February, the Hoosiers were 23-0 and concerned. The challenge laid before them at the start of the previous year was not to win but to "play to potential," and in winning, they felt they were falling short of that.

May listened to a writer suggest that this year's team might have developed a more valuable quality by being exposed to tough situations and surviving them than the previous Hoosier team had in its remarkable consistency, its purring precision that produced so many routs.

While scrambling, the theorist went on, perhaps this team had developed a gutty confidence in its ability to stare down a challenger when the pressure was highest.

"Yeah," said May, deflating the line of logic-

rationalization with one comment: "But the game is not *played* like that.

"We've been on a roller coaster, not on an incline going straight up. What we have to do now is get going in the right direction.

"The little things are going to count. That's what's going to make us or break us — little mistakes. We've got to get them out of the way."

It was May who dealt most realistically with the eternal comparison between 1974-75 and 1975-76 Hoosiers.

"At times, when we're playing a game the way we can play it, I think we are (better than last year)," he said. "And yet, there are times . . .

"We used to beat people offensively. This year, we don't have the shooting we had last year with Laz and Greeno (John Laskowski and Steve Green, whose abilities were shown by their selection in the

---

Quinn Buckner

'Feelings about teamwork really fit in well'

Phoenix, Illinois, July 27, 1972

Quinn Buckner, a high school all-American in both football and basketball and the top-ranked prep athlete in the nation this year, signed a Big Ten tender from Indiana University today and said he will attend IU.

Buckner plans to compete in both sports in college, just as he did — brilliantly — at Thornridge High School in Dolton, Ill., a southwest Chicago suburb.

Best known as a basketball player, the 6-3, 210-pound Buckner was a guard and "quarterback" on two straight state championship teams at Thorn-

ridge, which went 33-0 on its way to the title last year.

He averaged 25 points, 11 rebounds and 6 assists per game while shooting 55 per cent from the floor and 71 per cent from the free-throw line. He averaged 21 points and 11 rebounds as a junior, and an Illinois sports writer covering that year's state tourney called Buckner "the most exciting prep basketball player in Illinois."

His coach, Ron Ferguson, called him the heart of Thornridge's pressing defense, and as a junior, it was his steal and fast-break pass in the last 30 seconds that shot the Falcons away to a 63-58 semifinal victory. Last year, Thornridge steamrollered all opponents.

"He has charisma," Ferguson said. "His mere appearance brings out the best in everybody. Watch when things get tough, they all look to him . . . and he's always so cool . . ."

"He's unquestionably one of the best athletes in the nation," IU basketball coach Bob Knight said, "and certainly we feel he is one of the very best basketball players.

"His feelings about teamwork and team play really fit in well with the kids we have recruited. His talent should go very well with the talent we have on hand."

Quinn Buckner — 'One of very best'

QUINN BUCKNER

	G-S	FG	Pct.	FT	Pct.	R	Avg.	Hi	A	PF-D	TP	Avg.	Hi
1972-73	28- 27	130- 318	.409	41- 69	.594	134	4.8	13	82	104- 9	301	10.8	24
1973-74	28- 27	103- 273	.377	23- 41	.561	106	3.9	8	150	101- 6	229	8.2	21
1974-75	32- 32	165- 335	.493	49- 84	.583	123	3.8	9	177	103- 2	379	11.8	26
1975-76	32- 30	123- 279	.441	40- 82	.488	91	2.8	8	133	105- 3	286	8.9	24
Career	120-116	521-1205	.432	153-276	.554	454	3.8	13	542	413-20	1195	10.0	26

second round of the National Basketball Association draft and their winning jobs with the Chicago Bulls and the St. Louis Spirits).

"That's a lot of points. This year, we have to pick up their points on steals, fast breaks, just playing good, solid defense.

"There have been times when I thought we were really playing well. I thought we were going to put it to 'em. Then we relaxed a little, and they caught right back up. We can't let that happen."

That was after the second Minnesota game, on the eve of the Iowa game that proved to be the take-off point for a late-season charge.

May stood as a suitable symbol of the Hoosiers because, at a time he was being recognized as college basketball's best player of this season, he was worrying about getting better, and building a stronger team.

"I just want to be known as a player — a *complete* player," May said. "I hope I can do other things when I'm not scoring — rebound, play defense, set screens, get a few assists."

It was a team on which Abernethy played well throughout the year and superbly at times, yet was the one Hoosier who never got all-tourney, all-league or all-America mention. And, just before the national finals, he dismissed the subject by saying:

"I couldn't ask for much more than I've gotten out of my four years here — the association with the coaches and my teammates . . . a few things we did . . . the good times we've had over the years. It all goes along with being happy."

And, in those national finals, a four-team meet that had as many top-flight college stars as any in recent years, Mr. Underrated, Abernethy, was

Kent Benson

'Big thing with Kent is his desire for ball'

New Castle, Indiana, May 3, 1973

Kent Benson signed his application today for the wide-open center job on the Indiana University basketball team.

Benson, New Castle's 6-11 "Mr. Basketball,"

Kent Benson — 'Complete inside player'

announced his choice at Chrysler High School, where he has been the literal center of a success story for the last three years.

Benson said he picked Indiana after visiting IU, Purdue, Notre Dame and Kentucky. "When I visited Indiana, I had the feeling in my heart this was the place I wanted to go," he said.

He said he feels the Hoosiers "have started an era, and with the personnel they have back, they're going to keep it going. I hope I can fill in Steve Downing's shoes. It's going to be a big step, but I hope I can do that."

IU coach Bob Knight said he was "naturally very happy about his choice. We think he can fit in very well with the kind of kids we have at Indiana."

"Kent's a complete inside player," New Castle coach Cecil Tague said. "A lot of big people like to go outside part of the time. We just never let him do that, although he always wanted to go outside, to be honest.

"Another big thing with Kent is his desire for the basketball. He goes after the ball on the boards better than any big man I've ever seen. He stays after the ball like a shark going to blood — good second, third, fourth and fifth effort, not only offensively but defensively.

"When he went to IU on his visit, he was very much impressed with the players, and that wasn't the case everywhere he went. And I know he was impressed with Knight and the discipline he has in his program. I really think that appealed to Kent."

KENT BENSON

	G-S	FG	Pct.	FT	Pct.	R	Avg.	Hi	A	PF-D	TP	Avg.	Hi
1973-74	27- 24	113- 224	.504	24- 40	.600	222	8.2	15	25	81- 2	250	9.3	20
1974-75	32- 32	198- 366	.541	84-113	.743	286	8.9	23	40	97- 0	480	15.0	33
1975-76	32- 32	237- 410	.578	80-117	.684	282	8.8	15	52	93- 0	554	17.3	38
Career	91- 88	548-1000	.548	188-270	.696	790	8.7	23	117	271- 2	1284	14.1	38

voted to the five-man all-tournament team. Nothing, until the national finals.

It was a year when Buckner struggled through traumatic playing times and, after a series of tests showed there was nothing physically wrong, was ordered by Knight to give up fixing his own meals (in the apartment he shared with May) and return to dorm food.

The magic returned by season's end. Over the last 10 games, Buckner shot .532, averaged 12.2 points per game and led the Hoosiers as few college guards ever have or ever could have.

It was a year of manifold contributions from Wilkerson — shooting, rebounding, defense, ballhandling. A highlight was his last full game, when he pulled down 19 rebounds against tall UCLA in the national semifinals. He also finished No. 2 in the Big Ten in assists, with 14 in one of the victories over Michigan.

And Crews came on to play the best basketball of his IU career, including game-winning roles two straight Saturdays against Minnesota and Illinois, when the Hoosiers were struggling.

It was a notable and remarkable farewell year for a group of seniors that was around for 120 games and finished with an even 90 per cent winning record — 108-12.

Theirs is the legacy that is handed on to the Indiana teams to come, pressure handed out by them, for a change, not to them.

It's a winner's pressure, status won for Indiana University in their collegiate tenure.

FINAL IU BASKETBALL STATISTICS

WON 32, LOST 0

	G-S	FG	Pct.	FT	Pct.	R	Avg.	Hi	A	PF-D	TP	Avg.	Hi	M
Scott May	32-32	308- 584	.527	136-174	.782	245	7.7	18	68	95- 2	752	23.5	41	33
Kent Benson	32-32	237- 410	.578	80-117	.684	282	8.8	15	52	93- 0	554	17.3	38	34
Tom Abernethy	32-31	133- 237	.561	55- 74	.743	169	5.3	10	65	63- 0	321	10.0	22	32
Quinn Buckner	32-30	123- 279	.441	40- 82	.488	91	2.8	8	133	103- 3	286	8.9	24	24
Bob Wilkerson	32-29	111- 225	.493	29- 46	.630	156	4.9	19	171	77- 0	251	7.8	21	28
Wayne Radford	30- 2	49- 86	.570	42- 59	.712	63	2.2	9	42	44- 0	140	4.7	16	13
Jim Crews	31- 1	36- 78	.462	30- 35	.857	23	0.7	3	42	20- 0	100	3.2	9	10
Rich Valavicius	28- 0	29- 60	.483	10- 16	.625	49	1.8	6	8	42- 2	68	2.4	12	11
Jim Wisman	26- 3	22- 60	.367	21- 29	.724	21	0.8	4	58	41- 2	65	2.5	12	13
Bob Bender	17- 0	13- 23	.565	9- 12	.750	13	0.8	3	14	14- 1	35	2.1	12	6
Mark Haymore	13- 0	11- 27	.407	2- 7	.286	28	2.2	6	4	17- 0	24	1.8	7	5
Jim Roberson	12- 0	7- 12	.583	5- 6	.833	16	1.3	6	0	19- 0	16	1.6	7	4
Scott Eells	12- 2	4- 13	.308	3- 4	.750	9	0.8	2	0	3- 0	11	1.0	5	3
Team				0- 1		159								
Totals	32	1083-2094	.517	462-662	.698	1323	41.3	67	655	624-10	2628	82.1	114	
Opponents	32	837-1921	.436	400-572	.699	1140	35.6	48	325	651-14	2074	64.8	81	

BIG TEN

	G-S	FG	Pct.	FT	Pct.	R	Avg.	Hi	A	PF-D	TP	Avg.	Hi	M
Scott May	18-18	175- 342	.512	62- 84	.738	135	7.5	18	40	56- 2	412	22.9	41	33
Kent Benson	18-18	140- 231	.606	48- 72	.667	171	9.5	15	32	51- 0	328	18.2	38	35
Tom Abernethy	18-17	80- 153	.523	28- 38	.737	96	5.3	10	38	38- 0	188	10.4	22	32
Bob Wilkerson	18-15	67- 135	.496	15- 23	.652	82	4.6	12	105	50- 0	149	8.3	21	28
Quinn Buckner	18-16	54- 127	.435	10- 29	.345	39	2.2	7	79	57- 2	118	6.6	24	21
Wayne Radford	18- 2	36- 63	.571	24- 35	.686	44	2.3	9	28	31- 0	96	5.3	16	13
Jim Crews	18- 1	17- 35	.486	17- 20	.850	6	0.3	1	18	8- 0	51	2.8	8	9
Rich Valavicius	15- 0	21- 42	.500	7- 10	.700	40	2.7	6	5	25- 0	49	3.3	8	9
Jim Wisman	15- 3	14- 35	.400	12- 16	.750	13	0.9	2	42	25- 2	40	2.7	12	14
Jim Roberson	8- 0	4- 7	.571	3- 4	.750	8	1.0	4	0	7- 0	11	1.4	7	3
Mark Haymore	8- 0	4- 13	.308	1- 4	.250	15	1.9	5	1	10- 0	9	1.1	4	4
Scott Eells	8- 0	3- 11	.273	3- 4	.750	9	1.1	4	0	2- 0	9	1.1	5	3
Bob Bender	9- 0	3- 11	.273	2- 4	.500	11	1.2	3	5	7- 1	8	0.9	4	6
Team						83								
Totals	18	618-1205	.513	232-343	.676	754	41.9	67	393	367- 7	1468	81.6	114	
Opponents	18	471-1045	.451	244-342	.713	616	34.2	46	190	363-13	1186	65.9	81	

NCAA TOURNAMENT

	G-S	FG		Pct.	FT		Pct.	R	Avg.	Hi	A	PF-D	TP	Avg.	Hi	M
Scott May	5- 5	45-	88	.511	23- 28		.821	38	7.6	15	11	14- 0	113	22.6	33	36
Kent Benson	5- 5	40-	74	.541	14- 19		.737	45	9.0	13	7	16- 0	94	18.8	20	37
Quinn Buckner	5- 5	27-	54	.500	10- 19		.526	23	4.6	8	18	16- 0	64	12.8	16	36
Tom Abernethy	5- 5	20-	33	.606	12- 16		.750	27	5.4	6	9	10- 0	52	10.4	14	38
Bob Wilkerson	5- 5	10-	26	.385	11- 12		.917	37	7.4	19	24	7- 0	31	6.2	14	31
Jim Crews	4- 0	3-	6	.500	4- 5		.800	7	1.8	3	10	2- 0	10	2.5	4	10
Wayne Radford	4- 0	3-	8	.375	1- 1		1.000	7	1.8	5	2	3- 0	7	1.8	5	12
Mark Haymore	2- 0	2-	2	1.000	0- 0		.000	2	1.0	1	0	0- 0	4	2.0	2	1
Rich Valavicius	4- 0	1-	2	.500	1- 3		.333	2	0.5	2	0	0- 0	3	0.8	2	5
Jim Wisman	3- 0	0-	2	.000	2- 3		.667	1	0.3	1	6	4- 0	2	0.7	2	2
Jim Roberson	1- 0	0-	1	.000	0- 0		.000	0	0.0	0	0	0- 0	0	0.0	0	2
Bob Bender	2- 0	0-	0	.000	0- 0		.000	0	0.0	0	0	0- 0	0	0.0	0	1
Scott Eells	1- 0	0-	0	.000	0- 0		.000	0	0.0	0	0	0- 0	0	0.0	0	1
Team								13								
Indiana	5	151-	298	.513	78-106		.736	201	40.2	45	86	72- 0	380	76.0	90	
Opponents	5	137-	324	.423	40- 62		.645	179	35.8	37	48	107- 6	314	62.8	70	

Pop go the Hoosiers!

1975-76 All-America teams

UNITED PRESS INTERNATIONAL

Scott May(x), INDIANA
Kent Benson, INDIANA
Adrian Dantley, Notre Dame
John Lucas, Maryland
Richard Washington, UCLA
  (x) — Player of year.
  Coach of year: Bob Knight, INDIANA

ASSOCIATED PRESS

Scott May(x), INDIANA
Kent Benson, INDIANA
Adrian Dantley, Notre Dame
John Lucas, Maryland
Phil Sellers, Rutgers
  (x) — Player of year.
  Coach of year: Bob Knight, INDIANA

BASKETBALL WEEKLY

Scott May(x), INDIANA
Kent Benson, INDIANA
Adrian Dantley, Notre Dame
Phil Ford, North Carolina
Bernard King, Tennessee
  (x) — Player of year.
  Coach of year: Bob Knight, INDIANA

THE SPORTING NEWS

Scott May(x), INDIANA
Adrian Dantley, Notre Dame
Phil Ford, North Carolina
John Lucas, Maryland
Robert Parish, Centenary
  (x) — Player of year.
  Coach of year: Tom Young, Rutgers

NAT'L. ASS'N. OF BKB. COACHES

Scott May(x), INDIANA
Kent Benson, INDIANA
Adrian Dantley, Notre Dame
Phil Ford, North Carolina
Richard Washington, UCLA
  (x) — Player of year.
  Coach of year: John Orr, Michigan

U.S. BKB. WRITERS ASS'N.

Adrian Dantley(x), Notre Dame
Kent Benson, INDIANA
Bernard King, Tennessee
Mitch Kupchak, North Carolina
John Lucas, Maryland
Scott May, INDIANA
Phil Sellers, Rutgers
Willie Smith, Missouri
Earl Tatum, Marquette
Richard Washington, UCLA
  (x) — Player of year.

All-Big Ten
ASSOCIATED PRESS
First Team

Kent Benson, INDIANA
Terry Furlow, Michigan State
Rickey Green, Michigan
Scott May, INDIANA
Michael Thompson, Minnesota

Second Team

Billy McKinney, Northwestern
Eugene Parker, Purdue
Scott Thompson, Iowa
Bob Wilkerson, INDIANA
Ray Williams, Minnesota

UNITED PRESS INTERNATIONAL
First Team

Kent Benson, INDIANA
Terry Furlow, Michigan State
Rickey Green, Michigan
Scott May, INDIANA
Michael Thompson, Minnesota

Second Team

Wayman Britt, Michigan
Billy McKinney, Northwestern
Scott Thompson, Iowa
Bob Wilkerson, INDIANA
Ray Williams, Minnesota

Bob Hammel

Bob Hammel has verbally frozen the many marvelous moments that went into one of college basketball's grandest achievements. Sports editor of the H-T since the fall of 1966, he has been named as Indiana Sportswriter of the Year four times — 1971, 1972, 1975 and 1976. In 1973, he received the Chris Savage Award given annually to an outstanding Indiana journalist by the Indiana University Department of Journalism.

Larry Crewell

Chief photographer Larry Crewell followed the Hoosiers during a season that took him from a Big Ten game in Champaign, Ill. to the sparkling champagne of an NCAA championship in Philadelphia. Since joining the H-T staff in 1959, Crewell has been recognized in several Indiana news photography contests for his outstanding work.

Acknowledgements

Layout editor. . . . . Cheryl Magazine
Cover design. . . . . Mel Miller
Production superintendent . . . . Bob Ayers
Technical director . . . . Jerry Keller
Technical assistant . . . . Dale Hannum
Graphic arts manager . . . . Danny Wagoner
Computer systems director. . . . . Mike Kinerk
Writers . . . . Phil Coffin
                                Phil Bloom
                                Stephen Hofer
                                Bill Hammel
                                Greg Dawson
                                Jeff Smithburn
                                Rex Kirts
                                John Whisler
Publisher. . . . . Scott C. Schurz
Assistant to the publisher. . . . . . Mike Hefron

Copy editors . . . . Vee Kinzer
                                Stephen Hofer
                                John Harrell
Typists . . . . Joan Arnold
                                Shannon Hawkins

Photographers	
Phil Whitlow:	26, 29, 36, 41, 42, 54, 57, 71, 72, 80, 81, 89, 90, 139
Cheryl Magazine:	9, 13, 52, 70, 78, 79, 109, 123, 133, 135
Don Vandeventer:	133
Russ Cockrum:	47
David Mather:	75

The White House Rose Garden, April 20, 1976

A White House visit, a recruiting sweep

On April 20, a year that began with practice Oct. 15 and the Soviet Union game Nov. 3 was ended by an unprecedented visit to the White House, on invitation from President Ford. The President, a Michigan alumnus, met with the Hoosiers for almost a half-hour, joking about Indiana's three victories over Michigan ("Next year, please let us win one") and exchanging conversation with coach Bob Knight and several players in a low-key, informal atmosphere.

The same day, a "season" of a different sort ended when 6-8 forward Glen Grunwald of East Leyden High School in suburban Chicago took the last available IU scholarship. Grunwald joined two other all-Illinois players (6-11 Derek Holcomb of Peoria Richwoods and 6-4 Bill Cunningham of Dolton Thornridge), two all-Ohio (6-5 Butch Carter of Middletown and 6-7 Mike Miday of Canton Timken) and Indiana All-Star Mike Woodson (6-5, Indianapolis Broad Ripple) as Indiana's new additions.

. . . not the end of an era nor the beginning of one. Rather, the continuance.